Fighting the Slave Trade

Western African Studies

Willing Migrants
Soninke Labor Diasporas, 1848–1960
FRANÇOIS MANCHUELLE

El Dorado in West Africa
The Gold-Mining Frontier, African Labor, and Colonial Capitalism in the Gold Coast, 1875–1900
RAYMOND E. DUMETT

Nkrumah & the Chiefs
The Politics of Chieftaincy in Ghana, 1951–60
RICHARD RATHBONE

Ghanaian Popular Fiction
'Thrilling Discoveries in Conjugal Life' & Other Tales
STEPHANIE NEWELL

Paths of Accommodation
Muslim Societies and French Colonial Authorities in Senegal and Mauritania, 1880–1920
DAVID ROBINSON

West African Challenge to Empire
Culture and History in the Volta-Bani Anticolonial War
MAHIR ŞAUL AND PATRICK ROYER

Between the Sea & the Lagoon
An Eco-social History of the Anlo of Southeastern Ghana, c. 1850 to Recent Times
EMMANUEL AKYEAMPONG

'Civil Disorder is the Disease of Ibadan'
Chieftaincy and Civic Culture in a Yoruba City
RUTH WATSON

Smugglers, Secessionists, and Loyal Citizens on the Ghana-Togo Frontier
The Lie of the Borderlands since 1914
PAUL NUGENT

Eurafricans in Western Africa
Commerce, Social Status, Gender, and Religious Observance from the Sixteenth to the Eighteenth Century
GEORGE E. BROOKS

Lineages of State Fragility
Rural Civil Society in Guinea-Bissau
JOSHUA B. FORREST

Fighting the Slave Trade
West African Strategies
SYLVIANE A. DIOUF

*'Kola is God's Gift'**
Agricultural Production, Export Initiatives & the Kola Industry in Asante & the Gold Coast, c. 1820–1950
EDMUND ABAKA

*Slavery and Reform in West Africa**
Toward Emancipation in Nineteenth-Century Senegal and the Gold Coast
TREVOR R. GETZ

*Ouidah**
The Social History of a West African Slaving 'Port,' 1727–1892
ROBIN LAW

*forthcoming

Fighting the Slave Trade

West African Strategies

Sylviane A. Diouf, editor

Ohio University Press
ATHENS

James Currey
OXFORD

Ohio University Press
Scott Quadrangle
Athens, Ohio 45701

James Currey Ltd
73 Botley Road
Oxford OX2 0BS

First published 2003
First published in United Kingdom 2004

Ohio University Press books are printed on acid-free paper ♾

12 11 10 09 08 07 06 05 04 03 5 4 3 2 1

Published in the United States of America by
Ohio University Press, Athens, Ohio 45701

Chapter 12, "Shipboard Revolts, African Authority, and the Transatlantic Slave Trade," by David Richardson, appears by permission of the *William and Mary Quarterly*.

Library of Congress Cataloging-in-Publication Data
Fighting the slave trade : West African strategies / Sylviane A. Diouf, editor.
p. cm. – (Western African studies)
Papers presented at a conference held Feb. 2001 at Rutgers, the State University of New Jersey.
Includes bibliographical references and index.
ISBN 0-8214-1516-6 (alk. paper) – ISBN 0-8214-1517-4 (pbk. : alk. paper)
1. Slave trade—Africa, West—History—Congresses. I. Diouf, Sylviane A. (Sylviane Anna), 1952- II. Series.
HT1332.F54 2003
380.1'44'0966—dc21

2003056308

British Library Cataloguing in Publication Data
Fighting the slave trade : West African strategies. — (Western African studies)
1. Slave trade — Africa, West — History 2. Africa, West — History
I. Diouf, Sylviane A. (Sylviane Anna), 1952–
380.1'44'0966
ISBN 0-85255-447-8 (James Currey paper)
ISBN 0-85255-448-6 (James Currey cloth)

Contents

PART 2
PROTECTIVE STRATEGIES

PART 3
OFFENSIVE STRATEGIES

Preface

The essays included in this volume were presented at a conference entitled "Fighting Back: African Strategies against the Slave Trade" held at Rutgers, the State University of New Jersey, in February 2001. The conference was sponsored by the Rutgers–New Brunswick Department of History; the Center for African Studies at Rutgers; the Rutgers Research Council; the Social Sciences and Humanities Research Council of Canada and the UNESCO Slave Route Project on the Nigerian Hinterland at York University; December Ventures, Inc.; and the Schomburg Center for Research in Black Culture of the New York Public Library. It was made possible in part by a grant from the New Jersey Council for the Humanities, a state partner of the National Endowment for the Humanities.

Introduction

Sylviane A. Diouf

BETWEEN THE EARLY 1500S AND the late 1860s, an estimated twelve million African men, women, and children were forcibly transported across the Atlantic Ocean.[1] About seven million were displaced through the Sahara desert and the Indian Ocean, in a movement that started in the seventh century and lasted until the twentieth.[2] If the idea that the deported Africans walked quietly into servitude has lost ground in some intellectual circles, it is still going strong in popular culture; as are the supposed passivity or complicity of the rest of their compatriots and their lack of remorse for having allowed or participated in this massive displacement. In recent years, a few works have investigated the feeling of guilt apparent in some tales and practices linked to the Atlantic slave trade, but the Africans' actions during these times, except in their dimension of collaboration, have hardly been explored (Iroko 1988; Austen 1993; Shaw 2002).

This collection of essays seeks to offer a more balanced perspective by exploring the various strategies devised by the African populations against the slave trade. It is centered on the Atlantic trade, but some chapters cover strategies against the trans-Saharan and domestic displacement of captives, and these analyses suggest that strategies against the slave trade were similar, irrespective of the slaves' destination.[3] The book focuses on a single area, West Africa, in order to provide a sense of the range of strategies devised by the people to attack, defend, and protect themselves from the slave trade. This evidences the fact that they used various defensive, offensive, and protective mechanisms cumulatively. It also highlights how the contradictions between the interest of individuals, families, social orders, and communities played a part in feeding the trade, even as people fought against it. Therefore, this book is not specifically about resistance, which is arguably the most understudied area of slave trade studies—with only a few articles devoted to the topic (see Wax 1966; Rathbone 1986; McGowan 1990; Inikori 1996). Resistance to capture and deportation was an integral part of the Africans' actions, but their strategies against the slave trade did not necessarily translate into acts of resistance. Indeed, some mechanisms were grounded in the manipulation of the trade for the protection of oneself or one's group. The exchange of two captives for the freedom of one or the sale of people to acquire weapons were strategies intended to protect specific individuals, groups, and states from the slave trade. They were not an attack against it; still, they were directed against its very effects. Some strategies may thus appear more accommodation than resistance. Yet they should be envisioned in a larger context. Strategic accommodation does not mean that people who had redeemed a relative by giving two slaves in exchange were not at some other point involved in burning down a factory; or that the guns acquired through the sale of abductees were not turned directly against the trade. Resistance, accommodation, participation in the trade and attacks against it were often intimately linked.

But what precisely did people do to prevent themselves and their communities from being swept away to distant lands? What mechanisms did they adopt to limit the impact of the slave-dealing activities of traders, soldiers, and kidnappers? What environmental, physical, cultural, and spiritual weapons did they use? What short- and long-term strategies did they put in place? How did their actions and reactions shape their present and future? What political and social systems did they design to counteract the devastation brought about by the slave trade?

These are questions the literature has not adequately addressed. A large part of the studies on the Atlantic slave trade have focused instead on its economics: volume, prices, supply, cargo, expenses, profitability, gains, losses, competition, and partnerships. Because the records of shippers, merchants, banks, and insurance companies provide the most extensive evidence, economic and statistical studies are disproportionately represented in slave trade studies. But a great number, if not most, envision the Africans almost exclusively as trading partners on the one hand and cargo on the other. Viewed from another perspective, research based entirely or primarily on slavers' log books and companies' records are almost akin to studying the Holocaust in terms of expenses incurred during the transportation of the "cargo," profits generated by free labor, quantity and cost of gas for the death chambers, size and efficiency of the crematoria, and overall operating costs of the death camps. In the difference in historical treatment between the Holocaust and the slave trade, words may play a larger role than readily perceived.

If the word *Holocaust* is a fitting and immediately understood description of the crime against humanity that it was, the expression *slave trade,* by contrast, tends to let the collective consciousness equate this crime with a business venture. Naturally, genocide and other crimes against humankind are not commercial enterprises but, one may argue, the slave trade was only partially so. The demand for free labor in the Americas resulted in the purchase, kidnapping, and shipment of Africans by Westerners who entered into commercial relations with African traders and rulers. The violent seizure of people, however, did not entail any transaction; the affected African communities were not involved in business deals. Although important to our understanding of the events, the literature that focuses on the commercial part of the process does not capture the experience of the vast majority of the affected Africans. It is no stretch to assume that the tens of millions who suffered, directly and indirectly, from this immense disaster were primarily concerned with elaborating strategies to counter its consequences on themselves, their loved ones, and their communities.

Violence was an intrinsic—but not exclusive—component of these strategies, whether on the part of the direct victims or of the larger population. If nothing else, the need for shackles, guns, ropes, chains, iron balls, whips, and cannons—that sustained a veritable European Union of slave trade–related jobs—eloquently tells a story of opposition from the hinterland to the high seas. As explained by a slave trader, "For the security and safekeeping of the slaves on board or on shore in the African barracoons, chains, leg irons, handcuffs, and strong houses are used. I would remark that this also is one of the forcible necessities resorted to for the preservation of the order, and as recourse against the dangerous consequences of this traffic" (Conneau 1976). Western slavers were indeed cautious when taking people by force out of Africa. Wherever possible, as in Saint-Louis and Gorée (Senegal), James (Gambia), and Bance (Sierra Leone), slave factories were located on islands to render escapes and attacks difficult. In some areas, such as Guinea-Bissau, the level of distrust and hostility was so high that as soon as people approached the boats "the crew is ordered to take up arms, the cannons are aimed, and the fuses are lighted. . . . One must, without any hesitation, shoot at them and not spare them. The loss of the vessel and the life of the crew are at stake" (Durand 1805, 1:191).[4] Violence was particularly evident throughout the eighteenth century—the height of the slave trade—when numerous revolts directly linked to it broke out in Senegambia.[5] Fort Saint-Joseph, on the Senegal River, was attacked and all commerce was interrupted for six years (Durand 1805, 2:273). Several conspiracies and actual revolts by captives erupted on Gorée Island and resulted in the death of the governor and several soldiers. In addition, the crews of several slave ships were "cut off" (killed) in the Gambia River (Pruneau de Pommegorge 1789, 102–3; Hall 1992, 90–93; Guèye 1997, 32–35; Thilmans 1997, 110–19; Eltis 2000, 147). In Sierra Leone people sacked the captives' quarters of the infamous trader John Ormond (Durand 1807, 1:262).[6] The level of fortification of the forts and barracoons attests to the Europeans' distrust and apprehension. They had to protect themselves, as Jean-Baptiste Durand of the Compagnie du Sénégal explained, "from the foreign vessels and from the Negroes living in the country" (263). Written records of the attack of sixty-one ships by land-based Africans—as opposed to the captives on board—have already been found for the seventeenth and eighteenth centuries (Eltis 2000, 171).

The acts—or fear—of armed struggle may have seemed the most dreadful to the Europeans, but the Africans' struggle encompassed more than a physical fight. It was based on strategies in which not only men who could bear arms, but women, children, the elderly, entire families, and communities had a role. As exemplified in the following chapters, to protect and defend themselves and their communities and to cripple the international slave trade that threatened their lives, people devised long-term mechanisms, such as resettling to hard-to-find places, building fortresses, evolving new—often more rigid—styles of leadership, and transforming the habitat and the manner in which they occupied the land. As a more immediate response, secret societies, women's organizations, and young men's militia redirected their activities toward the protection and defense of their communities. Children turned into sentinels, venomous plants and insects were transformed into allies, and those who possessed the knowledge created spiritual protections for individuals and communities. In the short term, resources were pooled to redeem those who had been captured and were held in factories along the coast. At the same time, in a vicious circle, raiding and kidnapping became more prevalent as some communities, individuals, and states traded people to access guns and iron to forge better weapons to protect themselves, or in order to obtain in exchange the freedom of their loved ones. As an immediate as well as a long-term strategy, some free people attacked slave ships and burned down factories. And when everything else had failed, a number of men and women revolted in the barracoons and aboard the ships that transported them to the Americas, while others jumped overboard or let themselves starve to death.

People adopted the defensive, protective, and offensive strategies that worked for them, depending on a variety of factors and the knowledge they possessed. Although a culture of "virile violence" tends to place armed struggle at the top of the pyramid, it is rather futile to rate those strategies. They worked or not, depending on the circumstances, not on intrinsic merit, and they each responded to specific needs. Some people may have elected to attack the slave ships first and then resettle in hard-to-find places as circumstances changed. Others may have relocated as a first option. And, naturally, because the conditions could not have existed at the time, Africans did not use other mechanisms that contemporary hindsight believes would have been more efficient.

The idea that the slave trade would have stopped if a continental armed movement had been launched persists in contemporary popular culture and has negative repercussions on the relations between some African Americans and a growing community of African immigrants whose ancestors they accuse of collective passivity. The fact that Africans did not constitute one population but many whose interests and needs could be vastly divergent has not reached the general public. Although it seems acceptable that the French and the English, or the English and the Irish, fought one another for dozens of generations and did not see themselves as being part of the same people—not even the same race—such a notion is still difficult to grasp for many when it comes to peoples in Africa.[7] Their conflicts based on land, religion, politics, influence, dynastic quarrels, expansion, economy, territorial consolidation—which they considered as serious as the French and English did theirs when they launched, and doggedly pursued, their Hundred Years' War—appear trivial to many in the face of the onslaught of the slave trade and the rise of racism. Reflecting this idea, Guyanese poet Grace Nichols writes:

> But I was traded by men
> the colour of my own skin
> traded like a fowl like a goat
> like a sack of kernels I was
> traded
> for beads for pans
> for trinkets?
> No it isn't easy to forget
> What we refuse to remember
> Daily I rinse the taint
> Of treachery from my mouth. (1990, 18)

Although she expressively exposes a wound that aches in contemporary African Diaspora, the sentiments she describes are anachronistic because they could not have reflected the deported Africans' point of view. Their autobiographies and interviews clearly evidence that they did not think they had been sold by "black brothers and sisters." Omar ibn Said writes that he was captured in war by "infidels"; Ibrahima abd al-Rahman Barry was made a prisoner by "Heboes" and sold to "Mandingoes"; Job ben Solomon was kidnapped by "Mandingoes"; Ali Eisami Gazirmabe by "Fulbe"; Muhammad Ali ben Said by "Kindills"; Olaudah Equiano was abducted by "two men and a woman"; Abu Bakr al-Siddiq was captured by "Adinkra's army"; Joseph Wright was made a prisoner by "the enemies"; Samuel Ajayi Crowther by an army of "Oyo Mahomedans, Foulahs and foreign slaves"; William Thomas was sold by "people belonging to Pedro Blanco's slave barracoon"; Ottobah Cugoano—the only one who at one point refers to betrayal by "some of my own complexion"—was abducted by "great ruffians"; and Mahommah Gardo Baquaqua was made a prisoner by "enemies" (see Alryyes 2000, 91; Griffin 1828b, 365; Curtin 1967a, 40; 1967b, 326; Smith, Last, and Gubio 1967, 211; Said 1873, 40; Jones 1967, 85; Wilks 1967, 162; Ajayi 1967, 299; see also *Anti-Slavery Reporter* 4 [8 February 1843]: 22–23, cited in Blassingame 1977, 227; Cugoano 1999, 13; Moore 1834, 35).

Nowhere in the Africans' testimonies is there any indication that they felt betrayed by people "the color of their own skin." Their perspective was based on their worldview that recognized ethnic, political, and religious differences but not the modern concepts of a black race or Africanness. With time, when an encompassing African—no longer an ethnic—consciousness developed in America, the story passed on still was not that people had been sold by other Africans but that they had been individually tricked and abducted by whites enticing them from the slave ships with European goods.[8] For the most part these were not descriptions of actual events—although some certainly were—but allegorical tales that assigned blame where the Africans and their descendants thought it belonged: with the people who came to take them away not with their own. These "memories" of the elders turned into solid truths for their descendants, even though they mostly were, in an objective sense, symbolic constructions not the reflection of reality. Later generations developed the black betrayal model. It is no more historically true than the one it replaced. As has been evidenced elsewhere, the concepts of Africa, Africans, blackness, whiteness, and race did not exist in Africa, and they cannot be utilized today to assess people's actions at a time when they were not operative (Eltis 2000, 150; Inikori, this volume). In addition, for this paradigm of continental Africans' collective culpability—quite a dangerous and devious concept anyway—to make sense, it has to be based on the (inaccurate) belief that the slave trade removed only people who had no parents, spouses, children, and friends; that it did not kill, wound, or mutilate more people in Africa than it deported overseas; that there were never any shifts in the military balance of power; that only certain populations were victimized to the exclusion of others; and that those who became captives had never been involved in wars, raids, or abductions that had resulted in the deportation and enslavement of others.

With the sharp increase in African immigration, the African betrayal model has found new vigor. Contemporary Africans are frequently accused by some African Americans of having "sold us" and are expected to apologize.[9] Henry Louis Gates Jr. pursued the idea in his television series *Wonders of the African World* and went on to state that "others have wondered and I am thinking here of Yambo Ouologuem's great novel *Bound to Violence* (1971) if Africa was cursed because of the apparent willingness of so many African societies to participate in the slave trade, bartering what, to us here, appear to be their sisters and brothers, for a mess of pottage" (2001, 3). As explored by Joseph E. Inikori in this volume, medieval Europeans were also involved in bartering their own "brothers and sisters"—actions for which no divine curse is invoked—and the present is not exempt from similar attitudes. According to the U.S. State Department's *Trafficking in Persons Report* for 2002, traffickers throughout the world buy, sell, and transport between seven hundred thousand and four million individuals (mostly young women and children) every year for prostitution and slave labor. Twenty-six nations in Europe and the former Soviet Union, nineteen in Asia, ten in the Americas, sixteen in Africa, and six in the Middle East are involved as source, transit, or destination countries. It would be surprising if Africans from the sixteenth to the nineteenth centuries had been more politically, "racially," socially, and morally enlightened than any other people in the past, the present, and (probably) the future. As for their massive collaboration that many believe had been necessary to displace twelve million people, the current traffic in human beings yields some informative hints. The United States alone receives—as transit and destination country—about fifty thousand victims of the sexual traffic annually. Within 370 years—the length of the transatlantic slave trade—if the present rates were to be sustained, 18.5 million women and children could be introduced by networks that manifestly do not involve most Europeans, Asians, Africans, Middle Easterners, and Americans.

The destruction brought by the Atlantic slave trade was unprecedented, its impact on three continents has been enormous, and its consequences on African peoples have been devastating: it was unique. But its uniqueness should not hide the fact that some people's reactions to it (their participation in particular) were not exclusive to the continent; and that the Africans' various acts against deportation and enslavement were not frequently seen on other shores, even on a smaller scale commensurate with the lesser assaults other peoples faced. England's—and to a lesser extent France's—deportation and sale into indentured servitude of her own abducted indigent children, prisoners of war, prostitutes, and convicts is a case in point. Moreover, the idea that the British poor should be enslaved was passionately defended by distinguished intellectuals up to the mid-1700s (Rozbicki 2001). Aware of these parallels, a king in Dahomey remarked to a British governor, "Are we to blame if we send our criminals to foreign lands? I was told you do the same" (Durand 1807, 1:291). The English and French deportation policies did not elicit protest. There were no recorded attempts at freeing the convicts marching to the vessels bound for America and Australia, no assaults on ships to liberate the abducted, no moral outrage expressed at the evil of sending away other "whites" or brethren, no political attack on the institution of forced—quite distinct from voluntary—indenture itself, and virtually no rebellions on the ships. But, as shown in this volume, many of these actions were recorded in Africa. They were part of the reality not, evidently, all of it. Reality, over such an extended period of time and the breadth and length of a continent, was convoluted. As in other areas of the world, it was made of greed, tyranny, exploitation, abuse, and self-interest on the part of some; and of organized struggle, rebelliousness, selfishness, altruism, willing collaboration, fear, heroism, apathy, forced participation, panic-induced reactions, cowardice, and defiance on the part of others. Thus, the chapters in this volume explore a complex story of successes, failures, and contradictions.

In the end, the strategies had a positive effect: they did not stop the slave trade but certainly reduced it. Slave traders had to go further inland to look for captives whose offensive, defensive, and protective mechanisms resulted in more time spent to locate them; more casualties among the raiders; extra time en route to the coast, with greater risks for escape, injury, and death; and additional costly measures to ensure control over the barracoons and the ships. Resistance "held down the numbers entering the trade by raising the costs of carrying on the business" (Eltis 2000, 192). There is little doubt that millions were spared, although in some cases, it means that slave dealers turned their attention to more vulnerable peoples and areas (see Eltis 2000, 170–92; Richardson, this volume).

About the Sources

Because they appear in written records rather infrequently, the Africans' actions against the slave trade have been more difficult to track than the commercial transactions. However, the slaving records themselves provide suggestive information, not only on what transpired on the ships, such as conspiracies and revolts, but also on the attacks led on shore by the local populations (see Eltis 2000, 170–92; Inikori 1996; Richardson, this volume). In addition, as illustrated in most chapters, the testimonies of European slavers and travelers are an appreciable source on the Africans' actions—starting with the descriptions of individuals' and groups' attacks directed against the first Portuguese who sailed down the coast in 1441 and organized systematic abductions and continuing with the depositions and memoirs of slavers well into the nineteenth century (Gomes 1959; Zurara 1960).[10] Archeology is also of help. D. Kiyaga-Mulindwa's study of earthworks in the Birim Valley of southern Ghana revealed their role "as deterrent to small-scale attacks, petty slave-hunting forays and kidnappings" (1982, 73). E. J. Alagoa (1986) has detailed the manipulation of the environment, such as the diverting of rivers as well as the setting up of villages far from them in order to avoid the river traffic. Settlement patterns and distribution of population yield valuable clues. Hill settlements and regrouping—as well as the social cost of these defensive strategies in terms of epidemics and malnutrition—in the Middle Belt of Nigeria have been shown by Michael Mason (1969) and M. B. Gleave and R. M. Prothero (1971) as being a direct consequence of slave raiding. Following these early leads, several papers in this volume use archeology, demography, and settlement patterns to explore communities' responses.

The autobiographies, biographies, and interviews of Africans are another valuable source. The ransoming of captives is mentioned by Mahommah Gardo Baquaqua, Ayuba Suleiman Diallo (Job ben Solomon), Mohammed Said, Muhammad Kaba, and Olaudah Equiano. Baquaqua also describes fortified towns. Ibrahima abd al-Rahman Barry refers to people who used to burn down the ships that traded with Futa Jallon, a provider of captives to the Atlantic market. Barry fought them, and, interestingly, they beat his army with guns, most likely acquired from the Europeans in exchange for captives (Griffin 1828a, 79). This represents another example of the ambiguity of some strategies, of how resistance and participation in the trade could overlap and thus of how the concept of strategies against the slave trade rather than resistance per se gives a more accurate image of the African reality of the time. Ayuba Suleiman Diallo refers to the Islamic enclave scheme that provided protection from enslavement; and Olaudah Equiano, whether he observed them himself or was informed by others, mentions young men's militias.

Much has been made of oral tradition's supposed lack of memory about the slave trade or of its purely allegorical nature. As recently commented, "Most of the oral traditions concerning the slave trade that have survived among African and African-American communities cannot be used as empirical evidence because their narrative content is, by any modern standards, patently implausible." (Austen 2001, 237). But several studies have shown that African oral tradition can be, on the contrary, quite prolific, detailed, and clinical rather than symbolic. Revealing information on a wide range of African practices and actions has come to light. Oral tradition pinpoints forgotten caravan routes, markets, and escapees' villages; it has recorded—and used as a dating system—the spread of diseases and the rise of alcoholism due to the slave trade; it has kept the detailed memory of occult activities and practical exercises used to season the detainees before departure (Niane 1997; Guèye 2001; I. Barry 2001). Oral accounts reveal that in some barracoons, people were taught how they would have to sit and lie down in the slave ship they were going to board. We learn that on the Upper Guinea Coast, some Western slavers maintained occult centers, staffed by men they paid to "work on" the captives, in some cases with medicinal plants (Lefloche 2001). The objective was to kill any spirit of rebellion, to "tame" the detainees, and make them accept their fate. The existence of these centers shows the extent of the precautions taken to insure the slavers against rebellions: shackles and guns safeguarded the body, while the spirit was broken in. Oral tradition has also recorded the occurrence of attacks on caravans, often by members of the captives' age groups to free them; the recourse to occult means to protect villages; the use of plant camouflage to escape the slavers; the rituals that made the escapees who fled to the freedom enclaves officially free men and women; and the strategy of banditism, which pushed some groups to kill indiscriminately anyone who ventured close to their territory so as to discourage any incursion (Guèye 2001, 20). The Diola of Casamance remember the ransoming of captives, the establishment of work teams for protection, the paths left intentionally overgrown, the armed groups that guarded the vulnerable points, the construction of fortresses, and the covering of roofs with dry leaves to detect the footsteps of would-be kidnappers (Baum 1999, 71). Making provision for the usual shortcomings of oral tradition, it is clear that certain communities deliberately passed on the memory of the slave trade through discursive narratives, drum language, rituals, songs, proverbs, place names, migration stories, genealogies, name changes, chieftaincies, and so on. In eastern Nigeria, the fact-based—not symbolic—memory of the slave trade and enslavement has remained fresh, as Carolyn A. Brown explores in this volume. Not surprisingly, it appears that the people whose areas were most closely associated with the trade as providers—such as Futa Jallon—are the less loquacious. Informants in southern Senegal, Guinea-Bissau, Rio Pongo, and eastern Nigeria, by contrast, have either more to say or are more willing to express it.[11] Without discounting its allegorical references—including among the Africans and their immediate descendants enslaved in America—it is obvious, as several chapters attest, that oral tradition, when adequately mined, is quite helpful when it comes to providing detailed information about the Africans' strategies against the slave trade.

Defensive Strategies

Several essays in this volume examine, in depth or in passing, the role of the environment in the strategic response of the Africans. Research in the lacustrine villages of Benin, conducted by Elisée Soumonni, shows that people took advantage of the only ecological feature available: they built small towns on stilts at the edge of or in the middle of lakes. This innovation enabled them to clearly see approaching raiders and to take the appropriate measures.

Thierno Bah examines the defensive strategies devised by populations who were raided for enslavement in the Sokoto Caliphate (Nigeria) and the Ottoman Empire. A landscape of mountains, caves, underground tunnels, and marshes was cleverly used for protection and reinforced with the building of ramparts, fortresses, and other architectural devices and the planting of poisonous and thorny trees and bushes. These refuge sites enabled people to maintain their existence, their cultures, and their religions.

Dennis Cordell explores parts of the same region, as well as today's Central African Republic. Cordell revisits the myth of the inevitability of capture and the invincibility of slave raiders to show that resistance was highly organized and that migration and the regrouping and fortifying of settlements proved effective in many cases. While the strategy of relocation, he stresses, did not confront slave raiders and slave traders straight on, it hit at the very core of their activity by depriving them of people to capture and sell.

Another line of defense against the domestic and international slave trades was the habitat itself. Adama Guèye illustrates how people used their habitat as a safeguard by reconfiguring the disposition, size, and architecture of their houses, villages, and capital cities. Guèye's archeological research and the oral traditions she collected in Kayor and Baol, Senegal, give indications on how the aristocracy utilized the existence of relationships of domination and submission for its own protection by imposing new forms of habitat and land occupancy whose functions were to shield the powerful.

Focusing on Wasulu and Masina, Martin A. Klein examines how these societies evolved differently, in part to counter the devastation of the domestic slave trade, a pattern also observed in societies decimated by the Atlantic slave trade. Decentralized Wasulu made a concerted effort to erase all traces of social and professional hierarchy, a move meant to stimulate cohesion and facilitate resistance. Masina, on the contrary, developed a strong state based not only on the reinforcement of Islam as a liberating force but also on slave raiding, slave trading, and slave using that helped support its army and the state structure.

Protective Strategies

One strategy adopted throughout the continent to protect people from local enslavement or deportation was to redeem those who had been captured, as analyzed in my chapter. Redemption was a complex, difficult strategy that often failed and may appear, with hindsight, detrimental and controversial since it often deported two persons in the place of one; but it rested on the very human and universal rationale that people would protect their relatives from deportation and enslavement, even if it meant sacrificing strangers.

Protecting themselves and family members was also a major preoccupation of the African traders who were in business with Westerners. The mechanisms they used are analyzed by Paul E. Lovejoy and David Richardson, who focus on the port of Old Calabar. Ethnic, cultural, political, and institutional mechanisms were essential to the stability of the trade because they attempted to ensure that the African partners of the European traders could not be "legally" deported.

Offensive Strategies

Drawing on oral tradition, John N. Oriji examines a series of defensive and offensive strategies against slavers in Igboland. The mass mobilization of the populations and the various defensive and offensive strategies they designed, he contends, question the views of some scholars who argue that the slave trade was a normal commercial transaction, conducted in the hinterland largely by peaceful methods.

Focusing on the Balanta of Guinea-Bissau, Walter Hawthorne examines the defensive strategies of stateless and decentralized societies and their offensive movements that often consisted in raids on European vessels and in attacks on slave entrepôts. What enabled some groups to defend themselves and strike the slavers was the production and sale of captives in order to obtain guns or the iron bars needed to forge powerful weapons and tools.

Ismail Rashid relates and analyzes a series of domestic slave revolts that took place on the Upper Guinea Coast and illustrates how domestic slavery and the Atlantic slave trade were closely linked. The author asserts that antislavery and anti–slave trade discourses manifested themselves *concretely* in the rebellions, the creation of maroon villages, and "the appropriations and creative interpretations of hegemonic ideas by the enslaved." This analysis goes against the widely held notion that Africans did not challenge the institution of slavery.

Joseph E. Inikori presents the argument that political fragmentation facilitated the slave trade because small decentralized entities had difficulty protecting their members from capture and deportation. He notes that the European traders intervened in the political process to prevent the rise of the African centralized states that would have hampered their operations.

Using detailed data on slave ship voyages, David Richardson explores the unknown relationship of shipboard revolts to the structural characteristics of the slave trade and to the political economy of slavery within Africa. Richardson's study shows that reasons for the higher incidence of revolts aboard ships leaving from a particular region are to be found not in European management failure but in African political and social realities.

As an epilogue, Carolyn Brown describes an oral history project that seeks to document the ways that communities in the Biafran hinterland remember the slave trade. Some interviews show how involvement in the trade is called upon to explain present misfortunes and how enslavement was sometimes a reaction to social resistance by women. This project also reveals that memories of resistance play an important role in the consciousness of these communities.

As they were faced with a multidimensional assault, Africans tested various approaches to protect themselves from deportation and enslavement and to attack the slave trade. They sought immediate answers in situations of emergency and, at the same time, they devised long-term solutions, developed innovative plans, pondered difficult alternatives, and made choices that twenty-first-century hindsight may judge questionable. They succeeded and they failed, but all along they engaged in valiant and heroic acts to survive and stay free.

Notes

1. Estimates of the number of Africans deported and lost during the Middle Passage continue to produce controversy among scholars. Numbers proposed range from

about 12 million to 15.5 million. Curtin 1969, 1976; Eltis 1990, 2000; Eltis and Richardson 1997; Inikori 1976a,b, 1996; Inikori and Engerman 1992; Klein 1999; Lovejoy 1982, 1989; Richardson 1989; Eltis et al. 1999; Solow 2001.

2. For estimates on the numbers of Africans deported through the Saharan and Indian Ocean trades, see Austen 1979, 1989, 1992; Manning 1990.

3. In West Africa, people could be dispatched through the Atlantic or the Sahara, or be kept locally. In consequence, their strategies against displacement and enslavement applied to all the slave trades, not one in particular.

4. In 1785, M. de Lajaille saw, on one of Bissau's islands, one Constantine, a French sailor who had been enslaved for 28 years after his ship had been burnt down and the crew massacred.

5. For a tentative explanation of the reasons for this upsurge in violence against the slave trade, see David Richardson, this volume.

6. An account of the events published by Carl Bernhardt Wadström in *Essay on Colonization* presents a different story: "The buildings were all burnt, and the goods in them, amounting, it is said to the value of 12 or 1500 slaves (near 30,000 [pounds] ster.) were either destroyed or carried away" (88).

7. Indeed, as late as the 1920s, the U.S. Immigration service considered the Italians, the Jews and the Irish a separate, nonwhite race. For the formation of whiteness and integration into whiteness, see Roediger 1994, 1999; Ignatiev 1995.

8. For examples of these tales, see WPA 1986, 29, 76, 121, 145, 163, 164, 176, 184. For attempts at analyzing their meaning, see Piersen 1993, 35–52; Gomez 1998.

9. Research I conducted among West Africans in New York has revealed how widespread these accusations are. Many Africans believe that African Americans are expressing genuine feelings that reflect a deep wound, and although they generally reject the accusation, some showed understanding. However, others believe it is little more than a facade. People who resent the immigrants' success, they stress, or want to dissociate from the Africans because of the internalization of anti-African stereotypes use "you sold us" as a moral justification to their hostility, anti-immigrant feelings, or shame at being linked with Africa and the Africans. For discussion of this phenomenon, see Arthur, 2000, 83–85; Holtzman 2000, 15; Perry 1997, 250–51.

10. Also see the numerous testimonies gathered between 1789 and 1791 by the House of Commons in Lambert 1975–76.

11. For the reluctance to talk about the slave trade in Futa Jallon, see I. Barry 2001, 60–62.

Bibliography

Ajayi, J. F. Ade. 1967. "Samuel Ajayi Crowther of Oyo." In Philip D. Curtin, ed., *Africa Remembered: Narratives by West Africans From the Era of the Slave Trade.* Madison: University of Wisconsin Press.

Alagoa, E. J. 1986. "The Slave Trade in Niger Delta Oral Tradition and History." In Paul E. Lovejoy, ed., *Africans in Bondage: Studies in Slavery and the Slave Trade.* Madison: University of Wisconsin Press.

Alford, Terry. 1977. *Prince among Slaves: The True Story of an African Prince Sold into Slavery in the American South.* New York: Oxford University Press.

Arthur, John. 2000. *Invisible Sojourners: African Immigrant Diaspora in the United States.* Westport, Conn.: Praeger.

Atkins, John. 1970. *A Voyage to Guinea, Brazil, and the West Indies.* 1753. Reprint, London: Frank Cass.

Austen, Ralph A. 1979. "The Trans-Saharan Slave Trade: A Tentative Census." In Henry Gemery and Jan S. Hogendorn, eds., *The Uncommon Market: Essays in the Economic History of the Atlantic Slave Trade.* New York: Academic Press.

———. 1989. "The Nineteenth Century Islamic Slave Trade from East Africa (Swahili and Red Sea Coasts): A Tentative Census." In William Gervase Clarence-Smith, ed., *The Economics of the Indian Ocean Slave Trade in the Nineteenth Century.* Totowa, N.J.: Frank Cass.

———. 1992. "The Mediterranean Slave Trade out of Africa: A Tentative Census." *Slavery and Abolition* 13:214–48.

———. 1993. "The Moral Economy of Witchcraft: An Essay in Comparative History." In Jean Comaroff and John L. Comaroff, eds., *Modernity and Its Malcontents.* Chicago: University of Chicago Press.

———. 2001. "The Slave Trade as History and Memory: Confrontations of Slaving Voyage Documents and Communal Traditions." *William and Mary Quarterly* 58 (1): 229–44.

Barry, Boubacar. 1998. *Senegambia and the Atlantic Slave Trade.* Cambridge: Cambridge University Press.

Barry, Ismaël. 2001. "Le Fuuta-Jaloo (Guinée) et la traite négrière atlantique dans les traditions orales." In Djibril Tamsir Niane, ed., *Tradition orale et archives de la traite négrière.* Paris: UNESCO.

Baum, Robert M. 1999. *Shrines of the Slave Trade: Diola Religion and Society in Precolonial Senegambia.* New York: Oxford University Press.

Becker, Charles, and Victor Martin. 1982. "Kayor and Baol: Senegalese Kingdoms and the Slave Trade in the Eighteenth Century." In Joseph E. Inikori, ed., *Forced Migration: The Impact of the Export Slave Trade on African Societies.* London: Hutchinson University Library.

Blassingame, John W. 1977. *Slave Testimony: Two Centuries of Letters, Speeches, Interviews, and Autobiographies.* Baton Rouge: Louisiana State University Press.

Bosman, Willem. 1967. *A New and Accurate Description of the Coast of Guinea, divided into the Gold, the Slave, and the Ivory Coasts.* 1705. Reprint, London: Frank Cass.

Burton, Richard F. 1863. *Wanderings in West Africa from Liverpool to Fernando Po.* 2 vols. London: Tinsley Brothers.

Cadamosto, Elvise. 1937. *The Voyages of Cadamosto.* London: Hakluyt Society.

Conneau, Theophilus. 1976. *A Slaver's Log Book, or Twenty Years' Residence in Africa.* 1851. Reprint, Englewood Cliffs, N.J.: Prentice Hall.

Cugoano, Quobna Ottobah. 1999. *Thoughts and Sentiments on the Evil of Slavery and Other Writings.* 1787. Reprint, London: Penguin Books.

Curtin, Philip D. 1967a. "Ayuba Suleiman Diallo of Bondu." In Philip D. Curtin, ed., *Africa Remembered: Narratives by West Africans from the Era of the Slave Trade.* Madison: University of Wisconsin Press.

———. 1967b. "Joseph Wright of the Egba." In *Africa Remembered.*

———. 1969. *The Atlantic Slave Trade: A Census.* Madison: University of Wisconsin Press.

———. 1976. "Measuring the Atlantic Slave Trade Once Again: A Comment." *Journal of African History* 17:595–605.

Durand, Jean-Baptiste. 1807. *Voyage au Sénégal fait dans les années 1785 et 1786.* 2 vols. Paris: Dentu.

Eltis, David. 1990. "The Volume, Age/Sex Ratios and African Impact of the Slave Trade: Some Refinements of Paul Lovejoy's Review of the Literature." *Journal of African History* 31:485–92.

———. 2000. *The Rise of African Slavery in the Americas.* Cambridge: Cambridge University Press.

Eltis, David, and David Richardson, eds. 1997. *Routes to Slavery: Direction, Ethnicity, and Mortality in the Transatlantic Slave Trade.* Portland, Ore.: Frank Cass.

Eltis, David, Stephen D. Behrendt, David Richardson, and Herbert S. Klein, eds. 1999. *The Trans-Atlantic Slave Trade: A Database on CD-ROM.* Cambridge: Cambridge University Press.

Gates, Henry Louis, Jr. 2001. Preface to *William and Mary Quarterly* 58 (1): 3–5.

Gleave, M. B., and R. M. Prothero. 1971. "Population Density and 'Slave Raiding': A Comment." *Journal of African History* 12 (2): 320–21.

Gomes, Diogo. 1959. *De la première découverte de la Guinée.* Ed. T. Monot and R. Maury. Bissau: Centro de Estudos da Guiné Portuguesa.

Gomez, Michael A. 1998. *Exchanging our Country Marks: The Transformation of African Identities in the Colonial and Antebellum South.* Chapel Hill: University of North Carolina Press.

Griffin, Cyrus. 1828a. "Abduhl Rahahman's History." *African Repository,* May, 79.

———. 1828b. "The Unfortunate Moor." *African Repository,* February, 77–81.

Guèye, Mbaye. 1997. "Gorée dans la traite négrière." In Djibril Samb, ed., *Gorée et l'esclavage,* 32–35. Dakar: UCAD-IFAN.

———. 2001. "La tradition orale dans le domaine de la traite négrière." In Djibril Tamsir Niane, ed., *Tradition orale et archives de la traite négrière.* Paris: UNESCO.

Hall, Gwendolyn Midlo. 1992. *Africans in Colonial Louisiana: The Development of Afro-Creole Culture in the Eighteenth Century.* Baton Rouge: Louisiana State University Press.

Heuman, Gad, ed. 1986. *Out of the House of Bondage: Runaways, Resistance and Marronage in Africa and the New World.* London: Frank Cass.

Holtzman, Jon. 2000. *Nuer Journeys, Nuer Lives: Sudanese Refugees in Minnesota.* Needham Heights, Mass.: Allyn and Bacon.

Ignatiev, Noel. 1995. *How The Irish Became White.* New York: Routledge.

Inikori, Joseph E. 1976a. "Measuring the Atlantic Slave Trade: An Assessment of Curtin and Antsey." *Journal of African History* 17:197–223.

———. 1976b. "Measuring the Atlantic Slave Trade: A Rejoinder." *Journal of African History* 17:607–27.

———. 1996. "Measuring the Unmeasured Hazards of the Atlantic Slave Trade: Documents Relating to the British Trade." *Revue française d'histoire d'outre-mer* 83 (312): 53–92.

——— ed. 1982. *Forced Migration: The Impact of the Export Slave Trade on African Societies.* London: Hutchinson University Library.

Inikori, Joseph E., and Stanley L. Engerman, eds. 1992. *The Atlantic Slave Trade: Effects on Economies, Societies, and Peoples in Africa, the Americas, and Europe.* Durham: Duke University Press.

Iroko, Abiola Félix. 1988. "Cauris et esclaves en Afrique occidentale entre le quinzième et le dix-neuvième siècles." In Serge Daget, ed., *De la traite à l'esclavage,* vol. 1. Paris: Société Française d'Histoire d'Outre-Mer.

Jones, G. I. 1967. "Olaudah Equiano of the Niger Ibo." In Philip D. Curtin, ed., *Africa Remembered: Narratives by West Africans From the Era of the Slave Trade.* Madison: University of Wisconsin Press.

Kiyaga-Mulindwa, D. 1982. "Social and Demographic Changes in the Birim Valley, Southern Ghana, c. 1450 to c. 1800." *Journal of African History* 23:1.

Klein, Herbert S. 1999. *The Atlantic Slave Trade.* Cambridge: Cambridge University Press.

Lambert, Sheila. 1975–76. *House of Commons Sessional Papers of the Eighteenth Century.* Vols. 68–73. Wilmington, Del.: Scholarly Resources.

Law, Robin, and Paul E. Lovejoy, eds. 2001. *Biography of Mahommah G. Baquaqua.* Princeton: Markus Wiener.

Lefloche, Mamadou Camara. 2001. "Traditions orales, traitement occulte et domptage de l'esclave au Rio Pongo." In Djibril Tamsir Niane, ed., *Tradition orale et archives de la traite négrière.* Paris: UNESCO.

Lovejoy, Paul E. 1982. "The Volume of the Atlantic Slave Trade: A Synthesis. *Journal of African History* 23:473–501.

———. 1989. "The Impact of the Atlantic Slave Trade on Africa: A Review of the Literature." *Journal of African History* 30:365–94.

———. 2000. *Transformations in Slavery: A History of Slavery in Africa.* Cambridge: Cambridge University Press.

Manning, Patrick. 1990. *Slavery and African Life: Occidental, Oriental, and African Slave Trades.* Cambridge: Cambridge University Press.

Mason, Michael. 1969. "Population Density and 'Slave Raiding': The Case of the Middle Belt of Nigeria." *Journal of African History* 10:551 64

McGowan, Winston. 1990. "African Resistance to the Atlantic Slave Trade in West Africa." *Slavery and Abolition* 11 (1): 5–29.

Moore, Samuel. 1834. *Biography of Mahommah G. Baquaqua, a Native of Zoogoo in the Interior of Africa.* Detroit: Geo. E. Pomeroy.

Niane, Djibril Tamsir. 1997. "Africa's Understanding of the Slave Trade: Oral Accounts." *Diogenes* 45 (autumn): 75–90.

Nichols, Grace. 1990. *I Is a Long Memoried Woman.* London: Karnak House.

Omar Ibn Said. 2000. "The Life of Omar Ibn Said." Trans. Ala Alryyes. In Marc Shell and Werner Sollors, eds., *The Multilingual Anthology of American Literature.* New York: New York University Press.

Perry, Donna. 1997. "Rural Ideologies and Urban Imaginings: Wolof Immigrants in New York City." *Africa Today* 44:2.

Piersen, William D. 1993. *Black Legacy: America's Hidden Heritage.* Amherst: University of Massachusetts Press.

Pruneau de Pommegorge, Antoine. 1789. *Description de la nigritie.* Amsterdam: Maradan.

Rathbone, Richard. 1986. "Some Thoughts on Resistance to Enslavement in West Africa." In Gad Heuman, ed., *Out of the House of Bondage: Runaways, Resistance and Marronage in Africa and the New World.* London: Frank Cass.

Richardson, David. 1989. "Slave Exports from West Africa and West-Central Africa, 1700–1810: New Estimates of Volume and Distribution." *Journal of African History* 30:1–22.

Roediger, David. 1994. *Towards the Abolition of Whiteness: Essays on Race, Politics, and the Working Class.* New York: Verso.

———. 1999. *The Wages of Whiteness: Race and the Making of the American Working Class.* New York: Verso.

Rømer, Ludvig Ferdinand. 1989. *Le Golfe de Guinée, 1700–1750: Récit de L. F. Römer, marchand d'esclaves sur la côte ouest-africaine.* Trans. Mette Dige-Hesse. Paris: L'Harmattan.

Rozbicki, Michal J. 2001. "To Save Them from Themselves: Proposals to Enslave the British Poor, 1698–1755." *Slavery and Abolition* 22 (August): 29–50.

Said, Nicholas. 1873. *The Autobiography of Nicolas Said, a native of Bornu.* Memphis: Shotwell.

Shaw, Rosalind. 2002. *Memories of the Slave Trade: Ritual and the Historical Imagination in Sierra Leone.* Chicago: University of Chicago Press.

Smith, H. F. C., D. M. Last, and Gambo Gubio.1967. "Ali Eisami Gazirmabe of Bornu." In Philip D. Curtin, ed., *Africa Remembered: Narratives by West Africans From the Era of the Slave Trade.* Madison: University of Wisconsin Press.

Solow, Barbara. 2001. "The Transatlantic Slave Trade: A New Census." *William and Mary Quarterly* 58 (1): 9–16.

Thilmans, Guy. 1997. "Puits et captiveries à Gorée aux XVIIe et XVIIIe siècles." In Djibril Samb, ed., *Gorée et l'esclavage,* 107–20. Dakar: UCAD-IFAN.

United States. Department of State. 2002. *Trafficking in Persons Report.* <www.state.gov>.

Wadström, Carl Bernhard. 1794. "An Essay on Colonization Particularly Applied to the Western Coast of Africa with Some Free Thoughts on Cultivation and Commerce." London: Darton and Harvey.

Wax, Darold D. 1966. "Negro Resistance to the Early American Slave Trade." *Journal of Negro History* 51 (January): 1–15.

Wilks, Ivor. 1967. "Abu Bakr al-Siddiq of Timbuktu." In Philip D. Curtin, ed., *Africa Remembered: Narratives by West Africans From the Era of the Slave Trade.* Madison: University of Wisconsin Press.

WPA. Georgia Writer's Project, Savannah Unit. 1986. *Drums and Shadows: Survival Studies among the Georgia Coastal Negroes.* Athens: University of Georgia Press.

Zurara, Gomes Eanes de. 1960. "Chronique de Guinée." Trans. Léon Bourdon. *Mémoires de l'IFAN* 60.

Part I

Defensive Strategies

Chapter 1
Lacustrine Villages in South Benin as Refuges from the Slave Trade

Elisée Soumonni

The prominent role played by Dahomey (Benin) in the supply of captives for enslavement in the Americas is illustrated by the abundant literature on this old West African kingdom.[1] Ouidah (Whydah in the English documents), its port of trade, is a familiar name to students and scholars of the Atlantic slave trade. The extant literature however does not address several issues of Dahomey's involvement in the trade. The impact of the obnoxious traffic on the old kingdom and indeed on other contemporary sub-Saharan African polities is generally overlooked. Little attention, if any, is paid to the ways local populations resisted the slave trade and enslavement, thereby often giving the impression that any form of resistance began on board the slave ships or in the Americas.

Not much is known about the various forms of internal resistance to the traffic, thereby creating the assumption among many that captives surrendered like sacrificial lambs to their oppressors. By examining the primary form of resistance and protection provided by the nature of the environment, this chapter is an attempt at challenging such a view. The environment under consideration is made of a series of lacustrine villages in the southern region of the present-day Republic of Benin. Ganvié is the most important and the best known of these villages because of its exploitation as "one of the gems of the Republic of Benin's tourist and cultural heritage" (Zinsou 1994). Ganvié is also referred to as the Venice of Africa, extolled by Eustache Prudencio, the country's popular poet, in one of his famous poems.[2] But even the least attentive tourists visiting the site can easily understand from the guide's explanations that those living in the so-called Venice of Africa and other adjacent lacustrine villages were not attracted there in the early eighteenth century by the beauty of the landscape. The search for security in a period of violence and fear created by slave raiders and traders forced fleeing populations to seek a decent life in an environment that was then and still largely remains unattractive.

THE COUNTRY OF "THE MEN ON WATER"

During the era of the transatlantic slave trade, Lake Nokoué and the swamplands surrounding it provided an ideal refuge for various migrants who came to constitute a homogenous ethnic group, that of the Tofinu (see Bourgoignie 1972). This major historical factor in the establishment and relocation of villages in the area, though acknowledged, is yet to be the focus of investigation. In contrast, the physical environment in which various and successive generations of migrants settled, their social organization, and their economic activities have been the subject of significant research. The starting point and focus of these studies are generally the ecological dimension of human settlements. Geographers, botanists, geologists, and archaeologists, in an ethnographic perspective, have made outstanding contributions to our knowledge of what I shall call Tofinuland (see, for example, Pélissier 1963; Mondjannagni 1969; Paradis 1975; Barbier 1978; Pétrequin and Pétrequin 1984).

Tofinuland, the country of the Tofinu, is part of the lagoon system created along the entire Bight of Benin through the deposit of sand by the eastward-moving coastal current. It is located in the lower zone of the So River, a branch of the delta built up by the Weme (Ouémé), the most important river of Benin, about forty kilometers from the coast. While the So flows into Lake Nokoué, most of the delta waters flow into the lagoon of Porto Novo and, through a natural channel, into that of Lagos. Tofinuland is in an amphibian environment prone to flooding by the swelling So and Weme Rivers, as well as Lake Nokoué and the lagoon of Porto Novo. Indeed, floods, a characteristic feature of Tofinuland, have been used as a classification criterion of its villages:

- villages with cultivable lands because they are not often flooded: Gbessou-Gbegome

- villages regularly flooded, with poor lands for subsistence agriculture during a few months: Kinto, Zoungome, Ahome Lokpo, Ahome Oume, Ahome Gblon, So-Ava, Dekame Pave, Ouedo Aguekon, Vekky;
- villages entirely lacustrine: Ganvie, So Tchanhoue, So Zounko, Ouedo Gbadji. (Bourgoignie 1972, 33)

Access to these various localities, whether partially or entirely lacustrine, is difficult. The same goes for conditions of life. Canoe is the only means of transportation from village to village and even from door to door within the same village. Fishing is virtually the only viable economic activity. How do thousands of dwellers (70,000, of which 25,000 live in Ganvié alone, according to the 1992 census) manage to survive is one of the questions that have puzzled researchers in development studies over the last four decades. In this quest, areas of attention include fishing activities and techniques, habitat, social organization, ethnic and cultural identity, sanitation, and education.

The Tofinu are closely associated with fishing. Most fishing is carried out from two-man canoes, with one man propelling the craft and the other casting the net, a picture that has become a cliché of tourist advertising agencies. But the most-studied Tofinu technique of catching fish is undoubtedly that employing *akadjas*, refuges consisting of branches forced into the mud. The fish grow inside these refuges, which are harvested periodically by surrounding them with nets, pulling out the branches, and capturing the fish. As a result of the ever growing importance of this technique, fishing grounds, like land, became valuable properties over which contentions could degenerate into violent clashes. Drying, smoking, and selling the fish is the business of the Tofinu women. The Tofinu have also designed an original habitat, *habitat palafitte.* They live in homes built on stilts at the edge of the lake or in the lake waters, planned in such a way as to accommodate both human beings and animals, the latter moving from the bottom level to the top floor during a flood, while the former remain in the middle.

History is generally called upon to explain the evolution of the natural environment and political and socioeconomic institutions. But the reference to historical factors generally remains vague or superficial. A notable exception is the research of Canadian ethnosociologist Georges Edouard Bourgoignie, which integrates the historical dimension in a comprehensive study of Tofinu society. After nine months on the field among the men on water as well as several long interviews and discussions with them, Bourgoignie realized how inseparable history was from the way their society is structured and continues to function. However, his focus was not on the history of the Tofinu within the general context of violence created by the transatlantic slave trade, on the ways they reacted to and protected themselves against the slave trade and enslavement. Of course, Bourgoignie cannot be blamed for this shortcoming since his study is basically ethnosociological in its objective and perspective. In this respect, a history of the Tofinu, in the era of the transatlantic slave trade remains to be written. What is being attempted here, on the basis of my own investigations in Ganvié and of published works on the Slave Coast can be seen as a very modest contribution in this direction.[3]

The Historical Context

Oral tradition is a vital source for the reconstruction of the historical experience of the various migrants to the Lake Nokoué area during the transatlantic slave trade. It is however difficult to make proper use of the information collected without some degree of familiarity with the extant literature on the geopolitical setting of the Slave Coast of West Africa. It is indeed difficult to ask informants relevant questions on the issue of local resistance to the slave trade and enslavement, to cross-check contradictory or misleading statements, to correct obvious errors, and to arrive at a relative chronology of remembered major events. Although the same stories are told with significant different details, it is easy to identify the same underlining factors at the origins of major events. Similarly, ethnonymy and toponymy are often a digest of a historical process. That seems to be the case with many Tofinu place and personal names. The meaning of the names Tofinu and Ganvié is still a matter of controversy among specialists of the area (see Bourgoignie 1972; Iroko 1998). This is not the place to go into the details of semantic arguments resorted to in the controversy, but a consensus of sorts seems to have emerged. With respect to Tofinu, it is reflected in Bourgoignie's title: *Les hommes de l'eau* (The men on water). As for Ganvié, its widely accepted meaning is "safe at last." Most oral traditions collected from local populations seem to confirm this generally agreed upon meaning. They are also consistent with the outline of the geopolitical history of the Slave Coast. Any meaningful reconstruction of the process that led to the establishment, peopling, and development of the Nokoué lacustrine village complex must therefore be conceived from this wider perspective. The various stories of migrations to the area only make sense within the framework of the Bight of Benin in the era of the transatlantic slave trade.

The Tofinu traditionally trace the origin of their migrations to Tado, cradle and departure center of Aja ethnic groups to various destinations. According to the prevalent tradition, the earliest migration from Tado, led by Agasu, resulted in the establishment of the related kingdoms of Sahe (Savi, Ouidah), Allada, Abomey, and Hogbonou (Ajase, Porto Novo). Though it is imprudent to suggest a reliable chronology, it is generally assumed that the migration of the Tofinu—who started establishing themselves as refugees in the area of Lake Nokoué by the end of the seventeenth century—occurred later, probably a century or so after the Agasu-led movement. Despite the present state of our knowledge of the various aspects of these migrations, two facts appear clearly from the general picture. First, the core of the refugees, who moved to the lake area by successive stages, was made of the Aja-Tado cultural group. Tofingbe, the Tofinu language, is closely related to the Aja-Fon family (Hazoumé 1981). Second, the search for security took place within the context of violence and fear associated with the ongoing slave trade in Ouidah, Allada, and Abomey. This violence escalated with the conquest, by Dahomey, of Allada in 1724 and Ouidah in 1727, and forced more groups, including non-Aja, to move to the lacustrine area in order to escape slave raiders and enslavement. The trend was to continue nearly two centuries, since Dahomey remained committed to slave-catching activities till the end of the nineteenth century. And during this long period, the Aja peoples provided the great majority of the captives for enslavement in the Americas, notably through raids by Dahomey on its neighbors. The conquests of Allada and Ouidah were particularly brutal. That of Allada was followed by the capture in 1732 of Jakin, with over four thousand of its inhabitants taken captive. Many more were subjected to the same fate during the sack of Savi, capital of the old kingdom of Ouidah.

In the heart of a region disrupted by such an outbreak of violence, as rightly pointed out by Georges Edouard Bourgoignie, "The Tofinu country was to provide an ideal refuge. Its villages, established in the swamp of the So River, or even in Lake Nokoué waters, could serve as a sanctuary to those who took to flight to survive.[4]

Tofinu's Defensive Strategies

Oral traditions of the various villages, despite their inherent confusions, contradictions, and vague chronological framework are consistent with the historical background of the successive migrations to the area. They also show that concern for security and defense was the determining factor in the location and relocation of villages by refugees. For the Tofinu, the So River and its marshland constituted a natural barrier against Abomey's armies, who were unfamiliar with such an environment. But a village can become easily accessible and exposed to danger when the marshland dries up. In such a situation, the natural protection against external aggression is no longer guaranteed and the village must be relocated. Most of the villages established on the right bank of the So River were affected by this phenomenon. The move to relocate a village on the very waters of Lake Nokoué was determined by pressing danger. Thus, Ganvié and So-Tchanhoué were born out of the abandonment of the villages of Sindomè and Sadjo, respectively. The old sites continue to serve today as cemeteries for the new ones.

The reaction of the Tofinu to impending danger or actual aggression was not, however, limited to relocating their villages. Before resorting to this solution, they faced the danger and responded to it with the means at their disposal. The story of Ganvié is worth considering in this respect, as it is illustrative of the general trend of the lacustrine refuge-villages of southern Benin.

The foundation of Ganvié, the lacustrine metropolis of the Bight of Benin, was the last stage of the migration from Tado of two rival Aja groups. According to tradition, the Dakoménu and the Sokoménu, for reasons that remain unclear but not unconnected with factional disputes, left Tado during approximately the same period. They found themselves in the territory of the king of Allada, who apparently failed to reconcile them. It is worth noting that the kingdom of Allada itself was on the eve of its collapse under the advancing army of Agaja. The decision of the Dakoménu and the Sokoménu to proceed to a more secure environment might be connected with this impending danger. In the process, they found themselves under the protection of Agué Gbénu, chief of Sindomè, an island of the So delta. There, they were forced to coexist and cooperate. The growth of Sindomè, however, not only generated jealousy and hostility from neighboring villages, such as So-Ava, but drew the attention of Abomey to the site. A canoe loaded with soldiers was sent to take captives for the Atlantic slave trade. But the refugees took advantage of the raiders' inexperience and overturned their canoe. The incident proved that the natural protection of the island was inadequate. So, the tradition goes, the Dakoménu and Sokoménu decided to relocate their village, the present-day Ganvié, on Lake Nokoué's waters, very likely in the aftermath of the conquest of Allada. Sindomè became Ganvié's cemetery. The very spot where the canoe of Agaja's men sank is considered sacred, while Finondè, the Tofinu passenger—perhaps kidnapped as a guide—of the canoe who provoked the disaster to save his people, has been made a god. His cult is said to be the most important today in Ganvié.

The two major wards of the new city are known as Dakoménu and Sokoménu. Though both groups give a slightly different version of the legend in order to emphasize their specific role and position in society, the story, I believe, cannot be dismissed as a pure fabrication. The movement of a growing number of refugees toward Lake Nokoué was undoubtedly a reflection of increasing pressure from slave raiders during the eighteenth century. The new location could rightly be seen as more secure in view of the well-known fact that Abomey's soldiers were unfamiliar with canoes and were poor swimmers. Details of the Sindomè incident, recorded in different versions of local traditions, confirm this interpretation. Much more remains to be known on this episode of Ganvié's history and on Sindomè settlement itself. Remnants of a significant human occupation—pieces of pottery and broken bottles—are visible on the ground and archaeological investigations on the site are likely to yield interesting results.

The cohesive nature of the society of the various lacustrine villages was another dimension of their defensive strategies. The "conscious mixing" of the various ethnic groups that took refuge in the lacustrine area does suggest a positive reaction against the pervasive effect of the slave trade on their neighborhood.[5] If the core of the refugees consisted of the Aja-related ethnic groups of the Tofinu, the latter were joined by refugees of other ethnic groups, namely the Yoruba and the Nupe, better known in southern Dahomey as the Tapa. The Yoruba elements in Tofinu society, illustrated by the prominence of the deity Shango, is a reflection of another important geopolitical dimension of the Lake Nokoué area, subjected in its northern part to the influences and pressure of the slave trading polities of Oyo and Porto Novo. The Tofinu's relationships with the two polities were also conflicted. Clashes resulted in the influx into Tofinuland of refugees from the Yoruba, Nupe, and Gun. The social status of these new refugees is a matter of debate. It has been argued by A. Félix Iroko, on the basis of oral evidence, that unlike the Aja-Tofinu, the refugees could not be regarded as free men. In fact, the argument goes, the influx of Yoruba elements resulted from the military expeditions of the kings of Porto Novo into Nigerian Yorubaland with the participation of the Tofinu. In other words, the Yoruba of Ganvié were initially brought there as captives, intended to be sold. As for the Nupe, they were introduced in Ganvié in the mid-nineteenth century by a Yoruba slave trader named Koklokuku (dead chicken) (Iroko 1998, 75–76).

I got quite different information about the slave trade and slavery in Ganvié and its environs on several occasions.[6] My informants confirmed that the refugees included captives and probably already enslaved elements.[7] They also claimed that Ganvié's inhabitants from time to time mounted expeditions to kidnap women from the nearby mainland because they were needed, not as slaves, but as wives.[8] Once in Ganvié, newcomers became free (if they were not so before their arrival), and nobody was permitted to come in and take them away for the purpose of selling or enslaving them. This version of oral tradition seems to me consistent with Iroko's own assertion of a "conscious mixing" of different ethnic groups, to the point of considering themselves to be "the same and unique Tofinu people," within such a relatively short period. Can one really imagine such a process in a society of masters and slaves? The most striking feature of the Tofinu experience is undoubtedly the emergence of a coherent and homogenous society, a consequence to be credited to both the nature of the environment and the fear of permanent external aggression. The defensive and protective system built up by the lacustrine communities took into account these two basic factors. Their skill as canoeists dissuaded Dahomean armies, unfamiliar with the use of canoes, from repeated attacks.[9] They were also renowned for their expertise in naval warfare. Their weapons, according to Georges Edouard Bourgoignie, were varied and efficient: "They consisted of javelin launchers, sledgehammers, swords, harpoons, and locally made and imported guns. They also had a particularly ingenious kind of Molotov cocktail" (Bourgoignie 1972, 92). Dahomean armies and slave raiders were not, however, the only targets of the Tofinu weapons. Minor incidents among rival villages could develop into large-scale clashes. Captives could be made in the process, and female prisoners might become wives, but not slaves of the victorious men.

Gods were also associated with the defensive system of the Tofinu against close or distant enemies. Most, if not all, the deities of the various ethnic groups were integrated into their pantheon. Thus, the cult of the Yoruba deity Shango is one of the most popular traditional religions in Ganvié.

Because of the peculiarity of their environment, the Tofinu are credited with what has been termed an "ecological personality par excellence" (Bourgoignie 1972, 353), characterized by a remarkable adaptation to the lacustrine milieu they live in. Such a view tends to downplay the determining historical factor in the development of their strategies of defense against a pervasive danger. A long-term perspective is needed in the assessment of what has been called lacustrine heritage. Without such a perspective, it would be difficult not only to properly grasp the psychology and personality of the Tofinu but also to design and implement a coherent development project for these populations, which, in many respects, can still be regarded as refugees.

The Legacy of a Traumatic Experience

The claim that the "past and the present of the lacustrine villages and societies are safeguarded, only the future remains to be ensured" is questionable (Bourgoignie 1972, 361). The basic question of their survival is not just one of the retention of these villages but, more important, of the memory they represent. In this respect, the past is not safeguarded because it still remains insufficiently known. It needs therefore to be studied in its various aspects and, more important, in the context of the transatlantic slave trade, a significant factor in the history of population movements and displacements in precolonial Dahomey. If the role of this refuge zone in the struggle against the slave trade and enslavement was well documented, it would be possible to integrate this historical dimension into present and future plans for its development. Ganvié, in this perspective, cannot be the sole beneficiary of such plans, but its population should profit if the whole environment were perceived as a memorial to the slave trade. But the present is not safeguarded if the past is preserved as a museum piece. The celebrated adaptation of the Tofinu to their environment, illustrated by their fish-farming techniques and their architecture, calls for reconsideration in view of the recent demographic explosion and the disturbing deterioration of the conditions of daily life. It is no longer certain that natural resources, in spite of the ingenuity of the techniques of their exploitation, can sustain the ever growing population. Already, petroleum products smuggled from Nigeria through the waterway are fast becoming the major economic opportunity for Ganvié, to the detriment of the ecology. What then is the prospect for the future?

The nearly tragic situation of the lacustrine populations can only be grasped in a historical perspective. From the end of the seventeenth century to the 1880s, the delta of the lower So and the shores of Lake Nokoué were a refuge for various groups in search of security in a geopolitically turbulent environment. As a result, while developing manifold relationships among themselves within the amphibian milieu, refugees lived isolated from and in fear of the outside world, depending on a subsistence economy compatible with ecological equilibrium. No serious attempts have been made to put an end to this isolation in the interest of the concerned populations. The opening, in 1885, of the channel of Cotonou as a permanent outlet for Lake Nokoué to the sea ushered in an era of difficult times for the survival of the Tofinu. As a result of the salt brought to the lake waters, drinkable water became a rare commodity. Thus started, for Tofinu women, the lucrative business of fetching and selling water. The interest of the colonial administration in the area was motivated by administrative considerations and more particularly the collection of taxes, usually carried out by armed agents. Little wonder then that the lower So region, as admitted by the colonial administrator in charge, continued to be dominated by fear.[10]

The postcolonial administration did little, if anything, to address the situation, resorting to the same confrontational strategy in dealing with the local populations. The poor state of the service roads to mainland villages, the failure to dredge channels for easy transportation by canoe from one lacustrine village to the other, and the absence of telephone communications, have contributed to maintaining, indeed institutionalizing, their isolation. Despite official slogans touting the need to develop the tourism potential of the region, public opinion is unaware of the lacustrine phenomenon, and the Tofinu feel neglected or abandoned. This feeling is fueled by the drastic drop in the fishermen's catch from Lake Nokoué, the lack of schools and health infrastructures, and the growing insecurity and frequency of thefts. As a result, the Tofinu find no justification for paying taxes, the collection of which remains as difficult as during the colonial administration. Today, the area probably has the highest rate of infant mortality in Benin, estimated at 16.6 percent. Hardly one child out of two reaches the age of ten. How can one believe the poet who extols the "quiet life" of the people of Ganvié, "the happiest men in the world" (Prudencio 1969)?

These observations on the present condition of the men on water is only in appearance a digression from their history as refugees. Indeed, their present condition was the starting point of investigations into their past. Besides, the ever growing interest in the study of the transatlantic slave trade is not unconnected with its lasting impact. In this context, it is not improper to consider the present state of the lacustrine villages of Lake Nokoué as a reflection of their resistance against the slave trade and enslavement. This historical background is being buried by the official policy aimed at turning the area and its community into a tourist attraction for foreign visitors. It would be a pity if the descendants of the refugees who survived the trials of the era of the slave trade were allowed to slowly but surely die, isolated in their historical refuge.

Notes

In its present form, this essay was written at the University of Hull, Faculty of Social Sciences, where I was a Leverhulme Visiting Research Fellow from January to September 2001. The facilities I enjoyed in this position are hereby gratefully acknowledged. I was lucky in my field investigations to be guided by reliable indigenous resource persons, some of them performing important traditional or modern functions (or both). This was the case with Dorothée Ahissou, a native of Ganvié, a trained secondary school teacher, a former district officer of So-Awa, and now the current king of Ganvié (under the name Houéton Zimbè Alodiga—"darkness disappears when lights appears"). During our discussions, King Alodiga was assisted by members of his court, notably the griot, Zannou Ehouè, regarded as the living custodian of Tofinu's traditions. Of particular help was Onishango, the priest of Shango, on the significance of the various deities of the lacustrine region and the protection to the populations they were credited with in times of danger.

1. On the limitations of written materials for the study of precolonial Dahomey, see Soumonni 1997.

2. The following excerpt is worth quoting:

> The Adriatic has its Venice and its gondolas,
> The Atlantic has its Ganvié, so much envied.
> I will praise you everywhere, Ganvié,
> Venice of my country, you will soon be
> The center of the world, and men from all horizons
> Will be dying to come and dream on your waters,
> Around your magic and haughty huts,
> Amid your slender and light canoes.

3. The bibliography of the Slave Coast is so abundant that even a selection cannot be attempted within the scope of the present study. A few references particularly useful to this essay are Law 1989, 1991, 1997; Akinjogbin 1967; and Manning 1982.

4. For the conquests of Allada and Ouidah, see Bourgoignie 1972, 53; Law 1991, 278–300.

5. Iroko explains this conscious mixing as "the shared concern for a homogenous and coherent group in view of ecological constraints." However, the fear of a common danger was also an important, if not the most important, factor in this process of social integration.

6. The existence of a slave market in nearby Abomey-Calavi makes the issue of a possible involvement of Ganvié and other lacustrine villages in slave trading activities not entirely irrelevant. My research assistant, Gérard Tognimasso, and I kept asking questions about this hypothesis during the interviews recorded in Ganvié.

7. January 28, 2001.

8. A current tradition of customary marriage among the Aja-Tofinu-related ethnic groups, whereby the bridegroom "kidnaps" the bride at night, is probably reminiscent of such expeditions.

9. Robin Law points out how hinterland states, employing land-based forces and unfamiliar with the use of canoes, found it difficult to penetrate the coastal lagoons. *Slave Coast,* 20–21.

10. Administrator Komoroski to governor of Porto Novo, 6 September 1913; quoted in Bourgoignie 1972, 145.

BIBLIOGRAPHY

Akinjogbin, I. A. 1967. *Dahomey and Its Neighbours, 1708–1818.* London: Cambridge University Press.

Barbier, Jean Eude. 1978. "Sédimentologique de la lagune de Porto Novo (République Populaire du Bénin)." Doctoral dissertation, Université de Bordeaux.

Bourgoignie, Edouard G. 1972. *Les hommes de l'eau: Ethno-ecologie du Dahomey lacustre.* Paris: Editions Universitaires.

Hazoumé, M. L. 1981. "Une esquisse phonologique du 'Tofingbe,'" Paper prepared for the Commission Nationale de Linguistique, Cotonou, June.

Iroko, A. Félix. 1998. *Mosaiques d'histoire béninoise.* Tulle: Editions Corrèze Buissonnière.

Law, Robin. 1989. "Between the Sea and the Lagoon: The Interaction of Maritime and Inland Navigation on the Pre-Colonial Slave Coast." *Cahiers d'etudes africaines* 29:209–37.

———. 1991. *The Slave Coast of West Africa.* Oxford: Clarendon Press.

———. 1997. *The Kingdom of Allada.* Leiden University.

Manning, Patrick. 1982. *Slavery, Colonialism, and Economic Growth in Dahomey, 1640–1960.* Cambridge: Cambridge University Press.

Mondjannagni, Alfred. 1969. "Contribution à l'étude des paysages végétaux du Bas Dahomey." *Annales de l'Université d'Abidjan* (series G) 1, 2.

Oké, Finagnon Mathias. 1969. "Notice sur les villages lacustres du Dahomey." *Etudes dahoméennes* (new series) 13 (June).

Paradis, G. 1975. "Observations sur les forêts marécageuses du Bas-Dahomey: Localisation, principaux types, évolution au cours du quaternaire récent." *Annales de l'Université d'Abidjan* (series E) 8, 1.

Pélissier, Paul. 1963. *Les pays du Bas Ouéme: Une région témoin du Dahomey méridional.* Dakar: Faculté des Lettres et Sciences Humaines.

Pétrequin, Anne-Marie, and Pierre Pétrequin. 1984. *Habitat lacustre du Bénin: Une étude ethno-archéologique.* Paris: Editions Recherches sur les Civilisations.

Prudencio, Eustache. 1969. *Violence de la Race: Poèmes.* Cotonou: Editions ABM.

Soumonni, Elisée. 1997. "The Neglected Source Material for Studying the Slave Trade in Dahomey." In Robin Law, ed., *Source Material for Studying the Slave Trade and the African Diaspora.* Stirling: Centre of Commonwealth Studies.

Zinsou, Edgar Oriki. 1994. "Ganvié: Un example de cité-refuge." In Elisée Soumonni, Bellanmin Codo, and Joseph Adande, eds., *Le Bénin et la route de l'esclave.* Cotonou: ONEPI.

Chapter 2

Slave-Raiding and Defensive Systems South of Lake Chad from the Sixteenth to the Nineteenth Century

Thierno Mouctar Bah

Between the sixteenth century and the close of the nineteenth, the outskirts of Lake Chad were characterized by long-standing violence. This situation was due to the polities of central Sudan, situated at the crossroads of important trade routes across the Sahara, which led violent conquests and slave raids. It was particularly the case of the Bornu Empire, the kingdom of Bagirmi, and the Fulani emirate of Adamawa. After a long economic crisis and internal conflicts, a new era opened for Bornu during the reign of Mai Ali Gaji (1470–1503). The new era was characterized by the building of a new capital, Birni Ngazargamu, protected by strong fortifications. Yet it was under Idris Alaoma that Bornu turned itself into a political, economic, and military power. His first twelve years were characterized by the intensification of the slave trade, in connection with the numerous military campaigns he led near the outskirts of Lake Chad and beyond, to Mount Mandara.[1] Bornu's military supremacy was essentially based on the use of cavalry and firearms supplied by the Ottoman Empire, in exchange for cohorts of slaves driven through the Sahara. Bagirmi, located on the west bank of the Chari River, had consistently shown its intention to be politically autonomous from its two powerful neighbors, Bornu and Ouadday. The quest for and the supply of slaves were a major preoccupation in Bagirmi (Deschamps 1971, 168).

As soon as news of the jihad launched by Usman dan Fodio reached the Fulani emirate of Adamawa, several leaders left for Sokoto. There, dan Fodio appointed Modibbo Adama lieutenant. He was invested with full authority in 1809 and received the banner of the jihad with orders to spread Islam all over Fombinaland.[2] Adama established a strong army and drew his inspiration from the tactics, strategy, and armaments of Bornu. Instructors came from the Maghreb and the Ottoman Empire to drill some units (Bah 1982). The spearhead was undoubtedly the cavalry, with cuirassed horses and coats of mail. Led by Modibbo Adama and his successors, military campaigns intensified. From the mid-nineteenth century, the Fulani were the masters of a large geographical area that stretched from the outskirts of Lake Chad to the edge of the equatorial forest. This territory became an emirate and was given the name Adamawa. Throughout the nineteenth century, it was characterized by the intensification of the slave raids. Man hunts were led within the framework of great expeditions that benefited from rapid intervention made possible by the horse. Adamawa became the largest supplier of slaves to Sokoto (Burnham 1995, 168).

For four centuries the Bornu, Bagirmi, and Adamawa states, equipped with a strong military arsenal (horses, cuirasses, and muskets) fostered violence on the outskirts of Lake Chad and organized raids to acquire captives drawn from the decentralized populations handicapped by their division. War had a serious impact not only on the environment but on human habitats because the raided populations became obsessed with defense (Bah 1976, 5). The quest for security was the decisive factor in the choice of settlement. Habitats themselves were made more secure by a defense-oriented architecture. This chapter examines the various refuge sites and defense mechanisms that enabled several communities to protect themselves against the slave raids and to preserve their freedom and identity, in an often hostile environment.

Mountain Ranges

Mountains were ideal places for the populations to resist the Islamic states of the Sudan, whose main weapon was the horse; and similar groups are found all along the mountainous diagonal, behind the forest zone, from the heights of northern Togo to the Nuba Mountains in the Sudan through central Nigeria and northern Cameroon (Planhol 1968, 319–20). In northern Cameroon the ruins of several villages show the dramatic impact of the invasions and the significant modification in the occupation of space through the change in village sites: vertically, when inhabitants perched themselves on mountain heights; horizontally, when they fell back on a crest. This topographical discrimination is a reflection of the hostility that characterized the border separating two antagonistic entities: on the one hand, Kanem, Bornu, Mandara, and Adamawa, which had a firm policy of expansionism, and on the other, the paleonigritic populations, also called Kirdi, which formerly lived in the plains and now settled in successive waves in mountainous areas that were an impassable barrier to the dreaded cavalry.[3] Several heterogeneous populations, anxious to preserve their cultural identity and to shelter their tutelary gods, congregated in this mountainous zone, characterized by the narrowness of its spaces. Thus, peoples from the east sought refuge along the routes that make up the present Matakamland. They settled on steep mountains, where they used caves as their last refuge; from there it was easy to watch over the lowlands and incoming paths and ward off any warlike maneuver (Podlewski 1961, 13).

Similarly the Kongle region has served as a "sorting centre" from which families from the northern and western plains settled in the various hilly regions overlooking the Poli cirque (Mohammadou n.d., 11). As for the Mofou, pressure from the Fulani pushed them to seek an inaccessible refuge in the hills of Mikiri, then of Durumi (Mohammadou 1975). The Toupouri fled into the Tekem Mountains, in Chad, where they resisted by throwing stones at the enemy. This mountain range is made of twelve low summits, where each of the twelve Toupouri clans settled. Due probably to their role in the survival of the group and as receptacles for ancestral religions, the mountains are sacred and are worshipped as the Sô-doré. Every year, the chief of the mountain, the Wangdawa, or Wangdare, celebrates a ritual called the Masereo in its honor. Farther north, the Mandara Mountains have attracted many different populations. Their use as a valuable refuge site certainly accounts for the fact that the Wandala kingdom succeeded in preserving its autonomy. When Bornu attacked it, the sovereign of Wandala, May Bladi, consulted his council on the attitude to take. Some of the councilors believed, "Wandala is strong enough to face Bornu's armies, to fight them, and to protect our land and our wives from their reach and, finally, to make them turn back." But the majority expressed a contrary view: "We are not able to withstand the strength of Bornu. Let us get ready to go back to our mountains, because they are a secure refuge, with rivers that never dry up. Nobody will drive us out of these high mountains; on the contrary, it will be easy for us to repel any assailant by throwing a shower of rocks at them" (Adala n.d., 2).[4] Further south, the Fulani conquest caused part of the Duru to create a strong concentration point, stretching from the Adamawa cliffs to the north of the Mbang mountain range. Duru villages are generally located on small hill chains or on the back slopes of hills where the habitat is scattered along rocky peaks.

Therefore, it seems that for a long time the environment was used for safeguarding the populations fleeing slave raids (Planhol 1968). The chronological sequences of this phenomenon are historically established. The sixteenth century witnessed a turning point in the Bornu emperor's—Idris Alaoma (1564–1596)—warring activities. Several populations that used to live on the plain took refuge in mountain ranges. The phenomenon increased in the seventeenth and eighteenth centuries, with Mount Mandara becoming a refuge. The nineteenth century, marked by the Fulani jihad, witnessed a large-scale withdrawal of the Kirdi from the plains to mountain refuges.[5] It is symptomatic that with the colonial conquest and the end of the slave raids by the late nineteenth century, several communities who felt safer settled on piedmonts and again right on the plain. Thus, the quasi-endemic violence, which raged over centuries around the southern part of Lake Chad, had a significant impact on settlement patterns and the mapping out of the geographical space for defense purposes.

Caverns, Caves, and Refuge under Rocks

On the southern outskirts of the Lake Chad region, numerous shelters under rocks and in caverns and caves have been occupied more or less continuously since the Neolithic era by several human communities. These structures were located on cliffs or hill slopes, which made access more difficult. They were a natural defense that could be strengthened with stone walls if necessary (Bah 1976, 4). Among the Mofou of northern Cameroon, the caverns (*daldam*) that dot the mountains have served as a strategic retreat in the face of a more militarily powerful enemy. The largest caverns were used as food warehouses and for sheltering the cattle. They were impregnable, and the populations that had found refuge in them could peacefully wait for the weary assailants to turn back (Marchesseau 1945).

In Mount Jim is a typical cave that served as a refuge. There, the Nyem-Nyem entrenched themselves to escape the raids that raged on the Adamawa plateau in the eighteenth and nineteenth centuries.[6] These raids were first conducted by the Baare-Chamba, then by the Fulani Lamidat of Ngaoundere (Mohammadou 2001). The disruptive movement that caused the departure of the Baare-Chamba from the Upper Benue was linked to a climate fluctuation that affected the central African savanna in the eighteenth century and was especially severe from 1738 to 1762. Hunger due to long periods of drought led to a significant migration of many communities (Nicholson 1981, 260). It was within that context that the Baare-Chamba, riding ponies, indulged in man-hunting across a large territory, south of Benue, on the Adamawa Plateau and right on the edge of the forest. Through armed violence, the Baare-Chamba significantly upset the ethnodemographic map as well as the environment in central Cameroon. Their rides brought them closer to the Atlantic and they were active participants in the slave trade that flourished in the harbors of Douala and the Bimbia River.

The Nyem-Nyem, who probably came from Lake Chad, experienced several migrations that took them south into the Benue valley, then onto the Adamawa plateau, where they have occupied three different mountainous sites, during the eighteenth and twentieth centuries (see Fofou Mama 1994). The most impressive of these is the rocky Mount Jim, in the mountains of Galim, in western Ngaoundere, which contains endless caves. The main lookout point, at the highest point of the mountain (1,300 meters), can be seen from a distance. Secondary watch points are set around the main one. At the foot of the mountain is a small valley where the Nyem-Nyem grow millet and maize as provisions in case of siege. Near the farms, in the foothills, is a cattle ranch, stocked essentially from raids made on the people on the plains.

On the mountain an esplanade with a series of polished and hewn stones testifies to an early occupation. The Nong, a big, flat stone on which the Nyem-Nyem poisoned their arrows, is located there. Under a rocky shelter, in an area delineated by a series of stones, the Nyem-Nyem hold a big council, each clan head sitting on a stone seat (Fofou Mama 1994, 4). From the esplanade there is direct access to the caves that stretch for about twenty kilometers. The Nyem-Nyem set up new social structures there, with each of several clans in a different quarter. In case of alarm, people were rallied by the *year,* a gong whose sound was easily decoded by the members of the community. At the entrance to the caves, are two round holes with a radius of about a meter; oral accounts hold that they were the resting place of two mysterious stones, one male and one female, whose role was probably magical and religious. It is believed that the stones used to roll down to "bathe" in the two holes lower down. Whoever encountered them was sure to live longer, to be rich, to be protected from evil sprits, or to be cured of illness or barrenness (Adala n.d., 2).

In case of danger and in order to buy food, the Nyem-Nyem used to travel through an underground tunnel to Gadjivan, whose inhabitants were not hostile. The grain they purchased from them was then kept in two earthen granaries, one of which is still intact. Next to it lies a big maize-grinding stone. In the Jim caves, water flows abundantly from two perpetual springs, one of which was reserved for the chief. The caves of Mount Jim have played a decisive role for the survival of the Nyem-Nyem as a people and in the sheltering of their tutelary gods.

Mount Jim is considered holy and since the beginning of the twentieth century the Nyem-Nyem have worshipped it through the Mvoudwin, an annual festival that recalls ancient cosmogonic myths. The ceremony is led by the chief of the community, whom the Nyem-Nyem identify with the sun, called Tà-Ligh'i. The annual ritual is performed at a propitious time before the sowing of crops. It is conducted by the Master of the Mountain (Naw Ndwi). He collects a quantity of millet from each clan chief and from that beer is brewed for the celebration. The chief goes to the Sacred Rock, makes libations, and invokes God so that he will make the season favorable and protect the Nyem-Nyem.[7] A procession is organized around a pool in the cave whose waters are supposed to possess healing and magical powers.

The festival, which lasts for several days, is characterized by a multitude of dances and songs whose main theme is the exaltation of the God of the Mountain, who successfully ensured the freedom of the Nyem-Nyem, putting them out of reach of slave hunters. Behind the chief, who dances dressed in kingly regalia, men, women, and newly initiated young people form a large circle, in the middle of which are the men who wish to show off their manhood and virtuosity.[8] These dances are accompanied by drums, hand bells, and women's praising cries. Nyem-Nyem dances are warlike and their aim is to exhibit the community's power and invincibility. The Nyem-Nyem have thus succeeded in resisting not only the Baare-Chamba and the Fulani slave raiders but the German soldiers who attacked the mountains of Galim in 1901.

Plant Defense Systems

To supplement the natural defenses, the refugees built fortified structures from stones and plants. Christian Seignobos (1987) provides a detailed study of precolonial plant defense systems, of park landscapes and agrarian civilizations in northern Cameroon and Chad. Fences created from the branches of thorny trees or live hedges provided an effective defense; where they exist, their alignment dominates a landscape in which earth and straw houses have left no trace. Thorny euphorbias were planted for reinforcement along rock walls. The oldest fences are made of trees up to two meters high. People use double ladders to get over them.[9] The stone walls of the Mandara mountains are outstanding. They were used to block channels, valleys, and cliffs. They ran along the borders of foothills and in concentric circles around the summits. The addition of defensive plants helped suppress the momentum gathered by attacking cavalry.

Plants used for defense were sometimes strengthened by earthworks, as in Guegou in Moundangland; this pattern is found in the Chari-Logone interfluves, where there were two waves of migration. The one from the northeast used earthworks; the other, from the south, used plants in association with walls for defense. Recounting the assault of Kolik in Toumahland by the inhabitants of Bagirmi, Gustav Nachtigal (1971, 396) describes dense neighborhoods with a "war village" in the middle—a portion of low ground that constituted the perimeter with a bushy wood at its center that acted as the real fortress. The Mofou were constantly on the alert. Their houses on the mountain ranges looked like fortresses. Five or seven round walls ensured the defense of the summit; access was possible through an underground passage. The residence of the clan head, located behind the second wall, served as the main entrance to the defense structure.

Paludal Areas

While mountain ranges are typical refuges, other sites also provided shelter from the slave raids. In the wetlands around Lake Chad and its tributaries, the Logone and Chari Rivers, shepherd-farmers defended themselves against the expansionism and domination of the Islamic states (Planhol 1968, 323). There the peoples who had lived in the large plain of Chad a few centuries before retreated to small hills surrounded by tall grass and shut in by an inextricable network of *bahr*.[10] Peoples like the Massa, Musgu, and Boudouma succeeded, from their refuge islets, in braving the cavalry of Bornu and in escaping the Fulani slave raids (Tilho 1910–14, 2:48).

The relative security of the populations that settled in the Logone valley was ensured by the rainy season. When the water level rose, it was practically impossible to move without a canoe. Due to the flatness of the ground, rainwater refused to drain, the river quickly filled shallow depressions, and the entire territory became flooded (A. Lebeuf 1969, 16). The Logone area therefore became a huge lake, a quagmire, upon which Bornu's and Bagirmi's cavalries could not venture.

The Massa and the Musgu, for their part, settled peacefully on grounds from which the water had drained or on alluvial strips; from here they could challenge the powerless enemy. Iman ibn Fartua, historiographer of the Mai, gives us interesting clues on the strategies used by the Ngafata and Tatala Sao, who benefited immensely from the paludal area and from the draining phenomenon of Lake Chad to escape Bornu' s troops: "They ceased to leave their dwelling places, and kept close to Lake Chad; so when the lake retreated eastward, they advanced toward it and settled around it in order to save themselves and took that as their surest stronghold" (in Lange 1987, 93).

Heinrich Barth witnessed expeditions launched in the nineteenth century by the sovereign of Bagirmi against the Musgu, who, feeling secure behind natural defense lines (the numerous rivers and swamps), succeeded in preserving their independence from an enemy possessing a powerful army. "The Musgu nation is situated so unfavourably, surrounded by enemies on all sides, that, even if they were linked together by the strictest unity, they would scarcely be able to preserve their independence. How then, should they be able to withstand their enemies? Nothing but the number of swampy water-courses which intersect the country in all directions, and during the greater part of the year render it impassible for hostile armies, while even during the remaining part the principal rivers afford natural lines of defence" (1965, 359–60). This relative security certainly accounts for the various migrations toward the Logone valley, a region of high population density compared with the neighboring regions plundered by slave raiders.

CITY FORTIFICATIONS

War had a direct impact on habitat: villages that were scattered in peacetime regrouped in strongly fortified towns during war. They were sometimes large towns capable of dissuading the enemy. It was mostly in the savanna that the defense system based on the city wall reached its most elaborate form.[11] The classic Sudanese fortress is made up of a clay wall, high enough to protect the town. The fortress walls—sometimes including crenelles, loopholes, and platforms acting as covered walkways—often stood out on the horizon. At times several successive fences, generally concentric, could be found beyond the city wall. In some regions, the village had a number of small enclosures, veritable blockhouses linked by flanking structures to ensure an autonomous defense. These structures were separated by winding alleyways in which only the inhabitants of the area could find their way. In some places, a strongly built citadel at the center appears to have served as a last refuge.

There are significant discrepancies in the technical quality of the building; the most successful city walls show a great deal of adaptation. Their construction, sometimes the work of powerful political groups, required a lot of manpower: groups of men, women, and children, singing in unison with drums, flutes, and other musical instruments, dug ground and carried water from the rivers so as to mix the *banco*. In other cases, the wall was compartmentalized and the responsibility for each part was incumbent on a given dignitary or clan (Smith 1976, 132).

Fortified Cities among the Sao and the Kotoko

South of Lake Chad, the outstanding Sao civilization—which has disappeared today—emerged, probably in the tenth century. Legend depicts the Sao as giants and credits them with astounding feats. We are acquainted with the real Sao civilization thanks to the numerous archaeological excavations by J. P. Lebeuf. Apart from their bronze jewelry, iron objects, and earth figurines, the Sao distinguished themselves by their outstanding buildings. Krawa is mentioned in oral tradition as one of the oldest Sao cities. As is sometimes the case, it is surrounded by a wall and stands at the foot of an inselberg fortress that served as a last refuge (Mohammadou 1975, 216 n. 24).

Throughout the year Sao cities were completely encircled by high defense walls. The country had to be conquered inch by inch, by dismantling the successive fortified towns, because the entrenched Sao were able to fight effectively for a long time against well-armed troops (J. Lebeuf 1962, 26). During Idris Alaoma's conquest in the sixteenth century, Damasak was the most powerful Sao fortress. Ibn Fartua, has unfortunately not given us a detailed description; but one could agree with Eldridge Mohammadou that this large city was surrounded by thick, high, trapezoidal walls. It was from Damasak that Chief Gaya put up heroic resistance: he had the enclosure wall strengthened, secured crops, and made new food stores; and he dispatched messengers to the chiefs of distant Sao cities, instructing them to resist and in case of assault to gather most of their men at Damasak (Mohammadou 1983, 77).

In the long run, however, Kanem military power defeated the Sao; their territory was raided and the people scattered. These events gave birth to new ethnic groups, among which are the Kotoko. With their high walls, houses grouped around a main building, winding alleyways, and their division into quarters, Kotoko cities overlooked the plain and distinguished themselves from the types of farm houses found in neighboring cities. The enclosure wall was never straight but very sinuous, and could extend for a few hundred meters or several kilometers as at Makari (2km) or Goulfeil (3km). Shaped like a trapezoid with a base of six to eight meters, the wall was made of clay mixed with debris. It could be as high as ten meters and was sometimes crowned with crenelles; it had openings, known as *gebanien* (*ge* = mouth, *banni* = wall; the "mouths of the walls"). Each opening was named—for either the quarter into which it opened, the external place to which it led, or an important event. At nightfall, the openings were closed with heavy doors at which watchmen were posted (A. Lebeuf 1969, 81–84). At the center of the main cities stood a particularly significant edifice, the *gudu,* or *guti.* The Kotoko used the term for several types of buildings that sometimes resembled a tower or a colossal mound; unlike A. Lebeuf, I think that such buildings have a military characteristic, like the *dyonfutu* of western Sudan, which constituted a last refuge (ibid.; and see Bah 1985a, 116).

Among the Sao and the Kotoko, the city premises were always sacred; the destiny of the people they were to shelter depended on the choice of location, a choice that in the end rested with the gods . A propitious day was fixed for the creation of the city; it is traditionally reported that human sacrifices were made to insure that the walls would be invulnerable. The Kotoko country was subdivided into provinces, each with a resident governor living in its capital, or *birni* (fortified place). Thus, among the Sao and their Kotoko descendants the skills for building fortifications played a decisive role; the social structure was based on cities protected by fortified buildings. The Sao also had a strong military base that served as the main political and religious center.

The Dome-Shaped Houses of the Musgu

While the Kotoko were shielded from slave raids thanks to the grouping of houses protected by city walls, the Musgu lived in scattered hamlets along the Logone River. Houses initially looked like typical Sudanese homes; the lower part was round and covered with hard-packed banco, while the upper part consisted of a wood-and-straw roof, the whole structure being from five to six meters high. The Musgu's houses were an easy target for the armies of Bornu and Bagirmi, which during their raids destroyed whole hamlets by setting fire to straw-and-wood roofs (Barth 1965, 407).

The Musgu thus designed a new structure that gave them more security. The main building material was clay mixed with animal dung, dry grass, and much water. After kneading for up to a week, the sticky paste was used to build round, dome-shaped houses of various diameters. In Gamsay, a series of such houses ranged from three to nine meters in height. They were connected in a closed circle and only two structures could lead outside; each family had its own circle of dome-shaped houses (Lenfant 1905, 166). Each house had an opening on top, a sort of window that acted as a watchtower and from which it was easy to observe the enemy. To get there, a person climbed on a structure spaced out from 10 to 15 centimeters and attached to the outer surface of the house; it was used by the person climbing, with a rope (*balbal*) crossing right through the house (Schaller 1973, 16). The dome-shaped houses, seen from afar, look very much like termites' nests. This intended camouflage helped the Musgu escape capture by several expeditions. The decline of the trans-Sahelian slave trade and the collapse of predatory hegemonies around Lake Chad brought about the gradual disappearance of the dome-shaped house.

The war stories of Idris Alaoma provide us with vital details on well-devised siege tactics. The siege of Damasak has been immortalized in the chronicle of ibn Fartua, a prominent historiographer from Bornu. In the north of Mandara, in the clay plain of Yedseram, several centuries before, a large fortified village, Mamasak (or Amsaka), was founded and peopled by adventurers who created a lively city, free from Bornu's neighboring vassals (Urvoy 1949, 79). In the long run, Damasak became the main religious area in Sao Ngafata, and all the neighboring cities acknowledged it as their ancestor (Mohammadou 1983, 76–77). To Idris Alaoma, its destruction was imperative. After a failed surprise assault, the siege was carried out according to the rules. The ditches that surrounded the city were first filled up with millet straw gathered from neighboring farms. The enclosure wall was then attacked. The siege engines, which rose above the wall, had been constructed following Ottoman poliorcetic (related to the besieging of cities or fortresses, from the Greek *poliorkêtikos* ["of or for besieging"]: *polis* ["city"] + *erkos* ["fence or enclosure"]) patterns: from the top of mobile towers soldiers fired muskets and firebrands on the roofs of Damasak, causing devastating fires (74).

Idris conducted a classic war of attrition; he had a fortified camp set up and he instructed all the military leaders to live and store weapons there. Then he summoned all Bornu's subjects to come with cutlasses, leather shields, and arrows and made them fell all the trees to isolate the villages.[12] When the rains came, Idris had all the crops cut down and people driven out of farms; finally, all the Ngafata yielded. The strong fortress of Damasak collapsed on a Saturday, the last day of the Chaaban (eighth month of the Islamic calendar). The year, however, remains uncertain: 1582 or 1587 according to Urvoy (79), 1575 according to E. Mohammadou (1983, 80).

For four centuries, slave raids marked the sociopolitical atmosphere, the economic activities, the human habitat, and the environment around Lake Chad. The kingdoms and the states in the region—like Bornu and Bagirmi—possessed sophisticated military arsenals and had the propensity of making raids, of instituting violence with a view to acquiring the maximum number of war captives from communities that were less organized.

The slave raids led several communities to devise strategies to protect themselves: retreat strategies or defensive buildings. The geographical area around Lake Chad was thus marked by numerous resistance points that stood as a permanent challenge to the dominating powers. These resistance points constitute an eloquent testimony to the resilience of ancestral cultures confronted by the Muslim states and kingdoms of the region. Several refuge sites enabled the people to shelter their gods, the symbols of their attachment to their roots. Through their entrenchment in a territory that has become a place for the protection of their identity, the communities continue to be devoted to their rituals, like the Mofu, whose princes, every year before the rainy season, purify the mountain refuges that enabled them to escape the slave raids.

NOTES

1. Idris Alaoma's numerous expeditions are well-documented by Ahmed ibn Fartua, a court historiographer. The first translation from Arabic to English was done by Herbert Richmond Palmer (1928). Dierk Lange's translation (1987) features invaluable critical notes and appendices.

2. Fombina, equivalent to the Arabic term *yamin* (to the right), refers to the territories south of Lake Chad where the Fulani first settled peacefully and then through military conquests.

3. Yerima Yassi Jean, interview by author, Lara, March 1982.

4. Guido Adala has compiled several oral traditions on the Mount Jim.

5. Kirdi is a generic term that refers to people who have converted to Islam. The term Habe (sing., Kado; lit., slave) is also used but has a strong pejorative connotation.

6. Nyem-Nyem, an ethnographic term used by the colonial administration and found in ethnographic literature, is controversial. It designates a population that lived

in the Kanem Empire as early as the ninth century. According to some sources the name is derived from Nyam (sun) the title of the king. The Fulani conquerors derisively called him Nyam-Nyam (big eater). Today, to display its pride in its cultural roots, the population uses only the name Ni-Zoo (those from Zoo, a mythical ancestor).

7. Amadou Njika, testimony, Ngaoundere, 5 August 1993.

8. Guido Adala, former provincial delegate for culture in Ngaoundéré, testimony, Yaoundé, 3 July 2001. We had jointly programmed a mission for the production of a documentary film on the next Nyem-Nyem festival, in December 2002.

9. Information collected in the palace of the Bandjoun king, May 1980.

10. *Bahr* (Arabic for sea or large river) here refers to lagoon canals separating the various islands.

11. In western Sudan, this military structure is known as the *tata,* the focus of my doctoral thesis. A comparative study with central Sudan, the focus of this chapter, shows many similarities.

12. I discussed above the use of plants for defense purposes. It is possible that Idris's use of burning contributed to the disturbance of the Lake Chad ecosystem.

Bibliography

Ahmed, Ibn Fartua. 1970. *History of the First Twelve Years of the Reign of Mai Idris Alooma of Bornu, 1571–1583.* Trans. from the Arabic by H. R. Palmer. London: Frank Cass.

Austen, Ralph A. 1995. "Slavery and Slave Trade on the Atlantic Coast: The Duala of the Littoral." *Paideuma,* 128–50.

Bah, Thierno Mouctar. 1976. "The Impact of Wars on Housing in Pre-colonial Black Africa." *African Environment* 76, 3 (May).

———. 1982. "Les armées Peul de l'Adamawa au dix-neuvième siècle." In *Etudes africaines offertes à Henri Brunschwig.* Paris: Edition de l'Ecole des Hautes Etudes en Sciences Sociales.

———. 1985a. *Architecture militaire traditionnelle et poliorcétique dans le Soudan occidental* (*du septième à la fin du dix-neuvième siècle.*) Yaoundé; Editions CLE.

———. 1985b. Guerre, pouvoir, et société dans l'Afrique pré-coloniale, entre le lac Tchad et la Côte du Cameroun." 2 vols. Doctoral thesis, Sorbonne.

Barth, Heinrich. 1965. *Travels and Discoveries in North and Central Africa in the Years 1849–1855.* 2 vols. 1860. Reprint, London: Frank Cass.

Bauvilain, Alain. 1989. "Nord Cameroun: Crises et peuplement." 2 vols. Doctoral thesis, Université de Rouen.

Bongfen, Chem-Langhëe, ed. 1995. "Slavery and Slave-Dealing in Cameroon in the Nineteenth and Early Twentieth Centuries." *Paideuma* 41.

Boutrais, Jean. 1987. *Le Nord Cameroun: Peul et Montagnards du Nord Cameroun.* Institut fondamental d'Afrique noire. Paris: ORSTOM.

Brasseur, Georges. 1968. *Les établissements humains au Mali.* Dakar: Mémoires de l'IFAN.

Burnham, Philipp. 1995. "Raiders and Traders in Adamoua: Slavery as a Regional System." *Paideuma* 41:153–76.

Carbou, André. 1912. *La région du Tchad et du Ouaddaï.* 2 vols. Paris: Leroux.

Chapiseau, François. 1900. *Au pays de l'esclavage: Mœurs et coutumes de l'Afrique centrale.* Paris: J. Maisonneuve.

Cuoq, Joseph. 1975. *Recueil des sources arabes concernant l'Afrique occidentale du septième au seizième siècle.* Paris: Centre national de la recherche scientifique

Denham, Dixon, Hugh Clapperton, and Walter Oudney. 1826. *Narrative of Travels and Discoveries in Northern and Central Africa in the Years 1822, 1823 and 1824.* London: J. Murray.

Deschamps, Hubert. 1971. *Histoire générale de l'Afrique, de Madagascar et des archipels.* Vol. 2. Paris: PUF.

———. 1972. *Histoire de la traite des noirs de l'antiquité à nos jours.* Paris: Fayard.

Fardon, Richard. 1998. *Raiders and Refugees: Trends in Chamba Political Development, 1750–1950.* Washington, D.C.: Smithsonian Series in Ethnographic Inquiry.

———. 1999. "Père and Chamba: A Report on Comparative Researches in Adamawa, North Cameroon." *Ngaoundéré Arthropos* 4:5–51.

Fisher, Allan Gorge Barnard, and Humphrey J. Fisher. 1971. *Slavery and Muslim Society in Africa: The Institution in Saharan and Sudanic Africa and the Trans-Saharan Trade.* New York: Doubleday.

Fofou Mama. 1994. "Monographie historique des Nyem-Nyem de l'Adamawa (Nord Cameroun)." Mémoire de DIPES II, Université de Yaoundé.

Fomin Efuenthkeng, S. D. 1984. "Slavery in Cameroon." Doctoral thesis, Université de Yaoundé.

Lange, Dierk. 1987. "A Sudanic Chronicle: The Borno Expeditions of Idris Alauma, 1564–1576." *Studien zur Kulturkunde* 86.

Lebeuf, Annie. 1969. *Les principautés Kotoko: Essai sur le caractère sacré de l'autorité.* Paris; CNRS.

Lebeuf, J. P. 1962. *Archéologie tchadienne: Les Sao du Cameroun et du Tchad.* Paris: Herman.

Lembezat, Bernard. 1991. *Les populations païennes du Cameroun septentrional.* 2 vols. Yaoundé: ORSTOM.

Lenfant, Eugène Armand. 1905. *La grande route du Tchad.* Paris: Hachette.

Lovejoy, Paul, ed. 1981. *The Ideology of Slavery in Africa.* Beverly Hills: Sage Publications.

Mahamat, Adam. 1998. "L'esclavage chez les peuples de la bordure du Logone: Le cas des Mousgoum du Nord Cameroun, dix-huitième–vingtième siècles." Mémoire de Maîtrise d'histoire, Université de Ngaoundéré.

Marchesseau, G. 1945. "Quelque éléments d'ethnographie chez le Mofu du massif de Dorum." *Bulletin de la Société d'Etudes Camerounaises* 10:21.

Martin, G. B. 1969. "Kanem, Bornu, and Fezzan: Notes on the Political History of a Trade Route." *Journal of African History* 1.

Mauny, Raymond. 1961. *Tableau géographique de l'ouest africain au moyen age.* Dakar: IFAN.

Meillassoux, Claude. 1986. *Anthropologie de l'esclavage: Le ventre de fer et d'argent.* Paris: PUF.

Mohammadou, Eldridge. 1975. *Le royaume du Wandala ou Mandara au dix-neuvième siècle.* Bamenda, Cameroon: Office national de la recherche scientifique el technique, Institut des Sciences Humaines, no. 3016.

———. 1978. *Les royaumes Foulbe du plateau de l'Adamoua au dix-neuvième siècle: Tignere, Tibati, Banyo, Ngaoundéré.* Tokyo: Institute of Languages and Cultures of Asia and Africa.

———. 1983. *Idriss Aloma du Bornou, seizième siècle.* Abidjan: Les Nouvelles Editions Africaines.

———. 2001. "Environnement, esclavage . . . invasion Baare-Chamba . . . au sud du Plateau bameliké, ca. 1750–1850." Paper presented at the Colloque Ecologie Humaine et Gestion du Milieu dans l'Ecotone Forêt-Savane d'Afrique Centrale, Yaoundé, 13–15 November.

———. n.d. *Le peuplement de la Haute Benoué.* Garoua; ONAREST, Centre National de la Recherche Scientifique.

Nachtigal, Gustav. 1971. *Sahara and Sudan.* Trans. Allan Fisher and Humphrey Fisher. 1879. Reprint, London: C. Hurst.

Nicholson, Sharon. 1981. "The Historical Climatology of Africa." In T. M. L. Wigley, M. J. Ingram, and G. Farmer, eds., *Climate and History: Studies in Past Climates and Their Impact on Man.* Cambridge: Cambridge University Press.

Njeuma, Martin Zachary. 1978. *Fulani Hegemony in Yola (Old Adamawa), 1809–1902.* Yaoundé: Centre de publication pour l'eseignement et la recherche.

Lara, Oruno D. 1976. "Esclavage et révoltes négro-africaines dans l'empire musulman du Haut Moyen Age." *Présence africaine* 98 (2d trimester): 51–103.

Palmer, Herbert Richmond. 1928. *Sudanese Memoirs.* Lagos.

———. 1970. *The Bornu, Sahara, and Sudan.* New York: Negro University Press (reprint of 1936 edition).

Planhol, Xavier de. 1968. *Les fondements géographiques de l'histoire de l'Islam.* Paris: Flammarion.

Podlewski, André Michel. 1961. "Etude démographique de trois ethnies païennes: Matakam, Kapsiki, Goudé." *Recherches et etudes camerounaises* 4, 13.

———. 1971. "La dynamique des principales populations du Nord-Cameroun: Piedmont et plaine de l'Adamaoua." *Cahiers ORSTOM* 2 (Paris; special issue).

Sanneh, Lamin O. 1976. "Slavery, Islam, and the Jakhanke People of West Africa." *Africa: Journal of the International African Institute* 46 (1): 80–92.

Schaller, Yves. 1973. *Les Kirdi du Nord Cameroun.* Strasbourg: Imprimerie des Dernières Nouvelles.

Sehou, Ahmadou. 1997. "La traite des esclaves dans le lamidat de Ngaoundéré (Cameroun) du dix-neuvième au vingtième siècle." *Héritages des tropiques* (Université de Yaoundé) 1, 1.

Seignobos, Christian. 1977. "L'habitat traditionnel au Nord Cameroun." in *Etablissements humains et environnement socioculturel.* Paris: UNESCO.

———. 1987a. *Le poney du Logone et les derniers peuples cavaliers essai d'approche historique.* Paris. Maisons-Alfort/IEMVT.

———. 1987b. "Les systèmes de défense végétaux pré-coloniaux: Paysages de parcs et civilisation agraires (Tchad et Nord Cameroun)." *Annales de l'Université du Tchad* (special issue; September): 3–59.

Smaldone, J. P. 1977. *Warfare in the Sokoto Caliphate.* Cambridge University Press.

Smith, Robert S. 1976. "Warfare and Diplomacy in Pre-Colonial West Africa." *Studies in African History* 15.

Strümpell, Kurt, and Lieutenant von Briesen. 1980. *Peuples et états du Fombina et de l'Adamaoua (Nord Cameroun).* Trans. from the German by Eldridge Mohammadou. Garma: ISH.

Taimou, Adji. 1994. "Les Kotoko des abords sud du Lac Tchad: Origines, migrations, et implantation." Mémoire de DIPES, Université de Yaoundé.

Tilho, Jean. 1910–14. *Documents scientifiques de la Mission Tilho.* 4 vols. Paris: Imprimerie Nationale.

Tremaux, P. 1862. *Le Soudan.* Paris: Hachette.

Urvoy, Yves. 1936. *Histoire des populations du Soudan Central (Colonie du Niger).* Paris: Larose.

———. 1949. *Histoire de l'empire du Bornou,* Paris: Larose.

Vincent, Jeanne Françoise. 1972. "Sur les traces du Major Denham: Le Nord Cameroun il y a cent cinquante ans, Mandara, Kirdi, et Peul." *Cahiers d'études africaines.*

Vincent, Jeanne Françoise, Daniel Dory, and Raymond Verdier. 1995. *La construction religieuse du territoire.* Paris; L'Harmattan.

Vossart, Jean. 1952. "Histoire du sultanat du Mandara, Province de l'empire du Bornou." *Etudes camerounaises,* no. 35–36.

Zeltner, Jean-Claude. 1980. *Pages d'histoire du Kanem, pays tchadien.* Paris: l'Harmattan.

———. 1987. *La traite des esclaves entre les pays du Tchad et la Méditerranée au dix-neuvième siècle.* Ndjamena.

Chapter 3
The Myth of Inevitability and Invincibility
Resistance to Slavers and the Slave Trade in Central Africa, 1850–1910

Dennis D. Cordell

Although mythologies surrounding slave raids and the slave trade in Africa would have it that slavers were all but invincible, enjoying superiority in numbers and technology, the reality for both the Atlantic and Muslim commerce was often otherwise.[1] African men and women employed a variety of strategies to resist attacks of slave raiders and later sale by slave merchants. Oral testimonies collected in north-central Africa in the 1970s, as well as travel literature from the nineteenth and twentieth centuries and early French colonial records, afford glimpses into the ways that peoples such as the Sara in today's southern Chad, and the Banda and Manza in today's Central African Republic (CAR) resisted the attacks of raiders: from the kingdoms of Bagirmi and Wadai in the Chad basin to the north in the 1870s, from the Khartoumers and their successors from the Nile basin to the east around the same time, and later in the century from bands of brigands associated with warlord Rabih Fadl-Allah and his client Muhammad al-Sanusi in the region itself. Indeed al-Sanusi became "sultan" of Dar al-Kuti, one of the last major slave-exporting states in north-central

Africa—before the tragic resurgence of slave raiding and slave trading in the area in the late twentieth century (Rone 1995; Weber 1999).

This essay explores the varieties and strategies of resistance to Muslim slave raiding and the Muslim slave trade in north-central Africa. Ranging from physical resistance that was perhaps more effective than the stereotypes of raiding usually suggest, to the adoption of new building styles, settlement patterns, and crops, and to strategies of hiding and flight, the peoples of this part of Africa attempted to protect themselves, their families, and their neighbors from the twin scourges of slave raiders and slave traders. These efforts were by no means always successful, but neither were they uniformly ineffective. Before examining the ways that individuals and groups resisted the depredations of raiders, however, it is necessary to contextualize and historicize the evolution of the slaving frontiers in this part of Africa.

THE EXPANSION OF MUSLIM SLAVING FRONTIERS IN NORTH-CENTRAL AFRICA

The broad chronology and geography of shifting Muslim slaving frontiers in north-central Africa are by now reasonably well known (Burnham 1980; Cordell 1979, 1983, 1985a,b, 1988; Dampierre 1967, 1983; Santandrea 1964, 1981; Sikainga 1991). Like the Judeo-Christian traditions, which preceded and coexisted with it, the Islamic *sunna,* or tradition, has not historically condemned either slavery or the slave trade (see Marmon 1999; Lewis 1990; Gordon 1987). Strictly speaking, however, Muslims were admonished against taking other Muslims into slavery. Moreover, Muslim slave owners were called upon to encourage their slaves to convert to Islam, grant them freedom in their wills, and consider the children of slaves who converted to Islam as free individuals. While such advice was by no means always heeded, it promoted both the removal of slave raiding to the limits of the Islamic world and an endlessly renewed demand for captives. With the initially rapid and subsequently steady expansion of Dar al-Islam (the land of Islam), then, the slaving frontiers shifted farther and farther away from the heartlands of Islam in the Middle East and North Africa—to Islamic border regions in the Mediterranean and southeast and central Europe, Central and South and Southeast Asia, and Africa south of the Sahara.

By the eleventh century, for example, the Muslim geographer al-Idrisi reported slave raiding in the Fazzan, in today's southern Libya—the borderland between Dar al-Islam and Dar al-Harb (the land of war) (in Levtzion and Hopkins 2000, 119). From there the Islamic frontier moved on to regions still farther south: Kanem, on the northern borders of Lake Chad, in the late eleventh or early twelfth centuries and again to the south to Borno[2] in the fourteenth (Nachtigal 1987, 142n3, 146; Levtzion and Hopkins, 428n8). In time, the ruling class of Borno proclaimed itself part of the Muslim world, and, with that, Borno slaving parties marauded in the lands along the middle Shari River, in today's southern Chad. Within north-central Africa, the state of Bagirmi arose by the sixteenth century and declared itself within the bounds of the Islamic world several centuries later (Nachtigal 1987, 398). Slavers from Bagirmi targeted regions to the southeast, the lands of the peoples whom today we call the Sara (Reyna 1990). By the seventeenth century the ostensibly Muslim state of Wadai grew up to the northeast of Bagirmi, in eastern Chad (Nachtigal 1971, 206–7, 207n1). The rulers of Wadai, too, cast in their lot with Dar al-Islam, and Wadaian raiders sought slaves in the southern hinterland among the Sara, but also among the Banda and the Manza. By the early nineteenth century, the state was well positioned at the southern terminus of a new trans-Saharan caravan route, an itinerary that fostered the export of increased numbers of slaves toward the Islamic heartlands (Cordell 1977). To the east, the kingdom of Darfur arose in the western region of today's Sudan. Darfur also lay at the southern end of a caravan route, Darb al-Arbaʿin, or Forty-Day Road, which became an important itinerary for exporting slaves (O'Fahey and Spaulding 1974; O'Fahey 1982; Barth 1965, 121). Borno, Bagirmi, Wadai, and Darfur, then, all competed for and carved out raiding zones to the south—in north-central Africa.

The expansion of Muslim slave raiding and slave trading in the nineteenth and early twentieth centuries also reflects another process—the expansion of the European world economy and European military technology into the Middle East and then indirectly, via Muslim intermediaries, up the valley of the Nile and southwest into north-central Africa. The focus here is on the Nile valley and the slave raiders and slave traders known as the Khartoumers and their successors. In a manner that paralleled the process described in the preceding paragraphs for the Chad basin west of today's Sudan and east of Lake Chad, the Islamic frontier moved up the Nile valley into the northeastern borderlands of north-central Africa. To be sure, local societies, both Muslim and non-Muslim, as well as the states that arose in the region, were different, but the process was somewhat similar.[3]

With Napoleon's invasion and occupation of Egypt in 1798 and the ensuing penetration of British political and economic influence in the Middle Eastern heartlands in the first half of the nineteenth century, the expansion of Dar al-Islam became intimately intertwined with the expansion of the European world economy and European military power. Regimes in the Islamic heartlands, and most notably that of Muhammad ʿAli in Egypt (1805–48), resorted to tactics of defensive modernization, importing European advisors, weapons, and forms of bureaucratic organization—initially to protect themselves from the growing European threat. They also soon mobilized these borrowings in an effort to dominate adjacent regions without direct access to European technology and organization. For Egypt, this led to designs on the upper Nile valley, as the government deployed imported European technology, advisors, and know-how to extend the Egyptian sphere of influence to the south. The Egyptians founded their "colonial capital" of Khartoum at the confluence of the Blue Nile and White Nile in 1824 (Bjørkelo 1989, 37).

By mid-century, slave raiders and slave merchants associated with Egyptian expansion launched ventures into southern and southwestern Sudan. They forged trade routes and founded fortified, armed camps, or *zaribas* (Arabic), along them. In so doing, they integrated these regions into the expanding Muslim economy adjacent to the Nile. Known as the Khartoumers because the Egyptian colonial capital on the Nile was a critical node in their commercial networks, these merchants employed armed bands to protect their centers and caravans. In this region, where people were the most valuable resource to be had, the Khartoumers and their mercenaries raided some local peoples for captives and enticed others to join in their enterprise, either out of a desire for gain or in an effort to protect themselves from the raiders. By the 1870s the German traveler Georg Schweinfurth (1874, 2:410–32) reported zaribas every twenty or thirty miles in Bahr al-Ghazal and farther south, in Azande territories.

Around this time, and propelled by British efforts to abolish the slave trade in the Nile Valley, the "zariba system," as Stefano Santandrea terms it, spilled over the divide separating the Nile basin from the Ubangi River basin to the west. In some cases, it was the Khartoumers themselves or their associates who exported the system beyond the borders of Sudan (Santandrea 1964). One of the most (in)famous was Rabih b. Fadl-Allah, a lieutenant of Rahma al-Zubayr, the most notorious Khartoumer of them all (Cordell 1986, n.d.). By 1876, Rabih had set up camp in today's eastern CAR (Dampierre 1983). At first Rabih maintained ties with the Khartoumer network based in the Nile Valley, whence he imported weapons and trade goods and towards which he exported captives. However, British pressure disrupted slave exports by way of the Nile Valley and via Darb al-Arbaʿin from Darfur in the latter part of the century. Rabih eventually redirected his attention toward the states of Bagirmi and Wadai to the north in an effort to tie his commercial operations into the existing slave-raiding and slave-trading networks that extended north into the Chad basin. Here the route from Bagirmi and Wadai to Libya remained free of European harassment—a perfect outlet for expanding exports of slaves. Hence the zariba system was reborn in the lands of the Sara, Banda, and Manza of north-central Africa.

Although a foreign seed, the zariba system found fertile soil in the region among local traders and raiders who hitched their fortunes to veteran Khartoumers such as Rabih. Foremost among these was Muhammad al-Sanusi, a Runga petty potentate in the northern part of today's CAR who became a client of Rabih. The outlines of al-Sanusi's career—along with the devastation he visited upon the area—are now known (Cordell 1985a). He used support from Rabih to establish himself, then made several bids for independence, finally succeeding once his patron had left the region for Bagirmi and Borno, where he was killed in 1900 in an encounter with the French at Kusseri in today's northern Cameroon. Al-Sanusi founded a permanent capital at Ndele in 1896 and set in motion an expanding spiral of violence that engulfed several tens of thousands of square miles by the time of his assassination by the French in 1911, leaving the northern CAR the very sparsely populated land that it is today. Al-Sanusi's resettlement of captives and refugees at Ndele created the largest city in north-central Africa by the time of the French conquest; so much so that early maps of the region identify it as the only substantial urban center between the Congo River and the central Sahara. Later cartographers copied their predecessors, so that Ndele remains prominently visible on today's maps of the area even though al-Sanusi's erstwhile capital of thirty thousand is today but a village of several thousand people.

Both contemporary observers and historians of the expansion of the Muslim slave trade in this part of Africa—including myself—have tended to emphasize the destruction wrought by slave raiders and the draining impact of the slave trade. All it takes is a glance at a population map of the region with its vast empty quarters and widely scattered settlements to understand that this tale of demographic disaster is not a figment of a too fertile imagination or simply a crusade to emphasize the horrors of slave raiding, slavery, and the slave trade (Pantobe 1984, 27). However, the historical sources that document this process also include numerous examples of the ways that local peoples defended themselves—from Muslim raiders from the north and east, as well as from locally born and raised brigands like al-Sanusi.

Slave Raiding, Mortality, and the Effectiveness of Resistance

Brought together, these tales of resistance make it clear that the Sara, Banda, Manza, and their neighbors were not simply tilting at windmills. Often successful and effective, in so far as they undermined the ability of the marauders to impose their will with complete impunity, some of these exploits were remembered with pride three-quarters of a century later. Taken together, they call into question the narratives of inevitability and invincibility promulgated by the raiders and traders themselves in efforts to weaken resistance, reported by the French to justify colonial conquest and their subsequent oxymoronic wars of pacification, and reproduced in oral accounts collected in the later twentieth century.

For example, near contemporary observers such as Al-Hajj Abdu, advisor to al-Sanusi, told French traveler Auguste Chevalier in 1903 that Rabih "ate the entire country, . . . where he passed he took all" (Chevalier 1907, 226). And Modat, the French resident in Ndele at the time of al-Sanusi's assassination in 1911, wrote that a popular cradle song went something like "*Rabi jo, razassa dugo*" ("Rabih came, bullets rained down") (1912, 226). Informants in Dar al-Kuti in the 1970s told stories they had heard all their lives about Rabih and his raiders: "When they headed down the way and came upon a tree, they ran right over it and it disappeared; they were as numerous as swarming termites"; or, "When they crossed a stream, so much water splashed on the banks that the water level plummeted" (Oral Account 22.3; OA21.4). Similar stories were told in the 1970s about al-Sanusi: that he was the "first sultan" in the area, meaning that his likes had not been seen before; that he was frightfully cruel, filling caves around Ndele with the skulls of clients and captives who displeased him; that he alone was responsible for the demographic desert of today's north-central Africa (Cordell 1985a).

While there is no doubt that slave raiding and the slave trade had a devastating impact on all aspects of life in north-central Africa, data at hand intimate at the same time that the story may be more complex—and the devastation somewhat less one-sided—than suggested by these tropes of total war. For example, the slavers' tactics did not convey total confidence and disdain for the capacity of non-Muslims to protect themselves. Both local and European accounts of slave raiding in Dar al-Kuti and the southern Chad basin for the period report that the raiders frequently resorted to surprise, attacking at daybreak just after the *fajr* (morning prayer) with guns blazing to frighten their targets (OA21.4; Julien 1929, 55–56; "Le saharien" 1908, 285; ANT). (And given that the most common firearm in this part of Africa in the late nineteenth century was the flintlock, which required considerable time to reload, the raiders' guns probably "blazed" only once.) Other usual tactics embodied subterfuge. Brigands first approached villages openly, giving people ample opportunity to flee into the brush. The raiders then withdrew, leading their would-be captives to return to their villages, thinking that the danger had passed. The marauders then returned surreptitiously, attacking and quickly subduing the settlement (Decorse 1906, 174).

Beyond these descriptions, there are also examples of raiding gone awry. For example, the Manza defeated al-Sanusi's banners outright in 1892 or 1893 (Vergiat 1937, 28; Gaud 1911, 95–96; Kalck 1970, 2:449–50). The Sara Ngama inflicted substantial casualties on another raiding party in 1896—although the expedition still returned with substantial numbers of prisoners. During a *ghazzia* against the Banda Linda five years later, the Banda attacked al-Sanusi's men, forcing many of them to throw themselves in the nearby Ouaka River, where they drowned (OA22.1; OA23.1; Julien 1925, 142–43; 1928, 65–66; 1929, 49, 56, 80). Mortality rates among raiders during the handful of ghazzias for which we have data confirm the ability of "victims" to turn the tables on their attackers. Accompanying al-Sanusi's men on an expedition in Sara country in June 1903, Chevalier (1907, 281–82) recorded that the sultan's force lost fifteen men in one attack on a village of about 120 people; in another ghazzia against a village of similar size, the raiders lost two men. To be sure, casualties among the raided were substantial, and, more often than not, their villages were burned. Moreover, it is also the case that the more advanced repeating rifles that appeared in the region after 1900 led to more lethal raids (Cordell 1988, 153). Nonetheless, large numbers of people managed to flee—presumably to return once the Muslim raiders went on their way.

Refuge and Relocation: *Kagas*, Caverns, and Fortified Villages

If active resistance to raiding of the sort described above was probably somewhat out of the ordinary, a more usual way of "fighting back" was simply to abandon the terrain in the face of a more powerful foe. Since the objective of the raiders was to take captives, refuge and relocation were effective forms of resistance. Most ghazzias took place in the dry season, when rank-and-file raiders were not tied down by the demands of agriculture and when travel was easier. Moreover, raiding expeditions did not return each year to the same locales.[4] Therefore, if people hid for a few days or weeks, or a month or two, the raiders tended to move on, not to return for the remainder of the season.

The wooded savanna of north-central Africa lent itself to this strategy. Although largely open, rainfall was greater than farther north in the Sahel, giving rise to numerous rivers and streams and promoting the growth of extensive stretches of dense brush and light forest. The peculiar geology of north-central Africa also facilitated refuge. From the northern part of today's CAR to southern Kordofan, in central Sudan, the vast plains are punctuated by enormous, almost surreal, outcroppings of rock riddled with caves and crevasses and are not easily accessible on foot, much less on horseback (Escayrac 1851, 371; Courtet 1907; Bruel 1935, 38, 54). Erosion produced these formations, as more porous surrounding laterite soil was washed away, leaving islands of denser rock. The languages of all peoples in the region include terms for these specific formations. Many individual outcroppings had their own proper names. Known as *kaga* among the Banda and *mbia* among the Azande farther southeast, some of these massive protrusions had their own sources of water (Bruel 1935, 202).

Believed to harbor spirits as well as provide physical protection, the kaga were prime destinations for people seeking to escape slave raiders. Slave-raiding forces that wreaked havoc in the region—from those of Muhammad ʿAli of Egypt, which marauded in Kordofan in the mid-nineteenth century, to the banners of al-Sanusi, which wreaked havoc farther west half a century later, to Fulani forces still farther west, in today's northern Cameroon—laid siege to these refuges (Escayrac 1851, 371; Bruel 1935, 202). At times, the outcroppings also served as bases for attack. Kaga Kazembe is a case in point. Rabih laid siege unsuccessfully against a Manza force lodged at Kazembe around 1885. An attack by al-Sanusi's men in 1892 or 1893 led to an outright Manza victory. And in both 1894 and 1901, Banda Ngao forces allied with the sultan failed to take the stronghold. Only in 1903 did a French force commanded by Capitaine Toqué force the Manza to abandon Kaga Kazembe (Vergiat 1937, 28). The oral traditions of numerous Banda and Manza groups in the region include tales of refuge in one kaga or another. Indeed the search for security led al-Sanusi himself to decide to locate his new capital at Kaga Ndele in 1896 (Cordell 1985a, 173, 245).

In addition to kagas, themselves frequently perforated by caves, the laterite soil also washed away below the surface in places, creating tunnels and caverns that afforded refuge from raiders. The written historical record from the turn of the last century, as well as oral accounts collected in the 1970s, include abundant references to such hideaways and routes of escape. A few years after 1900, for example, the French traveler Prins recorded communities of "troglodytes" in the Bamingui River region, including a community of three families consisting of eight adult men, four young men, five women, and two babies. The small number of women and children was due to the fact that al-Sanusi's forces had surprised them working in their fields and had taken other women and children captive (1909, 17–18). A few years later, and farther east in Kresh country in the eastern

Ubangi basin near the Ubangi-Nile divide, the French resident Modat observed that at one time people built their villages and cleared fields adjacent to Jebel Mela, a huge rock formation where in times of danger they hid in a labyrinth of tunnels and caves (Modat 1912, 185). Much later, in 1974 and 1975, tales of tunnels and caves continued to circulate among people in the area. Informants told me about and led me to tunnels that connected open areas once occupied by villages to kagas many yards away (OA3.2; OA4.1; OA5.2/6.1; OA6.2; OA9.2/10.1; OA13.1; OA15.2/16.1; OA22.1). In these areas the ground resounded with my steps as I walked above subterranean passages. One informant even maintained that a tunnel north of al-Sanusi's capital at Ndele led to Koudou, twenty-five kilometers to the southwest (OA14.2)!

Beyond seeking refuge in kagas and caverns, people in north-central Africa also protected themselves by banding together in larger settlements. Around 1850, most peoples, from the Gbaya in the west to the Manza and Sara in the center, and on to the Banda and Kresh farther east, tended to live in dispersed settlements. They practiced shifting cultivation and resided in scattered small hamlets near their fields. The intensification of slave raiding—in the middle third of the century from Muslim states to the north such as Bagirmi, Wadai, and Darfur, and then later from the Khartoumers from the east—led people to abandon these residential patterns. Early examples of larger villages were found among the Sara, who lived closest to Bagirmi and Wadai, the earliest sponsors of slave raiding in the area. Among the Sara, these larger concentrations of people also promoted a greater centralization of authority (Magnant 1986, 62, 163–66, 182–84, 189–206). This shift toward larger, fortified settlements spread south from the Chad basin and southwest from the Nile regions with the progression of the Muslim slaving frontier.

Larger settlements were the logical outgrowth of more common and more violent raiding. They also reproduced the fortified camps, or *zawiyas,* of the slave raiders themselves. The camp of the Kresh chief Saʿid Baldas in the Ubangi-Nile border region, visited by the Frenchman Prins in 1901, was a prime example of this phenomenon:

> We can call the large town that is the capital of the Sultanate of Saʿid Baldas a city; a city enclosed by a circular adobe wall five meters thick at the base and a meter thick at the top, [a wall] five meters high with an open space bordering the circumference on the inside, [a wall] pierced by loopholes and topped off with a frieze of sharpened bamboo stakes. A moat between six and ten meters wide and between five and eight meters deep runs around the

> foot of the wall [on the outside]; three gates on the west side are capped with tree trunks seven meters tall that serve as observation towers; gates three meters wide and four meters tall can be hermetically sealed in the blink of an eye by beams always at the ready.
>
> This enclosure, whose equivalent I have only seen at Maïnfa in Bagirmi, is nothing other than the headquarters of the sultan, who brought together there, around his own residence, the residences of his major chiefs and sharpshooters, who numbered about 150. It also sheltered at the time of our visit a settled population of two thousand souls, but certain areas of the settlement were deserted that could easily accommodate a population of equivalent size. . . . Total population was between four and five thousand. (Prins 1925, 138–39, 140)

While most of the fortress villages in north-central Africa were not as well fortified, peoples throughout the area abandoned earlier scattered patterns of residence for denser settlements in locales not always chosen for their proximity to ample supplies of water or agricultural land.

New Crops and a Return to Old Agricultural Practices

Along with refuge, relocation, and new types of settlements—all aimed at resisting Muslim slave raiders in the late nineteenth and early twentieth centuries—people returned to older sources of food and adopted newer agricultural practices. Peoples of this region were probably the first to domesticate millets and sorghums, crops known for their high protein content (Stemler, Harlan, and deWet 1975). By the mid-nineteenth century numerous varieties of the plant provided a rich sustenance.

However, the cultivation of sorghums and millets also made people particularly vulnerable to raiders. First, the plants were grown in large cleared fields that made them very visible to passersby and signaled the presence of farmers not too far away. Second, the crop demanded substantial care throughout the growing season, and so it could not be abandoned for very long without jeopardizing the harvest. Third, because the ripened grain develops in dense clusters at the top of the plant, the heads of grain were easily stolen. Finally, the mature crop must be harvested within a narrow window of time or else be lost to birds and rodents or fall over in the fields to rot (Prioul 1981, 93–96; ENA; Prioul n.d.). Continued cultivation of the crop, then, was not particularly well suited for populations besieged by violence.

Local peoples countered the vulnerabilities posed by sorghum cultivation with two strategies. The first can hardly be called resistance, although it served to protect farmers fleeing slavers: they simply stopped growing sorghum and relied more completely on hunting and gathering, earlier practices that had become only supplements to farming after the spread of sorghum. Examples of this behavior are numerous in the historical record of the period, but Prins, once again, offers a salient description. During his sojourn in and around Saᶜid Baldas's capital, he visited the Banda village of Joungorou (or Yango Hourou.) The settlement lay very near a dense gallery forest and could only be reached by crawling through tunnels in the dense surrounding brambles. There were no visible paths nearby to give away the presence of a village. Moreover, the people had no fields because they feared that these signs of habitation would also betray them. They survived by hunting, gathering wild honey, and trading dried meat from hunting for grain with the people of the neighboring village of Mouvou (Prins 1925, 157).

The other strategy was more active than passive and changed the agricultural history of the region. Beginning with Banda groups in the south and spreading north to the Manza and the Sara, local peoples began cultivating manioc. A root crop of dubious nutritional value, manioc was, nonetheless, suited for times of insecurity. First, it could be planted in small plots and the mature crop was not very tall; hence, manioc patches were easy to conceal. Second, once planted, it required very little care. The root of the plant is the part that is eaten. Hidden below the ground, it is relatively safe from marauders. Neither did the plant have to be harvested within a specified period of time. The yield is substantial, between six and forty tons per hectare, depending on the quality of the soil (Schlippe 1956, 66). Schweinfurth (1874, 1:526–27) described some of these characteristics of the plant in the 1870s, and also noted that the easternmost population to cultivate the crop at the time were the Mangbetu in the northeastern Ubangi basin. Later, Michel Georges (1963, 346), an agricultural economist, confirmed the observations of the German traveler, noting that manioc was commonly planted at the beginning of the second year of a four-year cycle, left in the ground through the third and fourth year, and harvested at the end of the fourth or beginning of the fifth year.

In the late nineteenth century manioc cultivation became common. Charles Tisserant (1953, 215–18) suggests that in 1850 the crop was cultivated only in the southwest part of today's CAR, whence it spread north and northeast, reaching the Banda of the Bambari region in the eastern Ubangi basin (and north of the Mangbetu) in 1880. Manza informants reported that in earlier times they ate millet exclusively, and that they borrowed manioc from the Banda. Indeed the importance of millet in Manza ritual—for circumcision and ancestor ceremonies—suggests that it, and not manioc, was the primordial crop among them (Renouf-Stefanik 1978, 50n118). Shortly before 1900, in fact, traveler Félix Chapiseau (1900, 102) reported that the Manza grew both manioc and millet. In 1974, when asked about manioc cultivation in earlier periods, Banda informant Yadri Sali in Ndele replied "*gozo mafi, kalla bes*" ("there was no manioc, only millet") (OA9.1).

The irony of the tale of the diffusion of manioc is, of course, that the plant was domesticated as a food crop in the Americas (Tisserant 1953, 217). It later spread to Africa with the rise of the Atlantic slave trade and made its way into the African interior by following, in reverse, the itineraries used by slave raiders and slave traders to take their caravans of captives to the coast. In north-central Africa it helped people conceal themselves from Muslim raiders. And they took it with them in what was, in all probability, the most common form of resistance—flight and resettlement in another region.

MIGRATION OR FLIGHT AS RESISTANCE

Of all the types of resistance surveyed in this chapter, migration or permanent relocation was perhaps the most common. While this strategy did not confront slave raiders and slave traders head-on, it hit at the heart of their enterprise by depriving them of people to capture and sell. The historiography of north-central Africa—oral, written, and material—testifies to the frequency with which individuals, families, and villages fled their attackers. Much of this story is told elsewhere, so a summary will suffice here (Cordell 1983, 1:69–70; 1985a, 23–30; Giles-Vernick 1996, 257).

Oral testimonies collected from the peoples of north-central Africa abound in the bibliography below—from Browne (1806) in the late eighteenth century, el-Tounsy (1845, 1851) shortly thereafter, Barth (1965) in the mid-nineteenth century, and Nachtigal (1971, 1987) a generation later, to early French travelers and military men around 1900, the colonial authorities and scholars that arrived with colonial rule, and on to the foreign and African researchers of the independence era. They all recorded tales of flight and migration as people migrated to escape slave raiders. The catalogue is both impressive and overwhelming.

For example, the Binga, the Yulu, and the Kara, who lived south of Darfur in the early twentieth century, reported that they had once lived farther north, but migrated southward to avoid ghazzias from Darfur and later attacks of the

Khartoumers (Santandrea 1964, 229–30; Modat 1912, 193). This tale of flight is repeated farther west among the Goula of Lake Mamoun and Lake Iro in today's southeastern Chad. People who remained either retreated into the swamps on the lake margins or paid tribute in slaves to Wadai and Darfur (Modat 1912, 277; Browne 1806, 356; Barth 1965, 2:657; Fresnel 1849, 19). The Sara, too, once lived farther north and migrated south and southwest in the nineteenth century to avoid enslavement. Unfortunately, they moved into the area that would later become al-Sanusi's prime raiding territory (Delafosse 1930).

Farther south, in the region of the Nile-Ubangi divide, the Kresh peoples migrated west in the 1870s, 1880s, and 1890s to escape Rabih, later to find themselves within the reach of al-Sanusi; so they fled back toward the east around 1900. By the 1970s they were but a memory in the region (Santandrea 1964, 191, 207; Modat 1912, 285). The stories of the Manza and the Banda are similar (Gaud 1911, 97, 107; Julien 1925, 106; Modat 1912, 224–28; Prioul 1981, 16–17; Giles-Vernick 1996). Buffeted by ghazzias from the north, the Banda migrated from south of Darfur to the southwest, where they found themselves within the reach of Rabih and al-Sanusi. They moved farther to the west, where they met the Manza and Gbaya, themselves migrating to the south and the east to avoid Fulani raiding expeditions from the Borno region as well as predators from Bagirmi to the north. As a result, the Banda, already made up of a large number of populations, splintered into still smaller groups and headed south down the valleys of the Ubangi River tributaries to just north of the Ubangi itself. The population density in the region in 1958 tells the tale. The population of the Mobaye district of the southeastern CAR, home to many Banda, averaged 12.1 people per square kilometer; while that of Ubangi-Shari colony as a whole was 1.9 people per square kilometer (Kalck 1970, 1:171–72, 212–13, 244). The north central, eastern, and northeastern parts of the country—prime targets for Muslim slave raiding and slave trading between 1850 and 1920—were all but deserted. They remain so today.

The Myth of Inevitability and Invincibility Revisited

At the end of this tale of violence and resistance, what might be said about the premise proposed at the beginning? Just how effective was resistance to Muslim raiders and ghazzias among the peoples of north-central Africa? To what extent were tales of the inevitability of capture and the invincibility of slave raiders more myth than reality—products of the hyperbole of historical memory and exaggeration by Europeans preaching the need for a *mission civilisatrice?* In responding to these questions, it is very important to acknowledge, but also not to overemphasize, the effectiveness of resistance. Many people were killed or carried off, and the lives of countless others were disrupted and forever scarred. The first objective, then, must be a more nuanced understanding of both raiding and resistance. A second aim must be to separate the immediate and long-range impacts of slave raiding and slave trading and resistance to both.

As for physical resistance to the raids themselves, the limited anecdotal information presented in this essay underscores the need to cull the historical sources for more descriptions of episodes of slave raiding and slave trading. While specific examples from north-central Africa may be more numerous because slave raiding and the slave trade persisted (and indeed expanded) through the late nineteenth and early twentieth centuries, examples from other regions and earlier eras may be more common than we suspect. In any case, the data presented in the preceding pages, as well as the literature on firearms in Africa more broadly, strongly suggest that until the introduction of repeating rifles in the second half of the nineteenth century, guns were not terribly effective. A review of collected incidents will probably show that local people who chose to stand and fight still paid a terrible price for their decision to resist. At the same time, however, slave raiders were not invincible and the capture of their "victims" was not inevitable. Moreover, resistance by people under attack may have also exacted of their attackers a price substantial enough to affect the way the raiders carried out their labor of violence.

It is also crucial to assess the indirect implications of raiding and resistance. In the case of north-central Africa, for example, many of the forms of resistance led people to leave their homelands either temporarily or permanently. Today's demographic desert, then, is not entirely the result of physical decimation; it is also the product of effective resistance. In addition, strategies of resistance that privileged settling in larger villages also had major consequences for health, reproduction, and survival. Larger, more compact settlements in less accessible locales created threats to the health of their inhabitants—such as the proliferation of disease through contaminated water supplies and the accumulation of waste, both animal and human. The epidemiological implications of larger settlements also demand exploration. Historical records and recollections from this part of the continent include numerous examples of outbreaks of smallpox and other contagious diseases rendered more frequent and virulent by the creation of larger concentrations of population (Cordell, Gregory, and Piché 1992, 39–70; Cordell 1985a; see also Austen and Headrick 1983; Headrick 1994). An assessment of the impact of raiding and the effectiveness of resistance, then, requires estimations of the numbers of people lost to the former as well as an appreciation of the gains and losses associated with the latter. The task is formidable but possible. It also demonstrates that a real, if not always effective, alternative to submitting to slavers and traders was indeed fighting back.

Notes

I dedicate this essay to the Muslims and non-Muslims of Ndele and the sous-préfecture of Dar al-Kouti in the Central African Republic, who in 1974 were making a decided effort to live together, despite the history of slave raiding and slave trading that so profoundly divided them three-quarters of a century earlier. I also wish to acknowledge my partner, the late Gary W. Irvin, for his encouragement and balanced advice about juggling the demands of research, teaching, and administration.

1. In this essay I use the expression "Muslim slave trade," to refer to slave raiding and slave trading by slavers on the Islamic frontier in Central Africa who identified themselves as Muslims, and who identified the people they enslaved as nonbelievers (usually *kirdi* or *kafir* in the oral testimonies recorded by visitors to the region at the time). I intentionally do not use the term Islamic, for two reasons. First, I focus attention on the raiders and traders themselves, and on how they distinguished themselves from their captives. Second, I wish to avoid the impression that I am implying that there is something inherent to Islam that sanctions slavery. To do so would be to make an essentialist argument that is inaccurate. While Islamic doctrine has in the past condoned enslaving some categories of non-Muslims, interpretations of proper behavior—and hence definitions of what is Islamic—have changed through time. For elaboration, see Brunschvig 1960; Juynboll 1913; Philips 1985, 66–87, 195–217. The same may be said of Christianity. Although historical convention today refers to the European commerce in captives to the Americas as the Atlantic slave trade, European slavers also often thought of the trade and their activities in religious terms, setting themselves as Christians against their captives, whom they described as non-Christians or "pagans" or "heathen." See Davis 1984, 32–39, 42–44, 51–52, 55–71, 91–93, 107, 112, 146. In that sense, for earlier periods at least, it would make sense to describe the European trade as the Christian slave trade. Throughout the world, in all epochs, slavers employed a variety of psychological means of dehumanizing the people they enslaved, thus justifying their ill treatment of fellow women and men.

2. Borno is the current official Nigerian spelling for this state.

3. For a history of the kingdom of Sinnar, see O'Fahey and Spaulding 1974, 15–104, and, on slave raiding, 56, 80.

4. For lists of raids by Rabih and al-Sanusi between 1879 and 1911, see Cordell 1985a, 54–55 (fig. 1), 105–8 (fig. 4).

BIBLIOGRAPHY

Oral Accounts

For a more lengthy description of the informants whose testimonies were collected in the former sultanate of Dar al-Kuti in 1974, see Cordell, *Dar al-Kuti,* 246–51. All of the following interviews were conducted by the author in Chadic Arabic in the presence of Muhammad Abakar, a research assistant who spoke Chadic Arabic and French.

OA3.2. Yadjouma Pascal, Banda Mbagga, about 76 years old when interviewed on 16 May 1974 in Ndele.

OA4.1. Yadjouma Pascal, Banda Mbagga, interviewed on 18 May 1974 in Ndele.

OA5.2/6.1. Yacoub Mahamat Dillang, Runga, about 80 years old when interviewed on 20 May 1974 in Ndele.

OA6.2. Abakar Tidjani, Runga-Nduka, about 55 years old when interviewed on 23 May 1974 in Ndele.

OA9.1. Yadri Sali (Salih), Banda Ngao, about 85 years old when interviewed on 5 June 1974 in Ndele.

OA9.2/10.1. Mahamat Ngouvela Dodo, Banda Ngao-Bulu (Buru), about 55 years old when interviewed on 5 June 1974 in the village of Mbollo.

OA13.1. Khrouma Sale (Salih), Runga Bagrim, about 80 years old when interviewed on 19 June 1974 in the village of Koundi.

OA14.2. Khrouma Sale (Salih), Runga Bagrim, interviewed on 21 June 1974 in the village of Koundi.

OA15.2/16.1. Yadjouma Pascal, Banda Mbagga, interviewed on 21 June 1974 in Ndele.

OA21.4. Al-Hajj Abakar Zacharia, Runga, about 80 years old when interviewed on 29 September 1974 in the village of Mbangbali.

OA22.1. Adoum Oumar, Runga, about 50 years old when interviewed on 29 September 1974 in the village of Manga.

OA22.3. Yahya Issa-Din, Runga Tunjur, about 75 years old when interviewed on 30 September 1974 in the village of Birbatouma.

OA23.1. Abdoulaye Oumbra, Sara Dinjo-Banda Linda, about 80 years old when interviewed on 1 October 1974 in the village of Djamssinda.

Archives

ANT (Archives Nationales du Tchad). N'Djaména. Series W. W53.27. Lucien, "Note sur les rezzous kirdis, miniminis, zevoix, etc." Biltine, n.d. (ca. 1911–15).

ENA (École nationale d'administration). The library of ENA includes archival documents from the Circonscription du Kémo-Gribingui.

Published Sources

Austen, Ralph, and Rita Headrick.1983. "Equatorial Africa under Colonial Rule." In David Birmingham and Phyllis Martin, eds., *History of Central Africa,* 2:27–94. London: Longman.

Barth, Heinrich. 1965. *Travels and Discoveries in North and Central Africa.* 3 vols. 1853. Reprint, London: Frank Cass.

Bjørkelo, Anders. 1989. *Prelude to the Mahdiyya: Peasants and Traders in the Shendi Region, 1821–1885.* Cambridge: Cambridge University Press.

Browne, William George B. 1806. *Travels in Africa, Egypt, and Syria from the Year 1792 to 1798.* London: T. Cadwell.

Bruel, Georges. 1935. *La France équatoriale africaine: Le pays, les habitants, la colonisation, les pouvoirs publics.* Paris: E. Larose.

Brunschvig, R. 1960. "ᶜAbd." In H. A. R. Gibb et al., eds., *The Encyclopaedia of Islam: New Edition,* 24–40. Leiden: E. J. Brill.

Burnham, Philip. 1980. *Opportunity and Constraint in a Savanna Society: The Gbaya of Meiganga, Cameroon.* New York: Academic Press.

Chapiseau, Félix. 1900. *Au pays de l'esclavage: Moeurs et coutumes de l'Afrique centrale, d'après les notes recueillies par Béhagle.* Paris: Maisonneuve.

Chevalier, Auguste. 1907. *Mission Chari-Lac Tchad, 1902–1904: L'Afrique Centrale Française: Récit du voyage de la Mission.* Paris: Augustin Challamel.

Cordell, Dennis D. 1977. "Eastern Libya, Wadai, and the Sanusiya: A Tariqa and a Trade Route." *Journal of African History* 18:21–36.

———. 1979. "Blood Partnership in Theory and Practice: The Expansion of Muslim Power in Dar al-Kuti." *Journal of African History* 20:379–94.

———. 1983. "The Savanna Belt of North Central Africa." In David Birmingham and Phyllis Martin, eds., *History of Central Africa,* 1:30–74. London: Longman.

———. 1985a. *Dar al-Kuti and the Last Years of the Trans-Saharan Slave Trade.* Madison: University of Wisconsin Press.

———. 1985b. "The Labor of Violence: Dar al-Kuti in the Nineteenth Century." In Catherine Coquery-Vidrovitch and Paul E. Lovejoy, eds., *The Workers of African Trade.* Beverly Hills: Sage Publications.

———. 1986. "Warlords and Enslavement: A Sample of Slave Raiders from Eastern Ubangi-Shari, 1870–1920." In Paul E. Lovejoy, ed., *Africans in Bondage: Studies in Slavery and the Slave Trade,* 335–69. Madison: African Studies Program, University of Wisconsin Press.

———. 1988. "The Delicate Balance of Force and flight: The End of Slavery in Eastern Ubangi-Shari." In Suzanne Miers and Richard Roberts, eds., *The End of Slavery in Africa,* 150–71. Madison: University of Wisconsin Press.

———. n.d. "Rabih b. Fadlallah." In Valentin Y. Mudimbe, ed., *The Encyclopedia of African Religion and Philosophy.* New York: Garland Publishing. In press.

Cordell, Dennis D., Joel W. Gregory, and Victor Piché. 1992. "The Demographic Reproduction of Health and Disease: Colonial Central African Republic and Contemporary Burkina Faso." In Steven Feierman and John M. Janzen, eds., *The Social Basis of Health and Healing in Africa.* Berkeley: University of California Press.

Courtet, H. 1907. "Géologie et minéralogie." In Auguste Chevalier, *Mission Chari-Lac Tchad, 1902–1904. L'Afrique centrale française. Récit du voyage de la mission,* 621–55. Paris: Augustin Challamel.

Dampierre, Eric de. 1967. *Un ancien royaume Bandia du Haut-Oubangui.* Paris: Plon.

———. 1983. *Des ennemis, des Arabes, des histoires . . .* Paris: Société d'ethnographie.

Davis, David Brion. 1984. *Slavery and Human Progress.* New York: Oxford University Press.

Decorse, Gaston Jules. 1906. *Du Congo au lac Tchad: La brousse telle quelle est, et les gens tels qu'ils sont (Mission Chari-lac Tchad, 1902–1904).* Paris: Augustin Challamel.

Delafosse, Maurice. 1930. *Enquête coloniale dans l'Afrique française.* Paris: Société d'Editions Géographiques, Maritimes et Coloniales.

Escayrac de Lauture, P. H. Stanislas d.' 1853. *Le désert et le Soudan.* Paris: J. Dumaine.

Fresnel, Fulgence. 1849. "Mémoire sur le Waday: Notice historique et géographique sur le Waday et les relations de cet empire avec la côte septentrionale de l'Afrique." *Bulletin de la société de géographie de Paris,* 3d ser., 11:5–75.

Gaud, Fernand. 1911. *Les Mandja (Congo français).* Brussels: A. de Wit.

Georges, Michel. 1963. "La vie rurale chez les Banda." *Les cahiers d'outre-mer* 16 (October–December): 321–59.

Giles-Vernick, Tamara. 1996. "Na lege ti guiriri (On the Road of History): Mapping Out the Past and Present in the M'Bres Region, Central African Republic." *Ethnohistory* 43:245–75.

Gordon, Murray. 1987. *L'esclavage dans le monde arabe.* Paris: Editions Robert Laffont.

Headrick, Rita. 1994. *Colonialism, Health, and Illness in French Equatorial Africa, 1885–1935.* Ed. Daniel R. Headrick. Atlanta: African Studies Association Press.

Julien, Émile. 1925–29. "Mohamed-es-Senoussi et ses états." *Bulletin de la Société des recherches congolaises* 7 (1925): 104–77; 8 (1927): 55–122; 9 (1928): 49–96; 10 (1929): 45–88.

Juynboll, T. W. 1913. "ᶜAbd." In M. T. Houtsma, R. Basset, T. W. Arnold, and R. Hartmann, eds., *Encyclopédie de l'Islam: Dictionnaire géographique, ethnographique, et biographique des peuples musulmans,* 16–19. Leiden: E. J. Brill.

Kalck, Pierre. 1970. "Histoire de la République centrafricaine, des origines à nos jours." 4 vols. Doctoral thesis, Sorbonne.

Lewis, Bernard. 1990. *Race and Slavery in the Middle East.* New York: Oxford University Press.

Levtzion, N., and J. F. P. Hopkins, eds. 2000. *Corpus of Early Arabic Sources for West African History.* Princeton: Markus Wiener.

Magnant, Jean-Pierre. 1986. *La terre sara, terre tchadienne.* Paris: L'Harmattan.

Marmon, Shaun E., ed. 1999. *Slavery in the Islamic Middle East.* Princeton: Markus Wiener.

Modat, Capitaine. 1912. "Une tournée en pays Fertyt." *Afrique française: Renseignements coloniaux* 22 5 (May): 177–98; 6 (June): 218–317; 7 (July): 270–89.

Nachtigal, Gustav. 1971. *Sahara and Sudan.* Vol. 4, *Wadai and Darfur.* Trans. Allen G. B. Fisher and Humphrey J. Fisher. London: C. Hurst.

———. 1987. *Sahara and Sudan.* Vol. 3, *The Chad Basin and Bagirmi.* Trans. Allen G. B. Fisher and Humphrey J. Fisher. Atlantic Highlands, N.J.: Humanities Press, International.

O'Fahey, Rex. 1982. "Fur and Fartit: The History of a Frontier." In John Mack and Peter Robertshaw, eds., *Culture History in the Southern Sudan: Archaeology, Linguistics, and Ethnohistory,* 75–87. Nairobi: British Institute in Eastern Africa.

O'Fahey, Rex, and Jay Spaulding. 1974. *Kingdoms of the Sudan.* London: Methuen.

Pantobe, D. 1984. "Population." In *Atlas de la république centrafricaine.* Paris: Les Editions Jeune Afrique.

Philips, William D., Jr. 1985. *Slavery from Roman Times to the Early Transatlantic Trade.* Minneapolis: University of Minnesota Press.

Prins, Pierre. 1909. "Les troglodytes du Dar Banda et du Djebel Mela." *Bulletin de géographie historique et descriptive,* 11–26.

———. 1925. "Relation du voyage de l'Administrateur P. Prins à Said-Baldas et dans le Bassin de la Haute-Kotto (1901), precédée d'une note de M. l'Administrateur Bruel." *Bulletin de la société des recherches congolaises* 6:109–70.

Prioul, Christian. 1981. *Entre Oubangui et Chari vers 1890.* Paris: Société d'ethnographie.

———. n.d. "Notes sur la diffusion du manioc dans la partie centrale du territoire centrafricain." Bangui.

Renouf-Stefanik, Suzanne. 1978. *Animisme et Islam chez les Manza (Centrafrique): Influence de la religion musulmane sur les coutumes traditionnelles manza.* Paris: Société d'Etudes Linguistiques et Anthropologiques de France (SELAF).

Reyna, Stephen P. 1990. *Wars without End: The Political Economy of a Precolonial African State.* Hanover, N.H.: University Press of New England.

Rone, Jemera. 1995. *Children in Sudan: Slaves, Street Children, and Child Soldiers.* New York: Human Rights Watch.

Un saharien. 1908. "La question du Ouadaï." *Afrique française* 18 (August): 282–87.

Santandrea, Stefano. 1964. *A Tribal History of the Western Bahr el-Ghazal.* Bologna: Centro Librario dei Missionaria Comboniani.

———. 1981. *Ethno-Geography of the Bahr el-Ghazal (Sudan).* Bologna: Editrice Missionaria Italiana.

Schlippe, Pierre de. 1956. *Shifting Cultivation in Africa: The Zande System of Agriculture.* London: Routledge and Kegan Paul.

Schweinfurth, Georg. 1874. *The Heart of Africa: Three Years' Travels and Adventures in the Unexplored Regions of Central Africa, 1868–1871.* Trans. Ellen Frewer. 2 vols. New York: Harper and Brothers.

Sikainga, Ahmad Alawad. 1991. *The Western Bahr al-Ghazal under British Rule, 1898–1956.* Athens: Ohio University Press.

Stemler, A. B. L., J. R. Harlan, and J. M. J. deWet. 1975. "Caudatum Sorghums and Speakers of Chari-Nile Languages in Africa." *Journal of African History* 16:175–82.

Tisserant, Charles. 1953. "L'agriculture dans les savanes de l'Oubangui." *Bulletin de l'Institut des Etudes Centrafricaines* (Brazzaville), new ser., 6:209–74.

el-Tounsy, Mohammed ibn Omar [Muhammad ibn ?Umar al-Tunisi]. 1845. *Voyage au Darfour.* Trans. S. Perron. Paris: Duprat.

———. 1851. *Voyage au Ouaday.* Trans. S. Perron. Paris: Duprat.

Vergiat, A. M. 1937. *Moeurs et coutumes des Mandja.* Paris: Payot.

Weber, Olivier. 1999. *Soudan: Les enfants esclaves.* Paris: Editions Mille et Une Nuits.

Chapter 4

The Impact of the Slave Trade on Cayor and Baol

Mutations in Habitat and Land Occupancy

Adama Guèye

Throughout the Senegambian kingdoms the European presence gave rise to a new era, leading to the disruption of the economic, political, and social life of most of the states of this region. After the rerouting of trade from the Sahara, the Atlantic coast became the new focus of commercial exchange. The economy, up to that point dominated by agricultural activity, entered a new phase due to the slave trade organized by the Europeans based at trading stations along the coast: Gorée and Rufisque for Cayor, Portudal for Baol. Cayor and Baol, two political entities of northern Senegambia, participated in this trade. These two frontier states, their destinies sometimes linked, were from that time subjected to profound changes.[1] In addition to the destabilization of the economy, the political and social structures were severely shaken. Indeed, the insecurity encouraged by the hunt for human beings and the numerous ensuing wars caused both Cayor and Baol to sink into chaos for a long time. This situation reached its pinnacle in the seventeenth century under the reign of the Guedj family, who first took the throne in 1695. The leaders participated in the development of the slave trade with the assistance of a corps of warriors called captives of the crown, also known as *ceddo.* The ceddo, not always of slave origin, were granted privileges that allowed them to practice all sorts of exactions. Pillaged and kidnapped for ransom, the people of these kingdoms were at their mercy.

European sources, as well as the oral tradition, focus on the simmering crisis between the two kingdoms rather than the role played by the Europeans in the expansion of the slave trade. Information provided by the slaving powers, although substantial, contains gaps and biases. Today, at a time when certain reactionary theses are being developed, scholars of the slave trade cannot rely solely on written documents but need to turn to oral and archaeological resources as well. There is, for example, a close relationship between armed conflicts, the frequent abandonment of villages noted at the time of the slave trade, and the new habitat and modes of land occupancy created by the populations in response.

However, the people of Cayor and Baol were not passive agents; in the face of an increasingly dangerous situation, they devised strategies capable of slowing down the slavers. They created a new form of habitat and land occupancy based on separation by social class, following rules established by the aristocracy. It is in the transformation of their social structures that the impact of the slave trade is clearly visible. An archeological study completed with information from both the oral tradition and written documents from European sources permits us to determine the mechanisms used by the inhabitants of Cayor at Bayol to confront the rise of the slavers.

Armed Conflicts and Abandoned Villages

The ascent of the Guedj to power marks a great break in the history of this region. This new royal line, of which Latsucabé Faal is the first king,[2] came into contact with Europe quite early. The relationships that were woven between Africans and Europeans inscribed themselves within the framework of the Atlantic trade, which enabled the Guedj to "integrate the wider world trade" (M. Fall 1996–98, 2:82). The principal object of these transactions was the captive, who became a veritable financial standard. Since no group specialized in this type of commerce, as did the Juula in Manding country, the Wolof kings took this activity into their own hands. From the interior of the country, the captives were led to the trading sites established on the coast, where they were exchanged for goods imported from Europe. The nature of certain imported products, like firearms, contributed strongly to the expansion of the two kingdoms, completing the establishment of the hegemony of the Guedj. Yet this hegemony was contested by the other reigning families, resulting in a situation of latent crisis.[3] From that point on, one of the chief characteristics of this period is the frequency of wars between the two kingdoms. Armed confrontation extended beyond their frontiers as the kingdoms of Djolof, Walo, Siin, and Futa became serious threats.

With the intensification of the slave trade, war became the most lucrative industry and military aristocracies developed. The period that followed the death of the first reigning Guedj was particularly troubled. Armed conflicts reached their highest point with the wars between the line of Latsucabé and the Dorobé (1749–57) (R. Fall 1979, 79). The latter occupied the throne throughout this period and were later ousted by the Guedj, whose return to power did not succeed in bringing an end to the successive crises. It is from this perspective that we must situate the various opponents: first King Amari Ngoné Ndella, who was opposed to Birima Fatma Thioub; and then Thioub, opposed to Tié Yacine Dieng. These wars brought into conflict the two kingdoms and ended only in 1820. The battles, whatever their result, were profitable to the slavers since each defeat meant the capture and sale of prisoners by the victors.

Nonetheless, these conflicts sometimes impeded the development of the slave trade. In 1701, for example, André Brüe, director and commander of the French Compagnie du Sénégal, was captured by Latsucabé, resulting in an eight-month interruption of the slave trade. A few years later, the discord between Macodou Coumba Diarigne (1766–77) and another French agent, J. A. Le Brasseur, blocked the slave trade from February 1777 to January 1778 (Le Brasseur 1979, 86). The insertion of the Europeans in the internal affairs of different Senegambian kingdoms, explains in part the frequency of wars among the states. The latent crisis between Djolof and Cayor resulted in the occupation of the latter by the *burba* (king of) Djolof. As Father Jean Baptiste Labat recounted: "Capitalizing on the troubles of the country of the Damel, which was ruined by lengthy wars, [he] invaded it and exiled the young king" (1728, 4:116). But this victory was ephemeral and the people of Cayor reoccupied the throne. During the war, in order to escape captivity, the people "retreated into nearly impenetrable woods and abandoned their villages and fields to the Damel" (ibid.). The forest of Mboumoune, in particular, which separated the two kingdoms, served as a refuge for the inhabitants of Djolof.

On the northern frontier, the claims of Walo and, further away, those of Futa in the east became clear. Cayor, where the aftereffects of earlier battles were still visible, seemed an easy prey. In this area, the role of the French trading post of

Saint-Louis has to be taken into consideration. In order to safeguard their interests and fill their boats with captives, the Europeans encouraged these conflicts. The French and the British competed for a complete seizure of the region, but Cayor, relying on British power, was victorious in the war against Walo (Barry 1985, 172–75). The multiplicity of armed conflicts in the region, linked to the slave trade, meant that every free man or woman was a captive on reprieve since at any moment he or she could end up in the slave traders' nets. But not every war was fought for the ultimate benefit of the slavers, some were actually a rejection of the slave trade. The people fiercely opposed the predatory kings in order to escape servitude.

The impact of the slave trade on the patterns of settlement reveals itself in the frequency with which the inhabitants abandoned their homes and lands during this period. When facing an outbreak of violence, abandoning the land and resettling somewhere else was often the only weapon. But armed clashes also led to modifications in the patterns of settlement and the way the land was occupied. This trend is visible in the fragility of the frontier sectors, which were constantly being destroyed. At the same time, political centers, for the most part chief towns of the provinces, were strengthened.

The Destruction of the Frontier Sectors and Mobility of the Capitals

Written sources and oral tradition are virtually unanimous on the vulnerability of the frontier sectors. Since they were at risk, they were abandoned more often than other areas. Kany Samb, a traditionalist historian, confirms that villages such as Khamnâne, Keur Youga Thioro, Digne, Tiolane, Dieule Mbame, Djadj, and Soughère—situated at the frontier between Cayor and Baol—were part of the first zones attacked in case of conflict between the two states. Such villages were frequently abandoned as a result. The same phenomenon was observed at the frontier between Cayor and Djolof. During the war that opposed Macodou Coumba Diarigne and Madior Yacine Issa, the villages of Wakhale, Walalane, Khouma, and Ndiané were burned and deserted. This tactic, based on the destruction of the frontier sectors, found its most striking illustration in 1796, when it resulted in the stunning victory of Amary Ngoné Ndella over the troops of Almamy Abdel Kader Kane of Futa Toro. When the *damel-tègne* Amary Ngoné "learned that a levy en masse was being prepared against him, he did not hesitate to adopt the tactic required: completely destroy his frontier, seizing its provisions and filling its wells" (Roger 1829, 109). Nothing was left for the enemy, and numerous men, women, and children died of dysentery or hunger in front of the ruined and deserted villages and fields, where resupply was impossible. The prisoners from Futa Toro were sold to the European slavers and sent to the British West Indies.

With the destruction of the border areas, the relocation of the principal towns was a major characteristic of the fight against the insecurity brought about by the kings' involvement in the Atlantic trade. One of the most remarkable incidents of the Guedj dynasty was the transfer of the capital. Maka became the chief town of the two kingdoms, to the detriment of Mboule and Lambaye, the respective capitals of Cayor and Baol. This new residence was made famous by the oral tradition, written sources, and certain epic accounts (T. Fall 1977, 117). Founded by Latsucabé, Maka reached its height under Meîssa Teind Wedj (1720–48), son and successor of the first Guedj king. Maka was a simple village, created especially for the government of the two countries, a royal village, a village of princes and princesses who never knew manual labor. Maka was a village where everything remained precarious and provisional. This precariousness was evident in the fact that several capitals were chosen after this one. Macodou Coumba Diarigne took up residence at Khandane, while Amary Ngoné Ndella moved to Bardiale. This period was thus noteworthy for the mobility of the royal residences out of a concern for protection that proved to be the direct result of the slave trade. Beyond these royal capitals, secondary political centers developed, such as Kaba in Baol. This village was crossed by one of the ancient slave routes that started at Portudal, the principal trading point for the area, and ended at Lambaye, chief town of the kingdom.[4] Kaba reached its apogee under the rule of the Guedj. The *fara* Kaba, of slave origin, commander of the armies of Baol, lived there. He was named by the king to thwart the actions of the free-born *djaraf*.[5] The fara Kaba was an economic pillar, since he was responsible for the sale of the king's slaves. He was also involved in acts of pillage, the principal source of the aristocracy's income.

Defensive Strategies

The slave trade installed a veritable "civilization of violence" in the kingdoms of Cayor and Baol. The people, in order to escape this steamroller, used their habitat as a protective shield. The economic lag and technological stagnation this new situation induced were reflected in the people's way of life: obsessed with daily survival, they did not build any dwellings meant to last. The human habitat throughout this period was notable for its simplicity and precariousness, but it was always well structured and responded to deep strategic preoccupations. The defensive strategies the people of Cayor and Baol established essentially rested on precariousness, as already noted, but also on relief, vegetation, and separation. The aristocracy, confronting an outbreak of violence, managed spatial and social organization to its advantage. Each social category was assigned a village or a neighborhood with features that distinguish it from the others, a strategy that evidences the maintenance and perhaps strengthening of relationships of domination and submission, of command and obedience.

Interestingly, in the face of the ascent of strong military regimes, and in opposition to them and to the manipulation of the lower castes for the benefit of the aristocracy, Islam became an escape route for people victimized by various kinds of exactions. The marabouts (Muslim clerics) set themselves up against the tyranny of the ceddo. Two categories of marabouts emerged: the Serigne Fakk Taal, who fought for the respect of Islamic precepts, and the Serigne Lamb, who were linked to people in power (Guèye 1990, 54). In each kingdom, the marabouts founded villages for those who wished to escape the tyrannical yoke of the kings. As Brahim Diop has stressed, "It was in these village-refuges, these safe havens, that the people fleeing the zones of pillage came to settle, where the *ceddo* had no power. Security gave birth to prosperity. There were virtually never any shortages or famines or high mortality rates. Alcoholism and sexually transmitted diseases, quite common during the slave trade, were practically unknown there" (1997, 146). These Muslim enclaves were often established along wooded zones for enhanced security. Contrary to the rule followed in the villages of the aristocracy, the "lower castes" were not segregated and used as protective shields. The spiritual guides emphasized that Islam did not permit discrimination. The Muslim *sauvetés,* or safe havens, attracted refugees, who sometimes traveled great distances to reach them. Some of these refuges carry evocative names: "the village of free people," "here where no one can reach them anymore," "here where we speak of peace," or "place of abundance."

Throughout the region, the concern for defense was present in the pattern of settlement, its very precariousness being an essential element. The habitations were made essentially of straw and were thus susceptible to arson. Torching was a strategic response, as the inhabitants, sensing danger, elected to set their houses afire in order to slow the enemy's advance, allowing themselves time to flee and thereby escape captivity. In addition, because the habitat was precarious, it was also easily rebuilt. The materials, leaves and branches, were found in the immediate vicinity. A village destroyed as a defensive ploy could then be rapidly rebuilt as soon as the danger passed. Moreover, the building of each house was itself guided by strictly defensive considerations. The homes were usually accessed by only one door, which also served as a window. This opening was often placed so low that several individuals could not enter at the same time.[6] Whoever got in was required to bend over or crawl, so that he was easily neutralized by whoever was inside.

In addition to the precariousness of the structures, the aristocracy took into consideration certain elements of the physical surroundings. The political elite preferred to build its dwellings on small hills or, on the contrary, in the plains, where they were encircled by buttes that served as observation posts. The examples of Maka and Mboule are quite revealing. Nestled in the heart of a depression, these two royal capitals were surrounded by a chain of dunes that formed a natural barrier. Since the cities were well hidden, a stranger passing through the zone would not notice them.

Vegetation was also a determining element in the new organization of space. Villages were often situated at the heart of clearings, in the middle of forests, or abutting them. The woods served as a fall-back position where a counterstrike could be prepared. Of particular interest are the several defensive strategies mentioned by oral tradition, such as the cultivation of venomous plants to halt the advance of the slavers. Shrubs like Dedde (*Acacia ataxantha*) were also planted. They served as a hiding places, thanks to their thick branches entwined like vines to form a roof. And both written sources and the oral tradition confirm that the tops of certain tall trees were excellent observation posts. Epic stories reveal that at the battle of Maka a sentinel perched atop a tree, having caught sight of the enemy forces, sounded the alarm. In this way, the damel-tègne Meîssa Ten Wedj was warned of the danger, was able to organize a defense, and won the war.

In order to ward off any attack or enemy invasion, the aristocracy systematically modified how the land was occupied. This restructuring was directed by whoever commanded the village or neighborhood. It was his task to indicate to each social group which area they had to occupy. This reconfiguration of the settlements was far from accidental. In fact, based on the separation of different groups, it responded to strategic needs. Jacques Joseph Le Maire, who visited the palace of the king of Cayor in the seventeenth century recounted that "before arriving at the gate of the palisade that surrounded it, you find a spacious area where they coach the horses. Outside, next to these palisades were the houses of the great lords. You entered this square in the palace via a wide avenue. Those closest to the king had their dwelling along this avenue, their proximity or distance indicated their rank" (1695, 139–40).[7]

Both the written sources and the oral tradition refer to numerous courtyards that every visitor had to cross: the number given varies from three to seven. Baron Roger, governor of Senegal from 1820 to 1828, noted that "between each courtyard is a house that serves as guardhouse" (1829, 82). Oral tradition confirms the existence of this architecture. The traditionalist Kany Samb notes that visitors had to go through seven gates, called *fithiare* (vestibule), that opened on vast and shady courtyards. This layout was intended to shelter the king, whose dwelling was remote and well protected.

The spatial organization and establishment of the villages followed a defensive concern. The royal capitals were girdled by a crown of villages that served not only as both military cover and shield in case of outside attack but as a source of supplies. Khandane, the place of residence of King Macodou Coumba Diarigne, was surrounded by villages of captives such as Lissar, Tiar Khandane, and Khatta Keur Youga. Such was also the case with Lambaye, capital of Baol, enclosed by several villages, among them Mbotal, Mboubane, Sokano, Rew Mawo, Ndjackalack.

Within the towns and villages themselves, social segregation was strictly enforced for social and security reasons. The involvement in a particular occupation determined the existence of socioprofessional groups considered inferior. The west, sign of nobility, was the seat of power. The dwellings of the king or provincial ruler were established there. They usually abutted a forest where the king could retreat at the first warning of danger. The other cardinal directions had their own particular meaning (A. Guèye 1998, 79). The east was inhabited exclusively by the griots (musicians) or at times by slaves. The disdain for certain categories insured that their dwellings were never established near those of the king. The oral tradition emphasizes that sometimes even the mere shadow of their homes could bring misfortune. There was often a tall tree, a clear sign of power, between their dwellings and those of the king. Foreigners and captives occupied the north and south. At Laa, the patronymic Teugue gua (blacksmiths' place) was used to indicate the *guent* (deserted habitat) of the blacksmiths in the southern part of the province. Minorities, such as the Moors and the Fulani, were sometimes also housed in this area. At Khandane there are still traces of these divisions. Only the guent of the shoemakers still exists. It is surrounded by that of the griots and the *mabo,* a subgroup of the blacksmiths. These different social categories served as a shield for the nobility.

In order to maintain a certain level of resistance, the populations regrouped. One of the essential characteristics of the defensive strategy they devised was the restructuring of settlements into tightly knit groups of "around forty or fifty houses of straw abutting each other in a circle surrounded by palisades of thick trees" (A. Guèye 1998, 79). Lambaye at its largest would have comprised at least a hundred single-family. The homes were carefully grouped so as to take on the form of a labyrinth and were interconnected in order to permit their occupants to warn their neighbors when danger loomed. During the slave trade, isolation and dispersion were real dangers, which explains why the distance between villages was reduced. For this reason, whenever the villagers felt threatened, they sounded the alarm and regrouped to organize their defense.

The slave trade led to profound changes in Cayor and Baol. The political, economic, and social structures were deeply shaken. The violence brought about by the incessant wars, a direct result of the hunt for men, women, and children pushed the people to elaborate defensive strategies based on the rational management of their environment. At times this enabled them to halt the advance of the slavers.

An analysis of the changes in patterns of settlement and the way in which the land was occupied founded only on the written sources cannot adequately bring forth the various elements that characterized several centuries of Senegambian history linked to the development of the Atlantic slave trade. Oral tradition preserved by traditionalists, as well as the excavating of sites related to the slave trade—like the work presently being conducted on Gorée Island—help us better understand its deep impact on the kingdoms of the region and the many ways in which the populations organized their short- and long-term resistance to counteract its devastation.

NOTES

This chapter was translated from the French by Richard Serrano, Rutgers, the State University of New Jersey.

1. According to T. L. Fall (1974), only six kings were able to reign over both kingdoms. They were then conferred the title of *damel-tègne.*

2. This king, whose rise to power is considered a coup, reigned over Cayor and Baol from 1695 to 1719.

3. To be considered for access to the throne in Cayor, one had to belong to one of seven families: Bey, Dorobe, Guedj, Guelware, Mouyoye, Sogno, Wagadou.

4. Djiby Guèye and Abdou Guèye, notables at Kaba, insist on the importance of this route during the era of the Atlantic slave trade. Called *leffoum* Kaba, it made this village famous.

5. Unlike the fara, the djaraf was a free man chosen among his peers. According to Abdou Guèye, the djaraf had to be a Guèye.

6. Abdou Gora Diop, village chief at Khamnâne.

7. This is probably the new capital founded by Latsucabe, since Le Maire's sojourn took place during his reign.

Bibliography

Adanson, Michel. 1757. *Histoire naturelle du Sénégal avec la relation abrégée d'un voyage fait en ce pays pendant les années 1749,1750, 1751, 1752, et 1753.* Paris: Claude-Jean-Baptiste Bauche.

———. 1980. "Mémoire inédit sur le Sénégal et l'île de Gorée." Presented and commented on by Victor Martin and Charles Becker. *Bulletin de l'Institut fondamental d'Afrique noire* 37 (4).

Bah, Thierno M. 1985. *Architecture militaire traditionnelle polioacetique dans le Soudan occidental du dix-septième à la fin du dix-neuvième siècle.* Yaoundé: Editions Clé.

Barry, Boubacar. 1985. *Le royaume du Waalo: Le Sénégal avant la conquête.* Paris: Karthala.

Bathily, Abdoulaye. 1987. "La traite atlantique des esclaves: Ses effets économiques et sociaux: Genèse du sous-développement." *Annales de la faculté de lettres et sciences humaines* 17 (191): 83–93.

Becker, Charles, and Victor Martin. 1975. "Kayor et Baol: Royaumes sénégalais et traite des esclaves au dix-huitième siècle." *Revue française d'histoire d'outre-mer* 62:226–99.

———. 1988. "Les effets démographiques de la traite des esclaves en Sénégambie: Esquisse d'une histoire des peuplements du dix-huitième à la fin du dix-neuvième siècle." In Serge Daget, ed., *De la traite à l'esclavage: Actes du colloque international sur la traite des noirs.* Vol. 2. Paris: Société Française d'Histoire d'Outre-Mer.

Boilat, David. 1853. *Esquisses sénégalaises.* Paris: Bertrand.

Ca' Da Mosto, Alvise. 1895. *Relations de voyages à la côte occidentale de l'Afrique, 1455–1457.* Paris: Leroux.

Curtin, Philip D. 1974. *Economic Change in Precolonial Africa: Senegambia in the Era of the Slave Trade.* Madison: University of Wisconsin Press.

Demanet, M. l'abbé. 1767. *Nouvelle histoire de l'Afrique française.* 2 vols. Paris: Veuve Duchesne.

Dieng, Bassirou. 1989. "L'épopée du Cayor: Poétique et réception." Ph.D. dissertation, Université de la Sorbonne.

Diop, Brahim. 1985. "Les sites archéologiques du Baol: Sites dits protohistoriques: Villages désertés ou 'Gent.'" Master's thesis, Université de Dakar, Faculté de lettres et sciences humaines.

———. 1997. "Traite négrière, désertions rurales, et occupation du sol dans l'arrière pays de Gorée." In Djibril Samb, ed., *Gorée et esclavage: Mythes et réalités.* Etudes africaines no. 38. Dakar: IFAN.

———. 2000. "Introduction à l'archéologie de la traite négrière dans les pays wolof et sereer." In R. Vernet, ed., *L'archéologie de l'Afrique de l'ouest Sahara et Sahel.* Paris: SEPIA.

Diouf, Mamadou. 1990. *Le Kajoor au dix-neuvième siècle: Pouvoir Ceedo et conquête coloniale.* Paris: Karthala.

Doumet. 1974. "Mémoire inédit (1769): Le Kayor et les pays voisins au cours de la seconde moitié du dix-huitième siècle." Presented by Charles Becker and Victor Martin. BIFAN 36, 1B:25–92.

Ducasse, A. 1948. *Les négriers ou le temps des esclaves.* Paris: Hachette.

Fall, Cheikh. 1966. "La randonnée de Birima Fatma Thioub." *Notes africaines* (Dakar: IFAN) (116): 124–34.

Fall, Mamadou. 1996–98. "L'Etat post-atlantique entre terroirs et réseaux transculturels en Sénégambie dix-septième–vingtième siècles: Approche méthodologique." *Revue sénégalaise d'histoire,* new ser., 2–3.

Fall, Rokhaya. 1979. "La royauté et le pouvoir royal dans le Kajoor précolonial." Master's thesis, Université de Dakar, Faculté de lettres et sciences humaines.

———. 1994. "Traite négrière et mutations internes dans un royaume sénégambien: Le Bawol." Acts of the International Committee for Museums and Collections of Archeology and History, Congress held in Dakar, 14–19 March.

Fall, Tanor Latsoucabé. 1974. "Recueil sur la vie des damels." BIFAN 39, B:197–148.

Gaston-Martin. 1993. *L'ère des négriers, 1714–1774.* Paris: Karthala.

Guèye, Adama. 1998. "Les expressions matérielles du pouvoir dans l'habitat au Cayor et au Baol, seizième–dix-neuvième siècle: Approche ethnographique." Master's thesis, Université Cheikh Anta Diop, Faculté de lettres et sciences humaines.

Guèye, Mbaye. 1985. *L'Afrique et l'esclavage.* Quétigny: Marliusart.

———. 1990. "La transformation des sociétés wolof et sereer de l'ère de la conquête à la mise en place de l'administration coloniale, 1854–1920." Ph.D. dissertation, UCAD.

———. 1997. "Gorée et la traite négrière." In Djibril Samb, ed., *Gorée et l'esclavage: Mythes et réalités.* Etudes africaines no. 38. Dakar: IFAN.

Labarthe, P. 1802. *Voyage au Sénégal pendant les années 1784 et 1785—d'après les mémoires de Lajaille.* Paris: Dentu.

Labat, J. B. 1728. *Nouvelle relation de l'Afrique occidentale.* 5 vols. Paris: Cavelier.

Lamiral, M. 1791. *L'Affrique et le peuple affriquain.* Paris: Editions Dessenne.

Le Brasseur, J. A. 1979. "Détails historiques et politiques: Mémoire inédit." Published and annotated by C. Becker et V. Martin. 1778. Reprint, BIFAN, 39, B, 1.

Le Maire, Jacques Joseph. 1695. *Les voyages du sieur Le Maire aux îles Canaries, Cap-Verd, Sénégal, et Gambie.* Paris: Jacques Collombat.

Martin, Victor, and Charles Becker. 1984. *Inventaire des sites protohistoriques de la Sénégambie.* Paris: Kaolack.

Mbokolo, Elikia. 1998. "La dimension africaine de la traite des Noirs." *Monde diplomatique* 529 (April): 16–17.

McIntosh, S. K., and R. J. McIntosh. 1993. "Field Survey in the Tumulus Zone of Senegal." *African Archeological Review* 11:73–107.

Mollien, Gaspard T. 1820. *Voyage dans l'intérieur de l'Afrique aux sources du Sénégal et de la Gambie.* Paris: Courrier.

Pélissier, P. 1966. *Les pays du Sénégal: Les civilisations agraires du Cayor à la Casamance.* Fabrège: St. Yrieux.

Person, Yves. 1974. "La Sénégambie dans l'histoire." In *Senegambia: Proceedings of a Colloquium at the University of Aberdeen.* Aberdeen University Press.

Pruneau de Pommegorge, Antoine. 1789. *Description de la nigritie.* Paris: Maradan.

Rodney, Walter. 1972. *How Europe Underdeveloped Africa.* London: Bogle l'Ouverture.

———. 1966. "African Slavery and Other Forms of Social Oppression on the Upper Guinea Coast in the Context of the Slave Trade." *Journal of African History* 7, 3.

Roger, M. le Baron. 1829. *Kelédor: Histoire africaine.* Paris: Moreau.

Rousseau, R. 1929. "Etude sur le Oualo. Les cahiers de Yoro Dyâo." *Bulletin du Comité d'études historiques et scientifiques de l'Afrique occidentale française* 1–2:133–211.

———. 1933. "Etude sur le Cayor. Les cahiers de Yoro Dyâo." *Bulletin du Comité d'études historiques et scientifiques de l'Afrique occidentale française* 16:237–98.

Samb, Kany. Traditionalist interviewed in Thiaroye, 9 April 1999.

CHAPTER 5

Defensive Strategies

Wasulu, Masina, and the Slave Trade

Martin A. Klein

HISTORIANS LOOKING AT AFRICA during the period of the Atlantic slave trade have generally focused on the growth of slave-trading states and the extension of slave trade routes into the far interior. Writers like Patrick Manning (1990) have divided African populations into the raiders and the raided. While raiders often became raiders in order to acquire weapons, almost all raided societies learned how to defend themselves. The effectiveness of their defenses forced slavers to reach deeper and deeper into the interior (e.g., Miller 1988, pt. 1). It also forced them to develop new strategies. My thinking on this question has been focused recently by the work of two young historians trained at Stanford, Andrew Hubbell (1997; 2001) and Walter Hawthorne (1998; 1999; 2001; this volume).[1] Both Hubbell and Hawthorne argue that the societies they studied learned to defend themselves quite effectively, forcing slavers to develop increasingly complex strategies. I explore two other cases, Wasulu and Masina. One fits the Hubbell-Hawthorne model and the other is different.

The most important defense against slavers was the construction of walled and fortified villages. Here the work of Hubbell and Hawthorne merges with a masterful thesis about military architecture written by Guinean historian Thierno

Mouctar Bah (1985; see also this volume). Its central argument is that in the absence of cannons, African armies could not breech the walls of a fortified town or village. Even Samori, West Africa's most powerful military leader, could not break the siege of the fortress of Sikasso. Since reading Bah's book, I have analyzed the siege of a market town in Wasulu in southern Mali, Ntentu, which did eventually fall, probably because it was betrayed. But its siege took months and involved resources that few slavers had. Village walls were not monumental but were high enough to put off slavers, who usually lacked the resources to undertake sieges. In West Africa, while massive military campaigns took place, much of the slaving was done by small bands of raiders. Slaving, I may add, was not a highly remunerative business.

Before I discuss the defensive mechanisms, let me describe these two societies. Wasulu is a decentralized society in southern Mali. By the eighteenth century, it faced some very predatory neighbors, of whom the most powerful were Segu to the north and Futa Jallon to the west.[2] Wasulunke villages were organized in *jamana,* village confederations, which provided collaboration but had no fixed structures of authority. The Wasulunke speak a dialect of Bambara though they claim Fulbe origin. Wasulunke did serve in the armies of other states and their war leaders sometimes established an evanescent hegemony. The jamana often warred with and raided each other, and in fact there seems at times to have been conflict within various jamana. In 1882 the various jamana submitted to Samori, whose agents in Wasulu were largely Wasulunke, some of whom became chiefs. In 1888, Samori attacked Sikasso, the most formidable fortifications in West Africa. For fifteen months he tried unsuccessfully to maintain a siege. The demands he made for food and porters fell heavily on Wasulu, which revolted. Samori cracked down forcefully. Massive numbers of people were enslaved. Others fled, taking refuge in areas controlled by the French. The ultimate disaster involved Ntentu, the market town where Samori traditionally disposed of his slave booty. In 1893, when he ordered villages loyal to him to move further east, Ntentu refused. The siege was long and bitter and eventually succeeded. Local traditions claim that over three thousand people died at Ntentu. My concern here, however, is as much the success of Wasulu as its eventual failure.

Masina is a very different case. It is the inner delta of the Niger, a vast flood plain, where the river splits into numerous channels and floods every year. The area early produced an important rice surplus, but much of the land was wild until recent centuries, a refuge for hunters and fishermen.[3] Fulbe pastoralists began moving in as early as the thirteenth century, and from the sixteenth century systematic inroads were made by both Fulbe herders and Bambara agriculturalists

(Gallais 1967, 1:67; Sanankoua 1990, ch. 1). The Bambara concentrated on dry land areas, but the Fulbe found the alluvial plains ideal for transhumant cycles. Gradually they established an ascendancy over preexisting populations, reducing many to slavery or tributary relationships (Gallais 1967, 1:77–93).

Brown speaks of the Fulbe of the delta as "loosely bound in anarchic little clans and matrilineages" (1969, iii). This were probably not very different from the kinship-based structures that were fundamental in agricultural Wasulu. The leaders of fractions were called Ardos. Two processes began to transform them. First, each of the Ardos began to develop a group of warriors, often the sons of wives taken from neighboring agriculturalists. They fought on horseback, in contrast to the herdsmen, who fought on foot as they followed their herds (Gallais 1967, 1:92–93). As elsewhere, a warrior subculture emerged. According to Brown, "They developed an ideal model of the intrepid cavalryman, innovative and courageous in battle, unyielding toward foes, stoic in defeat, and magnanimous toward lower classes. . . . Military prowess, political power and material wealth did create something of a gap between the Dikko and the other Fulbe clans, and made the Dikko objects of envy and resentment" (1969, 102). Second, as the demand for slaves pushed deeper and deeper into Africa, slave raiding and slave use increased, and the Ardos were pulled into the slave-raiding economy as clients of Segu. The Dikko, Brown writes, "policed and taxed the Pulo regions in the interest of the Diarra; they campaigned widely with the armies of Segu. They inter-married with the Diarra, and adopted some of the trappings and social practices of the Bambara royal clan" (101). The Ardos also became dependent on the labor of slaves, both earlier inhabitants reduced collectively and those taken in slave raids. At the same time, Masina increasingly bore the brunt of both Bambara and Tuareg raids. Vulnerable to attack because of their transhumant cycles, the mass of Fulbe found themselves more prey than predator.

Thus, we see that both Masina and Wasulu were increasingly threatened by the slave raiders. We also see that one aspect of both situations was that ambition and greed led some men within both societies to ally themselves to predatory neighbors.

Defensive Strategies

The most important defensive strategy in much of Africa was the construction of walls and the development of architecture that made it difficult for attackers to take prisoners even if they succeeded in entering a fortified village. Hubbell writes that Samo villages in Burkina Faso had high walls and few points of entry. Town gates were few and often so small that people had to bend over to enter. Houses had several entries, so that even a successful enemy had to pursue his prey through houses and narrow alleys. Hawthorne (1998) describes the development of large fortified villages among the Balanta of the Upper Guinea Coast. All over, small villages disappeared as people sought security in larger and better-protected villages. Perhaps most startling to Europeans were the complex, elaborate, and beautiful villages of the Gurunsi, a people much victimized by slave raiders. The entrances to Gurunsi villages were sometimes as low as seventy centimeters (Duperray 1984, 34). One French scholar-administrator was so baffled by the Gurunsi building such complex structures that he attributed their genius to the influence of Songhai and ancient Egypt (Bourdier and Trinh, 1985, 26–29).[4] There were other approaches to security. Some Diola built "defensive palisades" (Mark 1985, 54). Others maintained a dispersed settlement pattern, but land around villages was uncleared, compounds were walled, and homes were hidden in the forest growth. Compounds had a single door, which could be bolted, and had no windows open to the outside (Baum 1999, 121). The Lobi also had dispersed homesteads, each of which was a small fortress (Bonnafé, Fiéloux, and Kambou 1982).[5]

Walls were not much help in Masina because of the importance of transhumant pastoralism, but they were important in Wasulu and served the Wasulunke well until the 1880s. The area had powerful neighbors, Segu, Futa Jallon, and then Samori and his rivals in Sikasso; slaves from Wasulu were regularly noted at St. Louis, Senegal. In Wasulu, I traced the remains of some of these walls, bits of which are still standing. In Bulukura, today a small village of about three hundred people, the wall was built of a combination of mud, pebbles, and *karité* (shea butter). Parts of it have lasted at least 120 years. It surrounded the village, contained holes that could be used by riflemen, and had a diameter of about two hundred meters. At Ntentu, there were two walls more than three meters high, the outer one more than a kilometer in length. Given the lack of artillery, such fortifications could not be breached. Most slave raiders were unwilling to pay the price of a siege.

Walled villages were common almost everywhere that slave raiding posed a threat and they were effective. The only weakness was that people had to leave to work the land. Defense was thus often coupled with major changes in the ways people lived. Most important in some coastal areas was a change in cropping patterns. Crops were planted close to the village and worked collectively. When I first did research in Senegal, almost forty years ago, old peasants told me that the one benefit they received from the French conquest was that they did not have to carry their guns into the fields. Robert Baum's Diola informants told him that people carried guns to their fields, worked only in groups, and rarely traveled far from their villages (Baum 1999, 120–21; see also Capron 1973, 86–88; Jonckers 1987, 24). In this volume Hawthorne describes the way such defensive strategies led to radical changes in social structure and to a shift from yams to rice. Purchase of iron from Europeans and the production of iron tools also facilitated rice cultivation among the Diola. Mark (1985, 27–30) argues that increased food production led to population growth and expansion as the Diola moved into nearby swampy areas suitable for wet rice and diets improved.

Where hills and forests were available, people used them (see Bah, this volume). Archeologists often use the existence of walls and hilltop locations as evidence of increasing warfare. In Cameroon, many Chamba moved to easily defensible sites in the hills, but where land was in short supply, they became vulnerable when they had to go down to the plains to cultivate (Fardon 1988, ch. 5). When threatened by outsiders, the inhabitants of the Birim valley in Ghana put their villages on hilltops and built earthwork fortifications (Kiyaga-Mulindwa 1982). Charles Piot (1996) refers to the Kabre of northern Togo retreating into mountainous locations during the seventeenth and eighteenth centuries, when they had to face the challenge of slave-raiders from three directions (see also Verdier 1982). Michael Mason (1969, 561) refers to people in the Nigerian Middle Belt retreating into defensible hilltop locations (see also Gleave and Prothero 1971, 321). David Dorward (1987) describes the fortresslike settlements of the Eggon of the Middle Belt. Throughout the Nigerian Middle Belt, fortified hilly locations were common (Gunn and Conant 1960, 25, 58, 65, 76, 93, 117; Gleave 1965). Some Gurunsi also sought out easily defended hilltop locations, as did many people in the Dar al-Kuti region of the Central African Republic, as described by Dennis Cordell in this volume (Cordell, p.c.).

The biggest problem such communities had was the limited amount and quality of the land available to them. Many responded creatively. Robert Cornevin (1962) speaks of the Kabre as "remarkable farmers," who constructed anti-erosion barriers, built terraces, and used manure. Michael Gleave and R. M. Prothero write of "a marked tendency toward the development of intensive systems of agriculture making the most of their rock-strewn soils, often on steep slopes, to support increasingly dense populations" (1971, 321; see also Dorward 1987, 203). They terraced their hill-sides, practiced crop rotation, and used animal and vegetable waste to enrich their soils. The problem was that to the degree that they were successful and population grew, they had to come out of their hills. The plains were empty, but often fertile. Dorward writes that when the Eggon descended into the valleys to collect firewood, to hunt or to farm, lookouts were maintained. Drums and trumpets signaled the appearance of an enemy and warned people to retreat to the hills, where an attacking force faced a hail of stones, spears, poisoned arrows and bee-hives, often from carefully prepared positions (Dorward 1987, 203). Eventually, many had little choice but to develop settlements on the plains, which were as elsewhere, concentrated agglomerations with defensive palisades (204; see also Gleave and Prothero 1971, 321–22). People in fortified villages had similar problems. They had to leave the village in order to cultivate and were at that time exposed to attack. Joseph Ki Zerbo's father, Alfred Diban, was taken prisoner when he was working in the fields (Ki Zerbo 1983).

The effect of all of this was to force slavers to shift to new mechanisms. Dahomey originally exported only slaves taken in its wars, but its capital, Abomey, gradually became the center of trade routes moving slaves from further north (Law 1991). Slavers gradually developed mechanisms for stimulating conflicts within target areas and formed alliances with key groups in those societies. If the trade led to resistance, then resistance led to slavers seeking new sources and new mechanisms for extracting slaves. This is one of many ways in which resistance changed the nature of the trade and of slavery itself. The argument made most articulately by Andrew Hubbell is that slave traders increasingly found it desirable to find alliances within the targeted society. The Ardos in Masina and the Wasulunke who joined Samori were part of this process. The more common process was the linkage of traders with young men and young men's groups frustrated by the control of their elders and willing to raid the next village and kidnap people within their own.[6]

Wasulu

There were, however, large areas where a different dynamic prevailed, where people parried, resisted, and sometimes submitted to the state but where they jealously guarded their autonomy, resisted the lure of hierarchical political systems, and held firm in the maelstrom created by the slave trade. Like the Balanta, the Wasulunke resisted differentiation and sought to maintain egalitarian and undifferentiated social structures. Wasulunke society is also very homogeneous. Unlike state societies, where different levels of migration are embedded in the state structure and can often be dated by reference to the migrating group's traditions or the titles their leaders acquired, Wasulunke traditions are difficult to date and are often simply designed to establish the primacy of different clans that arrived at more or less the same time and the links between them. Most traditions trace Wasulu to the four sons of Tinkalan.[7] Brothers often created similar communities. Thus, Basidibe traditions speak of migrations of four brothers, who founded different communities.[8] Gwanan tradition speaks of four founders arriving at the same time. Every jamana seems to have one or a few founders, and every village can trace itself to one of the founder's sons. Informants usually date the different migrations within a few years of each other. Basidibe was supposedly founded seven years before Bolon. The question of who came first can be important both to chieftaincy titles and disputes over control of land, but history is flattened out. Whatever migrations took place left little impact on social or political structure. Chronology is also impossible. One of the functions of tradition is to establish parity in each jamana. No man has greater rights or privileges. Only age gives authority or commands respect. Traditions also establish relative parity between the jamana and established bonds, which were important when the community faced external threats.

The claim of a common origin is the ideological basis of homogeneity. Most traditions allude to migrants coming from Futa Jallon, though sometimes by diverse routes, which suggests different origins. The Bagayogo, for example, claim to have originated in Timbuktu, but they came to Wasulu from the Futa.[9] The tradition of Saaba Jakite suggests that he may actually have been of Senufo origin (Amselle 1998, 126). They found a well-watered and fertile region inhabited by Bamana or Malinke speakers. Most traditions say that these earlier inhabitants were driven from the area, but if that happened, how do we explain the loss of language?[10] One informant suggested that they lost their language because their mothers spoke Bamana.[11] Only one other referred to cohabitation with Bamana.[12] It is more likely that the migrants inserted themselves into a preexisting society. The absence of both linguistic or structural evidence of Fulbe origins would suggest that the indigenous people were much more numerous, though the major clans all claim Fulbe origin. Increasingly, they took over the institutions of their neighbors. There is no evidence of any cataclysmic event or of any coordinated migration. Amselle (1998, 78) sees them as refugees from other conflicts, but I see no reason to doubt that Fulbe moved into the area as part of the quest for pasture that has driven their history.[13] The well-watered lands of Wasulu were probably an attraction. Interaction with earlier Bamana-speaking inhabitants would explain the Bamanization, but it does not explain why almost no one claims descent from the Bamana. It is clear, however, that the tradition of

Fulbe origin provides an ideological basis for collaboration, just as the tradition of a common ancestor provides an ideological basis for equality within the jamana. Both are linked to an ideological resistance to the forces that threatened their existence.

The Wasulunke practiced mixed agriculture and lived within communities that had little hierarchy. Some of the jamana were quite large. Gwanan and Cemala had fifty-five villages, but Bolon had only eleven. There were no permanent offices; the major figures were clan (*gwa*) heads. "Here, there was not a single chief worthy of the name," Basi Tumani Bagayogo told us, "the oldest man in the village had authority in the village." Decision making and conflict resolution seem to have involved negotiation between clan elders. Wasulu comes close to Horton's definition of a stateless society, though I prefer to see it as a highly decentralized state system.[14] Authority existed, but except in war, it was weak. In spite of these diffuse political structures, the Wasulunke were generally able to defend themselves against slave raiders from more centralized neighboring states. When there was an external threat, the Wasulunke could come together and choose a war leader.[15] In some cases, military leaders like Jeri Sidibe were able to establish their hegemony over a part of Wasulu (Person 1968, 1:157, 175, 192–93). It is clear that the decentralization, homogeneity and egalitarianism were crucial to Wasulu's effective resistance to the slave trade but also made the area vulnerable to new strategies and more powerful enemies.

The most important defense against slavers was without a doubt the construction of the walls, which existed in many Wasulunke communities and which I have already described.[16] Walls made of mud, stones, and shea butter were capable of resisting any weapons an African army could bring to bear on them. These enclosures were large enough that people, granaries, and stock could be gathered within. They could be taken only after extensive sieges, which were usually costly for both attackers and defenders.[17] The danger to ordinary people came from their neighbors, from internecine conflict within a jamana, or from hit-and-run attacks from both neighbors and outsiders, which could seize people when they were outside their walls. People thus had to fight small bands and to withdraw into a defensive position when faced with attack by larger forces. Samori's successes resulted from his ability to mobilize resources and feed his *sofa* (warriors) in the field—and even Samori failed before the massive walls of Sikasso in 1888.

Wasulu was a decentralized society with a high degree of segmentation.[18] The segmentation was both its strength and its weakness. Decentralized societies could defend themselves against external attack. People could pull together against a common enemy. Decentralized societies were also marked by internal conflict and were vulnerable when internal conflict was linked to external threats. Thus, the Igbo of eastern Nigeria were a relatively minor producer of slaves for the Atlantic market until the Aro were able to create a network of trading operations that could incite and exploit local conflicts during the eighteenth century (Nwokeji 1999; see also Hubbell 2001). It is not clear whether the operations of *juula* (merchants) within Wasulu were able to play the role that the Aro played among the Igbo, but it is clear that many of the Wasulu jamana had links with Segu. Several informants claimed that their jamana were under the informal hegemony of Segu. One claimed that opposed factions would sometimes turn to Segu for help.[19] Jamana seem to have sometimes paid tribute to Segu and individual young males occasionally served Segu as *tonjon* (warriors), just as many later served among Samori's sofa.[20] Wasulu was, however, most important to Segu not as a source of allies or tributaries but as reservoir of slaves. The area was regularly raided, though until Samori it seems to have remained populous. Wasulu thus was an area that until 1882 coped with very difficult challenges, suffering regular losses, but sustaining itself, sometimes resisting, sometimes yielding, sometimes actively seeking help.

Several aspects of the system are relevant to its success. It is here that traditions of common origin became important. There was a small number of clans and parity between clans and between jamana. Equally important, early residents or later migrants could easily be incorporated within the system by changing their names and by developing a fictional genealogy. One acquired a new name and new history. The differentiation that exists throughout West Africa between landowners and latecomers hardly exists in Wasulu. The early inhabitants did not become owners of the land but were clearly folded into the clan structures of the immigrants a long time ago (Horton 1971, 95–96). Tales I was told were full of examples of people changing their names. In some cases, it was the correspondence of names familiar to any student of the western Sudan, but in others, it was arbitrary. For example, I was told that many of those returning from the slavery in the Sahel did not remember their clan names and were simply assigned to clans by lot.[21] Security clearly came from being part of a clan. Descent was not necessarily a biological category. At the same time, the clan structure provided a high level of cohesion.

Thus, Wasulu was marked by large clans, and few if any persons were not part of one of those clans. In some villages there seemed to be only one name. In Ntentu it was Samake. There were also few status distinctions. In only two of the villages I visited were there griots and they were not my informants. They often played the role of intermediary, but they neither recited histories nor chanted praises. The only important artisan group was blacksmiths. Furthermore, traditions suggest that they came later than others. They were also the only group that found it desirable to remain distinct. More important than the flatness of the social structure was the alliance systems, which were underlined by joking relationships. The Wasulunke were exogamous, with fixed patterns of marriage alliance. The kinship ties thus set up were useful in mediating conflicts and mobilizing support whenever there was a threat.

Masina

In Masina, salvation was a social revolution led by a small group of rural Muslim clerics. It is one of several cases where a community threatened by slave raiding turned to Muslim leadership. Futa Toro is another and Futa Jallon probably a third. The solution to Masina's problems demanded a state structure capable of protecting the transhumant cycle. This not only led to the revolution but also shaped the course it took.

The only alternative elite in Masina was the clerics. A diffuse group of varying ethnic origins, they did not compare in learning to their counterparts among the Hausa or along the Senegal River. Most were either makers of amulets or modest teachers of the Qur'an (Brown 1969, 209; Sanankoua 1990, 93–100). As outsiders, they did not participate in the patronage of established states and increasingly attacked not only the Ardos but also the syncretism and compromises that marked cities like Jenne and Dia (Ba and Daget 1955, 23–28).[22] During the period before the jihad, a number of clerics built up communities of disciples, possibly influenced by Sokoto and the two Futas. By 1818 their leader, Seku Amadu, felt strong enough to challenge Dikko power. As the story goes, one of his followers, acting on orders, killed an Ardo who had seized a disciple's blanket. The Jenné ulema then drove Amadu out of Jenné and forced him to take refuge at Nukuma, where he gathered elements hostile to the existing order (Ba and Daget 1955, 23–28; Gallais 1967, 1:93–96; Sanankoua 1990, 42–48).[23] In 1818, Amadu's army defeated an attacking coalition of the Dikko and the Bambara of Segu. With victory, the Muslims suddenly found themselves heading a national coalition as neutral groups joined the revolution.[24]

It was not enough to defeat the Dikko and the Bambara. The Muslims still needed a state capable of dealing with the continuing threat of both Bambara and Tuareg. They needed an army and a state structure capable of taxing and supporting that military structure. Seku Amadu based the new order on the rule of the ulema, represented by a council of forty. He always transacted business with two other marabouts at his side (Ba and Daget 1955, ch. 4; Monteil 1932, 106–14; Gallais 1967, 1:93–96; Sanankoua 1990, ch. 3). The state moved actively to regulate economic life, asserting control over land and regulating transhumant rights. Every market was placed under the control of an official in charge of weights, measures and prices (Gallais 1967, 1:93–96; Marty 1920, 2:137–38; Johnson 1976). Islam was encouraged and its prohibitions strictly enforced. Every village was to have at least one person capable of teaching the Qur'an. Women were secluded. Alcohol and tobacco were prohibited and only the uncircumcised were allowed to dance. The most important change was sedentarization. One of Brown's informants explains: "all heads of families were commanded to choose a place where they could be found in the . . . [rainy] season. The heads of villages were to watch over them. Each person had to be with the head of his village at some season. . . . They changed from straw huts to towns; they followed his [Seku Amadu's] example: only one or two sons would go with the animals because of Seku and his example" (Brown 1969, 209; see also Sanankoua 1990, 93–100). Thus, only a small part of the community traveled with the herds. The rest remained in their villages, where they could study the Qur'an and supervise the labor of their slaves. Sedentarization made taxation easier and it altered relationships between the Fulbe and the slaves (*rimaibe*) (Johnson 1976). Before the jihad, rimaibe villages served as bases for nomadic migrations and slave use was probably focused in the hands of the Dikko. After, it became generalized. From the time of Amadu, Fulbe and rimaibe either lived in the same villages or in adjacent ones (Gallais 1967, 1:148ff.).

There is a certain irony about the question of slavery. Seku Amadu's jihad was a response to the inroads of slave raiding on the Fulbe pastoral life. Furthermore, rimaibe were probably a high percentage of his original supporters. Many free or noble Fulbe waited on the sidelines during the first stages. Oral traditions say that Amadu appealed for support to slaves and artisan castes. All slaves who fought at Nukuma were freed, but slavery itself was not abolished (Sanankoua 1990, 111; Brown 1969, 116, 126; Ba and Daget 1955, 40).[25] In later years, slaves who were conscripted received booty, but were freed only for valor. The regime used slaves from early days. Those taken from the Dikko were often reassigned to men who served faithfully. As Fulbe infantry became cavalry, the army moved further afield, first to establish the regime's control within the delta and then to raid for slaves outside the delta. The labor of these slaves freed their masters to devote themselves to military defense, administration, and study. Thus, as in Futa Toro, Islam started as a liberating force and ended up rationalizing slaving military activity. The rimaibe of the delta became as much like serfs as any group in West Africa. The Dina lasted less than a half century, falling to Umar's armies in 1862, but by that time the Fulbe of Masina had become sedentary, dependent on slave labor, and deeply committed to Islam.

I am convinced that the most important forms of resistance to slavery were first, resistance to enslavement, and second, flight from slavery. Within slave systems, scholarly analysis has focused too often on revolts and on day-to-day resistance, both of which tend to be romanticized. They did take place, but there was an underlying process, which is hard to describe but probably more important, by which masters were forced by the logic of the situation to recognize the slave's humanity. Nevertheless, the fact of resistance to enslavement is important. Scholars have too often referred to reservoirs of people, who were tapped by the trade, as if to say that there were people waiting to be swept up by a kind of remorseless and brutal vacuum cleaner. We have too often divided Africans into victors and victims. Life was certainly safest at the heart of the great slaving kingdoms, but those who lived in areas widely raided did not go willingly. They created defenses—not only walls, but alarm systems—just as maroon communities did. They changed the structure of their community, the crops they grew, the ways they related to strangers and to each other, all in the interest of protection. Their successes drove the slave traders deeper into the interior and pushed them to develop methods of commercial penetration, which played off people and groups within these communities. Ironically, the very egalitarian democratic nature of these societies often opened them up to the more subtle mechanism of market-driven forces. Often, in protecting themselves, they became part of the system, enslaving others to better protect themselves. There is probably some moral lesson in all of this.

Notes

1. See also my effort (2001) to extend this model to much of West Africa, as well as Hawthorne's contribution to this volume.

2. On the role of slaving in the rise of Futa Jallon, see Barry 1998, 95–102; Rodney 1968. On Segu, see Roberts 1987; Bazin 1975, 1982.

3. On Masina's importance as a rice producer, see Carney 2001, ch. 2.

4. On Minianka defenses, see also Jonckers 1987, 17–19. Colonial administrators often had difficulty understanding that so-called primitives could do some very sophisticated things.

5. See also discussions of defense in the savanna in Olivier de Sardan 1982, 213–16, 223; Pradelles de Latour 1982, 251–52.

6. See Baum 1999 on Diola; Warnier on Grasslands; Fardon 1988 on Chamba; Piot 1996 on Kabre.

7. Tinkalan is Tengela, the Fula founder of a fifteenth-century kingdom (Amselle 1998, 124).

8. Interview with Daouda Sidibe, Siekoroli, 18 February 1989.

9. Basi Tumani Bagayogo, Kosijala, March 1989.

10. Interviews with Tiemoko Doumbia, Bouloukoura, 1–11 February 1989; Lamini Sidibe, Gweleninkoro, March 1989; Jigiba Sidibe, 6 March 1989; Al Hajj Magran Bourama Sangaré, Sangarejin, March 1989; Birama Sidibe, Sangaréjin, March 1989.

11. Al Hajj Bou Diallo, Yoroubougoula, February 1989.

12. Basi Tumani Bagayogo, Kosijala, March 1989.

13. I like Amselle's view of a highly fluid history marked by transformations, but I think he tends to exaggerate the evidence for earlier centralization.

14. In Wasulu there was little concentration of authority and it affected limited sectors of the lives of the Wasulunke. There were, however, full-time authority figures. They tended to be very old and, except for the war chiefs, had very limited authority. The system was also able to settle disputes over large areas. See Horton 1971, 78.

15. Basi Tumani Bagayogo, Kosiyala, described the selection of war chiefs by elders. Bagayogo was an informant of great wisdom and learning. March 1989.

16. I was able to trace the remains of the wall in several villages. I estimated the diameter of the enclosure by pacing it off. I also estimated the height of remaining fragments of walls.

17. For an excellent collection of articles on African warfare, see Bazin and Terray 1982. At the time of massacre, French troops were marching toward the area. When they arrived, there was almost no one left and the stench of the rotting bodies was so unpleasant that they established their fort at Bougouni.

18. See Amselle 1998, which skillfully analyzes the way in which segmentation may have worked. The only problem with Amselle's analysis is that he focuses on the tradition of Farbalay Jakite, who served Samori and later became a French chief. Jakite traditions suggest more centralization than do other traditions. One of my informants, Joncoro Dumbaya, suggested that even in Gwanan, leadership before Farbalay came from clan chiefs. See also a rival tradition from Al-Hajj Bou Diallo in Yoroubougoula.

19. Daouda Sidibe and Moussa Sidibe; Lamine Sidibe, Gweleninkoro; Yoro Sidibe, Cenba, February 1989. It seems likely that the northernmost jamana were involved with Segu.

20. For studies of Bambara polities north of Wasulu that were incorporated within the Segu state, see Amselle 1988, 1998, ch. 6.

21. Amselle (1998, 133, 157–59) cites cases of name changes.

22. On Amadu's ambivalent links to Sokoto, see Stewart 1976.

23. Ahmed remained hostile to Jenné. Caillié wrote that "the great trade of that town

interfered with his religious duties and drew aside the true believers from their devotions" (1830, 1:461). Thus, he built his capital, Hamdullahi, off the major trade routes. On Ahmed's antimerchant orientation, see Azarya 1980.

24. Ba and Daget (1955, 32–35) report that at Nukuma, a thousand of Amadu's supporters, of whom only forty had horses, faced two hundred thousand of the allied army. This is undoubtedly an exaggeration, but many in the delta undoubtedly waited for the outcome of the battle before supporting Amadu.

25. Some of the new ulema may have been of slave origin. The ulema group was quite small at the time of the jihad but expanded dramatically soon after. Freed slaves had the option of advancing socially by seeking a Muslim education. It is unlikely that such information would ever get recorded by the oral tradition. All the tradition tells us is that slaves served and were freed.

Bibliography

Amselle, Jean-Loup. 1979. With Zumana Dunbya, Amadu Kuyate, and Mohammed Tabure. "Littérature orale et idéologie: La geste de Jakite Sabashi du Ganon (Wasolon, Mali)." *Cahiers d'études africaines* 19:381–433.

———. 1988. "Un état contre l'état: Le Keleyadugu." *Cahiers d'études africaines* 38:63–83.

———. 1998. *Mestizo Logics: Anthropology of Identity in Africa and Elsewhere.* Trans. Claudia Royal. Stanford: Stanford University Press.

Azarya, Victor. 1980. "Traders and the Center in Massina, Kong, and Samori's State." *International Journal of African Historical Studies* 13:420–56.

Ba, Amadou Hampaté, and Jacques Daget. 1955. *L'empire peul du Macina.* Dakar: Institut Français d'Afrique Noire.

Bah, Thierno Mouctar. 1985. *Architecture militaire traditionnelle et poliorcétique dans le Soudan occidental.* Yaoundé: Editions Clé.

Barry, Boubacar. 1978. "Crise politique et importance des révoltes populaires au Futa Dyalon au dix-neuvième siècle." *Afrika zamani* 8–9:51–61.

———. 1998. *Senegambia and the Atlantic Slave Trade.* Trans. from the French by Ayi Kwei Armah. Cambridge: Cambridge University Press.

Baum, Robert. 1999. *Shrines of the Slave Trade: Diola Religion and Society in Precolonial Senegambia.* New York: Oxford University Press.

Bazin, Jean. 1975. "Guerre et servitude à Ségou." In Claude Meillassoux, ed., *L'esclavage en Afrique précoloniale,* 135–82. Paris: Maspero.

———. 1982. "Etat guerrier et guerres d'état." In Jean Bazin and Emmanuel Terray, eds., *Guerres de lignages et guerres d'état en Afrique noire,* 319–74. Paris: Archives Contemporaines.

Bazin, Jean, and Emmanuel Terray, eds. 1982. *Guerres de lignages et guerres d'état en Afrique noire.* Paris: Editions des Archives Contemporaines.

Bonnafé, Pierre, Michèle Fiéloux, and Jeanne-Marie Kambou. 1982. "Le conflit armé dans une population sans état: Les Lobi de Haute-Volta." In Jean Bazin and Emmanuel

Terray, eds., *Guerres de lignages et guerres d'état en Afrique noire,* 73–142. Paris: Editions des Archives Contemporaines.

Botte, Roger. 1988. "Révolte, pouvoir, religion: Les Hubbu du Fouta Jalon (Guinée)." *Journal of African History* 29:391–413.

Bourdier, Jean-Paul, and Trinh T. Minh-ha. 1985. *African Spaces.* New York: Africana.

Brown, William A. 1969. "The Caliphate of Hamdullahi, ca. 1818–1864: A Study in African History and Tradition." Ph.D. diss., University of Wisconsin.

Caillié, René. 1965. *Journal d'un voyage à Toumbouctou et à Jenné dans l'Afrique centrale.* 1830. Reprint, Paris: Anthropos.

Capron, Jean. 1973. *Communautés villagoises Bwa: Mali-Haute Volta.* Paris: Institut d'Ethnologie.

Carney, Judith. 2001. *Black Rice: The African Origins of Rice Cultivation in the Americas.* Cambridge, Mass.: Harvard University Press.

Cornevin, Robert. 1962. *Histoire du Togo.* Paris: Berger-Levrault.

Dorward, David. 1987. "The Impact of Colonialism on a Nigerian Hill-Farming Society: A Case of Innovation among the Eggon." *International Journal of African Historical Studies* 20:201–24.

Duperray, Anne-Marie. 1984. *Les Gourounsi de Haute Volta: Conquête et colonisation, 1896–1933.* Stuttgart: Franz Steiner.

Fage, John D. 1969. *A History of West Africa: An Introductory Survey.* 4th ed. Cambridge: Cambridge University Press.

Fardon, Richard. 1988. *Raiders and Refugees: Trends in Chamba Political Development, 1750–1950.* Washington, D.C.: Smithsonian Institution.

Gallais, Jean. 1967. *Le delta intérieur du Niger: Etude de géographie régionale.* 2 vols. Dakar: Institut Français d'Afrique Noire.

Gleave, Michael. 1965. "The Changing Frontiers of Settlement in the Uplands of Northern Nigeria." *Nigerian Geographic Journal* 8:127–41.

Gleave, M. B., and R. M. Prothero. 1971. "Population Density and 'Slave-Raiding'—A Comment." *Journal of African History* 12:319–24.

Gunn, Harold D., and F. P. Conant. 1960. *Peoples of the Middle Niger Region of Northern Nigeria.* London: International African Institute.

Hawthorne, Walter. 1998. "The Interior Past of an Acephalous Society: Institutional Change among the Balanta of Guinea-Bissau, c. 1450–c. 1950." Ph.D. diss., Stanford University.

———. 1999. "The Production of Slaves Where There Was No State: The Guinea-Bissau Region, 1450–1815." *Slavery and Abolition* 20:97–124.

———. 2001. "Nourishing a Stateless Society during the Slave Trade: The Rise of Balanta Paddy-Rice Production in Guinea-Bissau." *Journal of African History* 42:1–24.

Horton, Robin. 1971. "Stateless Societies in the History of West Africa." In J. F. A. Ajayi and Michael Crowder, eds., *History of West Africa.* London: Longman.

Hubbell, Andrew. 1997. "Patronage and Predation: A Social History of Colonial Chieftaincies in a Chiefless Region—Souroudougou (Burkina Faso), 1850–1946." Ph.D. diss., Stanford University.

———. 2001. "A View of the Slave Trade from the Margin: Souroudougou in the Late

Nineteenth Century Slave Trade of the Niger Bend." *Journal of African History* 42:25–48.

Inikori, Joseph E., and Stanley Engerman, eds. 1992. *The Atlantic Slave Trade: Effects on Economies, Societies, and Peoples in Africa, the Americas, and Europe.* Durham, N.C.: Duke University Press.

Jonckers, Danielle. 1987. *La société Minyanka du Mali: Traditions communautaires et développement cotonnier.* Paris: L'Harmattan.

Johnson, Marian. 1976. "The Economic Foundations of an Islamic Theocracy." *Journal of African History* 17:481–96.

Kane, Oumar. 1986. "Le Fuuta Tooro des Satigi aux Almami (1512–1807)" Thèse d'état. University of Dakar.

Kiyaga-Mulindwa, D. 1982. "Social and Demographic Changes in the Birim Valley, southern Ghana, c. 1450–c. 1800." *Journal of African History* 23:63–82.

Ki Zerbo, Joseph. 1983. *Alfred Diban, premier chrétien de Haute Volta.* Paris: Editions du Cerf.

Klein, Martin A. 1998. *Slavery and Colonial Rule in French West Africa.* Cambridge: Cambridge University Press.

———. 1999. "Ethnic Pluralism and Homogeneity in the Western Sudan: Saalum, Segu, Wasulu." *Journal of Mande Studies* 1:109–24.

Law, Robin. 1991. *The Slave Coast of West Africa, 1550–1750: The Impact of the Atlantic Slave Trade on an African Society.* Oxford: Clarendon Press.

Lovejoy, Paul. 1983. *Transformations in Slavery: A History of Slavery in Africa.* Cambridge: Cambridge University Press.

Manning, Patrick. 1990. *Slavery and African Life.* Cambridge: Cambridge University Press.

Mark, Peter. 1985. *A Cultural, Economic, and Religious History of the Basse Casamance since 1500.* Wiesbaden: Franz Steiner.

Marty, Paul. 1920. *Etudes sur l'Islam et les tribus du Soudan.* 4 vols. Paris: Larose.

Mason, Michael. 1969. "Population Density and 'Slave-Raiding'—The Case of the Middle Belt of Nigeria." *Journal of African History* 10:551–64.

Miller, Joseph C. 1988. *Way of Death: Merchant Capitalism and the Angolan Slave Trade, 1730–1830.* Madison: University of Wisconsin Press.

Monteil, Charles. 1971. *Une cité soudanaise: Djenné, métropole du delta central du Niger.* 1932. Reprint, Paris: Anthropos.

Nwokeji, G. Ugo. 1999. "The Biafran Frontier: Trade, Slaves, and Aro Society, c. 1750–1905." Ph.D. diss., University of Toronto.

Olivier de Sardan, Jean-Pierre. 1982. "Le cheval et l'arc." In Jean Bazin and Emmanuel Terray, eds., *Guerres de lignages et guerres d'état en Afrique noire.* Paris: Editions des Archives Contemporaines.

Person, Yves. 1968–75. *Samori: Une révolution dyula.* 2 vols. Dakar: Institut Fondamental d'Afrique Noire.

Piot, Charles. 1996. "Of Slaves and the Gift: Kabre Sale of Kin during the Era of the Slave Trade." *Journal of African History* 37:31–50.

Pradelles de Latour, Eliane. 1982. "La paix destructrice." In Jean Bazin and Emmanuel Terray, eds., *Guerres de lignages et guerres d'état en Afrique noire.* Paris: Editions des Archives Contemporaines.

Roberts, Richard. 1980. "Production and Reproduction of Warrior States: Segu Bambara and Segu Tokolor." *International Journal of African Historical Studies* 21:169–88.

———. 1981a. "Fishing for the State: The Political Economy of the Middle Niger Valley." In Donald Crummey and Charles Stewart, eds., *Modes of Production in Africa.* Beverly Hills: Sage.

———. 1981b. "Ideology, Slavery, and Social Formation: The Evolution of Maraka Slavery in the Middle Niger Valley." In Paul E. Lovejoy, ed., *The Ideology of Slavery.* Beverly Hills: Sage.

———. 1987. *Warriors, Merchants, and Slaves: The State and Economy in the Middle Niger Valley, 1700–1914.* Stanford: Stanford University Press.

Robinson, David. 1975. "The Islamic Revolution of Futa Toro." *International Journal of African Historical Studies* 8:185–221.

Rodney, Walter. 1968. "Jihad and Social Revolution in Futa Jallon in the Eighteenth Century." *Journal of the Historical Society of Nigeria* 4:269–84.

———. 1972. *How Europe Underdeveloped Africa.* London: Bogle-L'Ouverture Publications.

Sanankoua, Bintou. 1990. *Un empire peul au dix-neuvième siècle: La Diina du Maasina.* Paris: Karthala.

Stewart, Charles. 1976. "Frontier Disputes and Problems of Legitimation: Sokoto-Masina Relations, 1817–1837." *Journal of African History* 17:497–514.

Verdier, Raymond. 1982. *Le pays Kabiyé: Cité des dieux—cité des hommes.* Paris: Karthala.

Warnier, Jean-Pierre. 1985. *Echanges, développement, et hiérarchies dans le Bamenda précolonial.* Wiesbaden: Franz Steiner.

———. 1989. "Traites sans raids au Cameroun." *Cahiers d'études africaines* 29:5–32.

Part 2

Protective Strategies

CHAPTER 6
The Last Resort
Redeeming Family and Friends

Sylviane A. Diouf

IN JUNE 1829 A CARAVAN LEFT Timbo in Futa Jallon and headed south toward Monrovia, Liberia, carrying $6,000 to $7,000 in gold to be remitted to Ibrahima abd al-Rahman Barry, a son of the late *almamy* Ibrahima Sori Mawdo.[1] The aging man had returned to Liberia two months earlier, after forty years of bondage in Mississippi. Upon arrival, he had sent word to his wealthy and influential family to help him redeem his five children and eight grandchildren still living on a cotton plantation near Natchez. One hundred and fifty miles from Monrovia, the caravan learned of Ibrahima's death. The men turned back, and, as a result, most of his descendants spent the rest of their life in servitude (Russwurm 1830, 60; Alford 1977, 184).

An African family in one country and their formerly enslaved kin in another had tried and failed to gain the release of children born in America with gold gathered through the labor, or perhaps the sale into the Atlantic trade, of domestic slaves in Africa. Ibrahima's story illustrates the contradictions of redemption, a double-edged tactic that saved many Africans from bondage to the detriment, sometimes, of others.

Captive redemption is a well-documented practice, depicted in two main categories of sources. One consists of the autobiographies and biographies of, and interviews with, Africans. They represent a range of experiences: some people had been redeemed before but ultimately failed to be ransomed; others had witnessed the ransoming of captives; still others had attempted to be redeemed. The testimony of men and women who had been the victims of ransoming—as they were exchanged for somebody's freedom—would be of immense interest, but research has not turned up any documentation so far. Anyhow, given the way transactions were conducted, it is probable that many if not most substitutes were not even aware that they were taking someone else's place, and therefore such testimonies may very well not exist.

Westerners' accounts are another font of information. They extend from the writings of witnesses to the transaction to statements by traders and officials who engaged in the practice. The slave trade's victims, organizers, and opponents offer perspectives on the practice that are very often of a personal nature, the type that is frequently missing in slave trade studies. But records of actual transactions were seldom kept, and when they were, they do not necessarily offer the kind of information that would help a quantitative study. The logbook of the slaver *Bruce Grove,* for example, has two entries on a redemption case that describes the circumstances of the transaction and the reactions of the protagonists, but does not give any indication as to what exactly the ransom was—money, goods, or people:

> Cape Coast 1 April 1802
> Two of the men purchased this day were lately taken in a kind of skirmish[,] brought on board and sold in the presence of some of the party for whom they fought which occasion'd a little fracas on board the ship.
>
> Cape Coast 10[?] April 1802
> The men which were sold a few days back that occasioned a Quarrele on board our ship[,] were this day redeem'd by three Friends. I need not attempt to describe the poor fellows joy on being released from their irons.[2]

Because detailed information on specific transactions is lacking, it may remain impossible to assess the number of people involved in redemption, either as ransomed or as "replacements." Nevertheless, the regularity with which redemption is reported in African and European sources—in passages such as "they are *frequently* redeemed from us by their Friends" (testimony of James A. Penny, in Lambert 1975–76, 69:33; emphasis mine) and "In many cases his family or his friends are at hand, who redeem him with a slave" (testimony of

Richard Miles, in Lambert 1975–76, 68:120)—suggests that this strategy, meant to deprive the traffic of certain people, was used often.

That the opportunity existed to buy back the freedom of people slated for deportation raises several questions. Were specific individuals or groups more likely than others to benefit from it? Were others systematically excluded? What factors were relevant in deciding who would and who would not profit from it? What were the obstacles to redemption and, on the other hand, the circumstances that facilitated it?

But, to begin with, why did slave traders even allow ransoming? Since their objective was to round up as many people as possible, it would appear this procedure was counterproductive and thus would have been quite exceptional. Simply put, slave dealers accepted captive redemption because it made good commercial sense. One could buy back someone's freedom for a higher price than the dealer had paid, which would enable the dealer to purchase more people. However, in many instances money was refused, and only another person (or more) was accepted. The directors of the Sierra Leone Company described such a case: "We offered him money, but then he said, No, he must have slaves for them, as he wanted slaves, and they must be four foot four inches high" (Wadström 1794, pt. 2, 81). At times, the dealer's objective was not to keep a specific individual but to have him or her ransomed. Fat Sam, a legendary slaver on the Gold Coast, sent his kidnapped victims on board slave ships but did not sell them immediately. According to a British Navy surgeon, he waited to see if family members would redeem them (83). The high status of some people did not deter dealers from purchasing or abducting them for the purpose of exchange; it may in fact have encouraged them. This is exemplified by a trader in Sierra Leone who had seized free sailors, "one of them the son of the king of Sallum [in Senegal]. Indeed, the British slave-factor who bought them was so good as to say, he would not send them off, so that their friends might redeem them with other slaves when they saw fit" (81). Whether through additional money or the exchange of one for two, redemption provided the traders with more captives at no additional cost.

Since the practice was established before the Europeans' arrival, its introduction into the Atlantic system was doubtless due to the Africans' initiative; but the foreigners imposed their own terms. Among other items fit for exchange, local people welcomed livestock, whereas Europeans, having no need for it, dealt only in money and captives.[3] An 1843 interview with William Thomas, a young Cameroonian enslaved in Cuba, gives an idea of the reasons for, the cost, and the workings of redemption. His older brother had had an adulterous relation and, as the husband was unable to arrest him, he had seized Thomas as a pawn and sent word to the boy's "brother to come and redeem me for 100 goats. My brother had not so many, but took my little sister, and through a friend offered her to the man for me, but he said it was not enough."[4] Another man, Nanga, lived a similar experience. At twenty-four he was given as a pawn by his mother for a brother of hers who had been sold on account of adultery. He was shipped away before she could redeem him (Koelle 1854).[5] These two cases underline a twist in the workings of redemption. By placing a pawn, families were probably buying time and calculating who would be more useful free. Thomas's brother may have thought that if the young man were released, he could help him get the goats needed for the ransom. Thus, once Thomas had been freed and the ransom paid with his assistance, the sister, in turn, could be released. The same may apply to Nanga: his mother may have believed that once her brother was freed, he would be able to assist efficiently in his nephew's discharge. In these instances, the fact that the people whose freedom was sought were older than their substitutes—and thus, one may assume, more apt to help gather a ransom—suggests such a strategy on the part of their kin.

For redemption to work, slave dealers had to be true to their word and effectively release their captives. Some, nevertheless, reneged on their promise, as in this episode in Sierra Leone: "Most of the free people, thus sold by the several captors, being natives of the neighborhood, were eventually redeemed. But the captors seem to have profited by their sale, and not have promoted their redemption" (Wadström 1794, 2:81–82). In all likelihood those were isolated cases, if not, the transactions would have stopped, to the detriment of both parties: African families and Western slave traders.

OBSTACLES TO REDEMPTION

Various circumstances, including kidnappings and raids, often made ransoming quite arduous. The first obstacle was to locate the captive. In the chance of being redeemed, a line of separation appears between those who had been captured or kidnapped near the coast and rivers and those from inland. When people who lived near the Atlantic disappeared, chances are they would be sold into the European trade. For example, after one party had returned with a "quantity" of slaves, the next morning, "several women and men [came] to see their friends who were imprisoned, and requested of Mr. Marsh, the resident at Secundee [Ghana], to release some of their children and relations" (testimony of Anthony Pantaleo, in Lambert 1975–76, 73:220). Clearly, they lived in the vicinity and were able to find their friends immediately, thus saving them from deportation. The men brought to the *Bruce Grove,* as described above, were released after nine days, and it is probable that ransoming could take place as long as the boats remained on the coast. However, the people who were sold right before sailing time were at a disadvantage since their families had little time to locate them.

For those in the interior, finding their kin or friend could prove even more difficult. In several parts of West Africa, at the point of capture, kidnappers and traders were involved in a multidirectional commerce. Some captives would end up on the Atlantic coast, others across the Sahara, and still others would remain in the area. A coffle that Mungo Park traveled with in 1796, from Mali to Gambia, provides an example. One man's fate depended on a chance encounter with a merchant desirous to exchange one of his slaves for one from the caravan: one man on his way to the coast therefore remained in Senegambia, while the other, held locally, was ultimately sent to Antigua. Later, a sick man was traded in for a villager's young domestic, who found herself thrust into the Atlantic trade. Finally, as the dealers learned there was little demand for captives on the coast, some decided to take theirs back to Gajaaga, as they "were unwilling to sell them to disadvantage" (Park 1971, 349, 350, 353). What these cases reveal is that for a family to go straight to an Atlantic port was a risky gamble because there was no assurance that their kin had been sent there.

The circumstances of capture were also a factor in the families' ability to redeem their loved ones. Many people seized during raids had lost family members in the process. Joseph Wright, captured in such circumstances, stated, "The enemies . . . did not care for the elderly, and old people: they killed them without mercy" (in Beecham 1968, 352). But family members were precisely those who could have ransomed the youngsters. As for the survivors, they had to tend to the wounded and try to survive among destroyed markets and fields. To look for the missing may not have been a priority, nor even a possibility. When families did find their kin, they could face the terrible dilemma described by Samuel Ajayi Crowther, who saw people "in search of their relations, to set at liberty *as many as they had the means of redeeming*" (1842, 377; emphasis mine). Families of modest resources could thus be forced to decide who would be saved and who would be sent away. The psychological repercussions on everyone involved were unquestionably dreadful.

Abductions too put obstacles in the way of redemption. By definition, they happened without witnesses who could inform the families, and as soon as they entered the factories the victims were cut off from the rest of the community.

Usually, "[s]lave-traders and kidnappers . . . bargain for and convey away the slaves in the night, and none of the natives around are permitted to see them" (Wadström 1794, 2:77). People had little or no opportunity of letting their families know where they were (testimony of Thomas Trotter, surgeon in the Royal Navy, in Lambert 1975–76, 69:90; Wadström 1794, 2:77). Ottobah Cugoano was on the lookout aboard the slave ship that sailed along the coast in search of additional captives, but he "could find no good person to give away information of my situation to Accasa at Agimaque" (1999, 15). If their families were not already on their way, the abductees' lot, for the most part, rested on chance: "They may have been seen in carrying off by people on shore, who have informed their connections" (testimony of Trotter, in Lambert 1975–76, 73:90).

Problems were compounded when people had been kidnapped while traveling. Several weeks could pass before their family realized they had disappeared. The well-known story of Ayuba Suleyman Diallo (later known as Job ben Solomon) of Senegal illustrates this particular problem. In 1731 the young husband and father had traveled to Gambia to sell slaves and buy paper. On his way home, he was captured and sold to the same captain he had dealt with earlier. Through acquaintances he sent word to his father and, as a result, a caravan was dispatched with "several slaves" to take his place (Moore 1738; Curtin 1967, 40; Grant 1968). The men arrived too late, however, and Diallo was shipped to Maryland. He had had access to the captain; his family was wealthy and knew of his fate; but time worked against him. As for countless others, this was ultimately the decisive factor that led to his deportation.

The low availability of captives at a specific moment could also be an essential determinant in many people's future, as the story of the daughter of a man "of some consequence" shows. In 1793 the father had asked the governor of Sierra Leone to help him redeem his daughter. The governor offered a choice of goods or money to the merchant, "who refused both, observing that slaves were now difficult to be got, and must not be easily parted with; and that as the girl seemed a favourite, he ought to have two slaves for her; but that in compliment to the governor, he would give her up for one prime slave" (Wadström 1794, 2:80). Even though the father was well connected and had some means, it took him a long time to find a "suitable replacement"; and when he came back to release his daughter, the boat had already left. One may imagine the hope, followed by agony, of those who knew their families were trying to ransom them but who were shipped away before their kin's efforts succeeded.

Manifestly, redemption could be a difficult process in which factors beyond individual will played a significant role; it would thus be erroneous to conclude that families who were not able to free their relatives were passive accomplices in their deportation. Contemporary reality is instructive in that regard. Hundreds of thousands of people are missing each year in the United States, and notwithstanding the involvement of local, state, and national agencies and the use of sophisticated technology and media, thousands are never found. That countless African families, several centuries ago, were unable to locate their missing relatives and friends should be expected. Failure to free them was no indication of callousness on the part of families, nor was it a sign of the captives' low standing in their community.

Slaves, Politics, and Sex

There were also other reasons why some individuals could not be redeemed. Slave status was one of them. Wars were fought with numerous captives, either as slave-soldiers or as porters and help. Mungo Park (1971, 289) observed that they were taken prisoners in great numbers because they were poorly armed and loaded with baggage. The reason for their not being redeemed is suggested by the testimony of a British slaver: "If [the prisoners] have been Freemen originally, they are frequently redeemed from us by their Friends, who give us other Slaves in return" (James Penny, in Lambert 1975–76, 69:33). Since the standard of exchange was a slave for the freedom of a prisoner, it would have made little sense, within the logic of a slaveholding society, to redeem one by putting another in his place. Ultimately, the fate of the prisoners of servile status was commonly to change owners. They were thus excluded from the benefit of a strategy designed as an alternative to the killing of prisoners. Along with people accused of witchcraft, they seem to have been the only category that could not, as a matter of policy, be ransomed. Their future was sealed by local laws even before they reached the foreigners' barracoons, but in other cases, it is the European and American traders who refused to release some categories of captives.

This was especially true when they were prominent and had displeased them. Captain Thomas Wilson, who resided on Gorée Island in 1783, recounted how the British governor disliked a particular marabout (Muslim cleric) and had him kidnapped. His brother offered "two or more slaves" for the man's release, "which was rejected with scorn" (in Lambert 1975–76, 73:12). There is no indication of the cause of the governor's refusal, but other records show that Europeans who had a quarrel with political or commercial associates or rivals did not hesitate to get rid of them by shipping them away. Between 1697 and 1701, for example, André Brüe, director-general of the Compagnie du Sénégal, had a commercial falling-out with the king of Kayor and Baol, Lat Sukaabe Faal, who was opposed to the French trade monopoly (B. Barry 1998, 83–85). The Senegalese even imprisoned Brüe for several months. Upon his release, the director planned to send Faal to the Caribbean. He had already taken all the necessary steps when he was abruptly recalled to Paris (Durand 1807, 1:111). It is highly probable that Brüe would have refused any ransom for the man he hated so much. Other political figures who had angered the European traders were actually put onboard slave ships. A brother of the Komenda king on the Gold Coast was sent to Dutch Guiana because he had not allowed his servants to fight for the Dutch (Daaku 1970, 84). That several slave dealers were eventually shipped away without being redeemed, even though they had captives at their disposal to take their place, indicates that the ultimate motivation of their European counterparts overrode the attraction of a short-term gain (Wadström 1794, 2:17, 76, 77, 113; Mannix and Cowley 1962, 92). Some European and American slavers also accommodated their African associates who did not want specific captives to be freed. William Snelgrave recounted how the king of Dahomey asked him to promise he "would not let [two women] be redeemed by anyone that should offer to do it" (1971, 98). An interesting case comes from the Danish island of St. Thomas, where a former slave dealer from the Gold Coast and eight of his servants were enslaved in the mid 1700s. They had been seized on the instigation of a family he had had a matrimonial quarrel with. As the man stressed to his interlocutor, "No amount of ransom that his wealthy family was willing to offer could purchase his freedom" (Oldendorp 1987, 210).

To definitely get rid of adversaries or former partners was not the only reason why Western slave traders would reject offers of ransom. Their motive was sometimes just the opposite: they wanted to keep specific individuals. The testimony of a ship's gunner gives a hint of the ultimate motivations of some slavers and of the profits they could expect from ransoming: "Capt. Hildebrand, who was master of a sloop belonging to Mr. Brüe, paid an extraordinary price for a woman, one of a man's wives, after making of him drunk; the man wished to redeem her the next day, and so did the person that I bought the man of, but we did not give them up, neither he nor I; and I suppose they would have given a third of the goods more than they had for them, but we did not chuse it" (James Morley, in Lambert 1975–76, 73:153). The slave dealer doubtless had a personal interest in keeping the woman. In Senegal, French traders and employees of the Compagnie du Sénégal, selected attractive slave women and girls—some brought to Gorée

Island and Saint-Louis to be shipped away—to be their lovers. Their mixed-race daughters, who were born free, became the legendary *signares,* a powerful group of wealthy slave merchants (see Bowditch 1825, 207–9; Lamiral 1789, 244–45; Villard 1943, 72; Brooks 1976, 19–44). It is likely that attempts by family members to redeem the first generation of captives, the signares' mothers, would have met with rejection by their European owners or lovers.

Redemption was thus not a simple quid pro quo that systematically favored the powerful. Political, business-related, and personal considerations also weighed in the slavers' decision. High status and connections with the Westerners were no guarantee that one could be released.

Redemption's Victims

Enslaved Substitutes

In cases when redemption was possible, families had to make the exchange as attractive as possible. Brüe recounted how the wife of a chief officer at court had been sold on suspicion of "intriguing": "The Wife's Relations came to the General, and begged him to change her for a younger Slave, whom they would give him for her, who should be more for his Purpose" (1745–47, 2:35). The alternative was appealing; the substitute was younger and had the added benefit of already being accustomed to enslavement. Because the sale of captives born in the household was generally forbidden in West Africa, these slave substitutes were commonly men and women captured during raids and held, in Senegambia and Futa Jallon, in captives' villages—*gallo* among the Wolof, *runde* in Fulani areas—where they were agricultural workers.[6]

As mentioned earlier, to ransom one individual several substitutes could be needed. L. F. Rømer (1989, 163), a Danish factor, reported an incident he witnessed in Accra in the 1730s: Corrantryn, a local dealer, had captured two men and sent them to a ship scheduled to leave the same night. But the captives' friends sent a boat after her with two slaves for each man, and obtained their release. A more dramatic episode, in terms of numbers, involved Nankedabar, an old man who "redeemed himself, by selling twenty-two of his domestics. The rest were so terrified, that they all ran away from him, and are now (1791) living among the mountains of Sierra Leone" (Wadström 1794, 2:17). In the same vein, French slave trader Theophile Conneau (1976, 144–47) reported how an eighteen-year-old Futa Jallon princess was redeemed for ten slaves. The redemption of captives that sent slaves—sometimes in great numbers—in lieu of free people to the Americas clearly evidences inequality, exploitation, and domination. It would be unrealistic to expect that under the assault of the slave trade people would forgo social distinctions for the purpose of unity. Putting those deemed socially (or "racially") inferior in harm's way to protect oneself or one's family is a widespread stratagem exacerbated in times of war, when people are the most sanguine about unity and solidarity, but also the more at risk. In 1805, for example, France instituted the replacement system by which the drafted could pay poor young men to take their place during a war. During the American Civil War, wealthy men were allowed to offer $300 to escape the draft, thus sending poor Irish immigrants to fight in their place. The Vietnam War saw a similar model, with poor whites, blacks, and Hispanics disproportionately dispatched to the front, while most middle-class white students were shielded by school deferments.

Free People

Although men and women already enslaved may have been a common source of substitutes, free people were not excluded. In a deposition given in 1790, a former resident of the Gold Coast revealed that when people did not have slaves to give in exchange for their children's freedom, they sometimes purchased captives from the Europeans (Richard Miles, in Lambert 1975–76, 68:50). Among them were free people who had been captured in war or kidnapped.

People of free status were also the victims of abductions orchestrated in order to turn them into substitutes. Indeed, a Sierra Leone slave dealer "attributed the frequency of kidnappings among the Mandingoes to their head men getting into debt to the Europeans, and being then confined by them; in which case, their people were obliged to kidnap some person to redeem them" (in Lambert 1975–76, 68:77). These kidnap victims could be anyone: slaves, free persons of commoner status, craftspeople, traders, and notables.

The situation of emotional urgency under which families operated when trying to redeem their relatives turned some of them into participants in the slave trade. A forceful description of these kidnappers and of their motives has been left by Mungo Park:

> A few friends will combine together, and advance into the enemy's country, with a view to plunder, or carry off the inhabitants. A single individual has been known to take his bow and quiver, and proceed in like manner. Such an attempt is doubtless in him an act of rashness; but when it is considered that, in one of these predatory wars, he has probably been deprived of his

> child or his nearest relation, his situation will rather call for pity than censure. The poor sufferer, urged on by the feelings of domestic or paternal attachment, and the ardour of revenge, conceals himself among the bushes, until some young or unarmed person passes by. He then, tyger-like, springs upon his prey; drags his victim into the thicket, and in the night carries him off as a slave. (1971, 294)

It is likely that in those cases the captors were too poor to either possess their own slaves or to have enough resources to redeem their relatives in another way. Thus, in the context of redemption, the class factor—although definitive in the case of slaves—was not necessarily the most relevant for the rest of the population because the procedure, through kidnappings, did not systematically exclude the poor and those at the bottom of the caste system.

However, their strategies were limited, and some engaged in the ultimate sacrifice to save their relatives. Paul Erdmann Isert, who worked at trading posts on the Gold Coast, related the case of a man who, unable to repay a debt, was awaiting departure for the Caribbean. One of his sons asked to take his place and, "[s]ince the latter was a handsome young man who had many more years ahead of him than did his father, the exchange was very attractive" (1992, 141–42). The governor, however, arranged for the son to be released on condition that the family come up with money within a reasonable time. But such an involvement was exceptional, and substitutes who had redeemed their relatives with their own persons were shipped away, as was Oga, from Nigeria, who asked to take his son's place and was on his way to the Americas when his ship was intercepted by the British navy and directed to Sierra Leone (Koelle 1854, 18). As for the rest of the redemption cases, it is impossible to know the frequency of family swap, but there is no compelling reason to suppose a priori that it was exceptional.

Although redemption was essentially used by relatives and friends, in some instances, large communities and even a state would resort to it. Most reported—if not actual—cases concerned the Muslims. Islamic law states that free Muslims cannot be enslaved; and even though this interdiction was far from being followed to the letter, Europeans often mentioned that the Muslims often redeemed their own. The Islamic state of Futa Toro (Senegal) under almamy Abdul Kader Kane resorted to redemption and repeatedly closed the French and British slave trade passing through its territory.[7] Kane forcefully removed from slave coffles his subjects who had been kidnapped and, when necessary, redeemed them. But his strategy did not always work, as Carl Bernard Wadström reported: "On the

12th of January [1787], when I came to Senegal, the Moors had already begun their incursions, and had delivered 50 Negroes to the Company, who were taken in the dominions of King Dalmanny [almamy], and whom King Dalmanny sent down to the Directors of the Company to ransom. When the messengers from King Dalmanny arrived, the 50 slaves were already dispatched to Cayenne" (in Lambert 1975–76, 73–29). Kane probably attempted no additional action, but families tried to redeem their relatives who had already been transported overseas. This was a challenging endeavor that in all probability produced very few positive results.

REDEMPTION ACROSS CONTINENTS

Redemption, already difficult when the captives were still on African soil, was made all the more complicated when they had already left. The involvement of Western traders, slave captains, and slaveholders was a requisite, and only the most influential people could ask for and sometimes obtain it, as Paul E. Lovejoy and David Richardson state (ch. 7, this volume). King Naimbanna of Sierra Leone, who wanted them released, managed to get some information concerning "three distant relations . . . now in the West Indies. . . . Their names are Corpro, Banna and Morbour" (Wadström 1794, 2:16). An inquiry revealed that they lived in St. Croix, where one was a blacksmith and the other two were tailors (Fyfe 1962, 54). No mention was made of their release. Another family member was shipped to Jamaica, where he was able to get interviews with the governor. He was sent back when a letter asking for his release reached the island (Wadström 1794, 2:16). Similarly, in 1731, King Tom of Sierra Leone "begged of [Sir George Young] to apply to his brother George (meaning our king) to get [a young woman] restored to him" (Young, in Lambert 1975–76, 73:205); and a ruler in Bissau wrote to the king of Portugal in 1792 demanding the return of someone who had been deported (Rodney 1970, 258). John Corrente, a headman at Annamaboe (Ghana) had seen one of his sons, William Ansah Sessarakoo, shipped to Barbados in the late 1710s. The Royal African Company promised him that he would be recovered, and another of Corrente's sons sailed to the island to retrieve the captive, who was finally redeemed (*Royal African* 1720, 44–45, 47, 51). King Agaja of Dahomey requested and obtained the return, from Maryland, of Captain Tom, also known as Adomo Tomo (Snelgrave 1971, 67–72; Law 1991). Two brothers of Adandozan were sold in Demerara "by mistake" but were sent back to Dahomey in 1803, probably through payment to their owners (Dalzel 1967, 181). The propensity of the Dahomey kings to sell their rivals to the Europeans has been well documented, as have been a few cases of attempted and successful redemption. Fruku, also called Don Jeronimo, sold by King Tegbesu, spent twenty-four years in Brazil before being redeemed by King Kpengla (Dalzel 1967, 222–23; Akinjogbin 1967, 116, 171, 178–79; Law and Mann 1999, 318–20). The story of Agontime, presented as King Ghezo's mother—biological or otherwise—may also represent a successful redemption. After taking power in 1818, Ghezo sent two delegations to the Americas to look for her after she had been exiled by Adandozan with six hundred other men and women following a dynastic quarrel in 1797. In the early 1820s a woman named Agontime—said to have returned from the West—was named *kpojito* by Ghezo, the highest female position in the kingdom (Hazoumé 1937, 31–32; Herskovits 1938, 2:64; Akinjogbin 1967, 186; Bay 2001). Several contradictory versions of the episode exist, and what really transpired is unclear, but Agontime—whether the exiled mother or another woman by the same name—was probably ransomed from her place of exile if she had not freed herself before.

An extraordinary case of quasi-successful redemption comes from Georgia. Few details are available, but in 1936, Shade (Shadrach) Richards, a former slave interviewed by the Federal Writers' Project of the Works Progress Administration, revealed that his father Alfred, an African, was almost freed by his father. According to the interviewer's transcription, Shade's grandfather had come from Africa "to buy his son and take him home" (Federal Writers' Project vol. 4, pt. 3, 200). In reality, the protagonists must have been Shade's grandfather and great-grandfather because the 1870 and 1880 censuses state that Shade's father was born in Georgia. Unfortunately, both men died before they could leave. The casual manner in which the story was recounted suggests that this was not considered an amazing feat. However, for people in Africa to have been able to find out the exact whereabouts of their son enslaved near Zebulon in Pike County, Georgia, was a tour de force. It would be interesting to know the family's social background; whether the father was, for example, a trader or a notable who had a close relationship with the slavers. The fact that he was able to accomplish all the necessary steps to ransom his son could indicate that a few others might have succeeded.

Despite the unfavorable odds, ordinary people also tried intercontinental redemption. One such attempt was made by an old man from Timbo whose son, Amadou, had been seized four years earlier as he was coming back from the Rio Pongo with six friends.[8] They had been shipped off to the Caribbean "except one, who was recovered by the Foulah king. The old man said, he would willingly pay any ransom for his son" (Wadström 1794, 2:113–14). Although several years had passed, the father still had hopes of freeing his son and gave his name as well as those of the other young men to promote their release. Another man tried the same approach, as he endeavored to recover "his intimate friend, Famarah, a distinguished chief carried off the coast, some time ago as a slave." He also brought to the governor the case of a favorite young boy who had been shipped away (2:91, 107). Although transcontinental redemption commonly failed, the very fact that people attempted that strategy evidences the strong bond that continued to link people on both sides of the Atlantic and illustrates the love and concern of those who had remained in Africa.

A song heard on Gorée Island in the eighteenth century hauntingly expresses their feeling of irremediable loss and despair, as well as their strong will to be reunited with their loved ones, even if—when redemption was not possible—it entailed the ultimate sacrifice:

> Damel [king] has raided the village of Yene
> He has enslaved the woman I love
> Since then, I have so much pain
> That I cannot drink palm wine
> And I cannot eat couscous
> My love is going to be shipped to the islands
> I will ask to be made a slave to be with her
> I'd rather be a slave with her
> Than a free man in a place where she no longer is. (Verdun de la Crenne 1778, 158–59)

In the Americas, Africans from the same ethnic group or who shared the same religion also used that strategy. The most notable examples can be found in Trinidad (Truman 1844, 109–10; Campbell 1975–76, 467–95) and Brazil, where Muslim associations pooled their members' resources and redeemed Muslim captives off the boats or "anyone of their number who was the most respected" (Fletcher and Kidder 1866, 135). Africans came from cultures that used redemption as a matter of course, and they undoubtedly tried to use this classic strategy more routinely than documented. Ibrahima abd al-Rahman had immediately told his owner in Mississippi that his relatives would pay for his freedom (Alford 1977, 43). Similarly, in Saint Domingue, Tamerlan, the former private Qur'anic teacher of a prince, drew a French colonel's attention as he "talked a lot about his king's power; of the price he would pay to redeem him" (Malenfant 1814, 214). One may also speculate about the runaway Caesar's objective as he "boasts much of his family in his own country, it being a common saying with him, that he is no common negro" (Windley 1983, 2:127).[9] But contempt for the Africans, and the belief in their lack of human qualities, certainly made slaveholders highly skeptical of the readiness and financial capacity of "heathen and savage" parents to pay for their children's freedom. People in other parts of the world were better informed, and their willingness to release some captives for a ransom shows that the Africans used this strategy on an international scale. Mohammed Ali ben Said of Nigeria—a Union soldier in the Civil War, teacher, and lecturer—reported that while he was enslaved in Tripoli, Libya, as news reached the pasha that the group of young men captured with Said were "from the best families in Bornou, [the pasha] purchased the whole lot and held them for ransom" (1873, 73).

When their owners refused to take them seriously, Africans could try to reach their families or friends directly, like Ayuba Suleyman Diallo and Ibrahima abd al-Rahman, who both wrote letters in Arabic asking for their release (Curtin 1967; Alford 1977). It is legitimate to assume that through the centuries other men and women tried the same strategy. Almost all quite likely failed, as did John Homrn. The letters "he sent to his home, either never reached their destination, or his friends to whom they were addressed, were gone" (*Anti-Slavery Reporter* 2 [May 1847]: 74). Verbal communication could also be used through the intermediary of returnees and new arrivals. Those links have been well documented and are exemplified by the case of Dolore Real, a Nigerian Yoruba. Enslaved at ten, she spent thirty years in Cuba before going back home:

> Deponent knows she shall find her mother and her three brothers when she gets back. Has heard of them within the last four months through some Bozals, newly-imported from Lagos. These people who had not then been made slaves, had conversed with some self-manumitted Negroes who had gone back to Lagos from Havannah some time ago. This circumstance is not at all uncommon. The slaves in Havannah often hear of their relatives through the newly-imported Bozals. Self-manumitted slaves are also constantly going back home. . . . Through them many slaves sent news home to their friends. (*Anti-Slavery Reporter* 2 [2 October 1854]: 234–39, in Blassingame 1977, 314)

Given the widespread recourse to redemption in Africa, it is likely that the "news" sent home included requests for ransoms. What these examples clearly evidence is that the Africans knew they could count on their families, if communication was effectively established, to try to have them released. They probably were also aware that their kin may have tried to redeem them before departure. Muhammad Kaba Saganogo revealed to the Moravian brothers of Jamaica that he had been abducted at twenty while on his way to Timbuktu to finish his studies in 1777. He added that he knew "[h]is relations endeavoured to ransom him, but in vain" (in Buchner 1971, 50). Speaking of his folks, Cudjo Lewis, the last survivor of what is considered the last slave ship to the United States, stressed, "I know they hunt for me" (in Hurston 1942, 212). Their hunt may well have included an attempt at ransoming him.

Far from abandoning their relatives, African families who could, looked for them, pooled resources, walked to the slave ships, and tried to gain time and precious manpower by sometimes pawning a younger child in their place. Some offered themselves as substitutes, continued to promise money to the Westerners long after the ships had left, and collected funds to free or repatriate their unknown, American-born grandchildren. They also engaged in the trading of other men, women, and children as a means to protect their own from deportation.

The recourse to the strategy of redemption and the fact that it had some amount of success at no point suggest that the people who were swept into the Atlantic trade were either already enslaved, political prisoners, commercial rivals of the Europeans, or lived far from the coast. The workings of the slave trade were much more complicated, and the abilities of particular individuals, families, and communities to take advantage of redemption were often surpassed by larger-scale events and obstacles.

Redemption worked, but it was not meant to disrupt the slave trade; it worked within its framework. It was a strategy against the trade in specific people, a protective mechanism of last resort that legitimately sought to prevent it from affecting one's family and group. From a personal, familial, and communal standpoint—the level at which people operate—it rested on a rational and inevitable choice. It was a deeply human, if in some cases flawed, strategy. Ransoming ultimately exposes still another dreadful effect of the slave trade: it sometimes turned people who had been deeply affected and victimized by it into participants.

Notes

1. Oral tradition has not kept any memory of his sale and deportation, but mentions a disastrous raid during which several high-ranking chiefs' sons were captured and probably sold. Sori Mawdo's genealogy mentions two sons—among fifty—named Abdourahmane. See I. Barry 2001, 63.

2. Logbook of the *Bruce Grove,* Cambridge University Library. I am grateful to David Richardson for providing this source.

3. On the ransoming of captives in southern Senegal, see Baum 1999.

4. For pawning, see Lovejoy and Richardson (1999; and this volume).

5. For examples of pawns shipped to the Caribbean, when ransoming was offered a few hours late, see Oldendorp 1987, 209–11.

6. Among these captives, those who remained in the area were often part of the dowry offered by wealthy families. See Guèye 2001, 21.

7. For details on Kane's active opposition to the transatlantic slave trade, see Wadström 1790, 178; B. Barry 1972, 216; Pruneau de Pommegorge 1789, 14; Roger 1828, 238–39.

8. It is quite possible that he had traveled there to sell slaves. According to Wadström, who recounts the story, "It has been stated . . . that the Foulahs were often seized by freebooters, in returning from the factories to which they had been carrying the captives, taken in their predatory wars. This fact is confirmed by the following incident, among others of the kind that occurred in this journey" (1794, 2:113).

9. This notice was posted in the Annapolis *Maryland Gazette,* 17 August 1780.

Bibliography

Akinjogbin, I. A. 1967. *Dahomey and Its Neighbours, 1708–1818.* Cambridge: Cambridge University Press.

Alford, Terry. 1977. *Prince among Slaves: The True Story of an African Prince Sold into Slavery in the American South.* New York: Oxford University Press.

Atkins, John. 1735. *A Voyage to Guinea, Brasil and the West-Indies.* London: C. Ward and R. Chandler.

Barry, Boubacar. 1972. *Le royaume du Waalo: Le Sénégal avant la conquête.* Paris: François Maspero.

———. 1998. *Senegambia and the Atlantic Slave Trade.* Cambridge: Cambridge University Press.

Barry, Ismaël. 2001. "Le Fuuta Jaloo (Guinée) et la traite négrière atlantique dans les traditions orales." In Djibril Tamsir Niane, ed., *Tradition orale et archives de la traite négrière.* Paris: UNESCO.

Bay, Edna G. 2001. "Protection, Political Exile, and the Atlantic Slave Trade: History and Collective Memory in Dahomey." *Slavery and Abolition* 22 (April): 42–60.

Baum, Robert M. 1999. *Shrines of the Slave Trade: Diola Religion and Society in Precolonial Senegambia.* New York: Oxford University Press.

Beecham, John. 1968. *Ashantee and the Gold Coast.* 1841. Reprint, London: Dawsons of Pall Mall.

Blassingame, John W., ed. 1977. *Slave Testimony: Two Centuries of Letters, Speeches, Interviews, and Autobiographies.* Baton Rouge: Louisiana State University Press.

Bosman, William. 1967. *A New and Accurate Description of the Coast of Guinea, Divided into the Gold, the Slave, and the Ivory Coasts.* 1705. Reprint, London: Frank Cass.

Bowdich, Edward T. 1825. *Excursions in Madeira and Porto Santo, during the Autumn of 1823, While on His Third Voyage to Africa.* London: George B. Whittaker.

Brooks, George E., Jr. 1976. "The *Signares* of Saint-Louis and Gorée: Women Entrepreneurs in Eighteenth-Century Senegal." In Nancy J. Hafkin and Edna G. Bay, eds., *Women in Africa: Studies in Social and Economic Change,* 19–44. Stanford: Stanford University Press.

Brüe, André. 1745–47. "Voyages and Travels along the Western Coasts of Africa on Account of the French Commerce." In Thomas Astley, *A New General Collection of Voyages and Travels.* Compiled by John Green. 4 vols. London: T. Astley.

Buchner, J. H. 1971. *The Moravians in Jamaica.* 1854. Reprint, Freeport, N.Y.: Books for Libraries Press.

Campbell, Carl. 1975–76. "John Mohammed Bath and the Free Mandingos in Trinidad: The Question of Their Repatriation to Africa, 1831–38." *Journal of African Studies* 2 (winter): 467–95.

Conneau, Captain Theophilus. 1976. *A Slaver's Log Book; or, Twenty Years' Residence in Africa.* 1854. Reprint, Englewood Cliffs, N.J.: Prentice-Hall.

Crowther, Samuel. 1842. *Journals of Rev. James Frederick Schon and Mr. Samuel Crowther.* London: Hatchard and Son.

Cugoano, Quobna Ottobah. 1999. *Thoughts and Sentiments on the Evil of Slavery and Other Writings.* 1787. Reprint, London: Penguin Books.

Curtin, Philip D. 1967. "Ayuba Suleiman Diallo of Bundu." In Philip D. Curtin, ed. *Africa Remembered: Narratives by West Africans from the Era of the Slave Trade.* Madison: University of Wisconsin Press.

Daaku, Kwame Yeboa. 1970. *Trade and Politics on the Gold Coast: A Study of the African Reaction to European Trade, 1600–1720.* Oxford: Clarendon Press.

Dalzel, Archibald. 1967. *History of Dahomy, An Inland Kingdom of Africa.* 1793. London: Frank Cass.

Durand, Jean-Baptiste. 1807. *Voyage au Sénégal fait dans les années 1785 et 1786.* 2 vols. Paris: Dentu.

Federal Writers' Project. 1941. Slave Narratives, a Folk History of Slavery in the United States from Interviews with Former Slaves. 17 vols. Washington, D.C.

Fletcher, James, and D. P. Kidder. 1866. *Brazil and the Brazilians Portrayed in Historical and Descriptive Sketches.* Boston: Little Brown.

Fyfe, Christopher. 1962. *A History of Sierra Leone.* Oxford: Oxford University Press.

Grace, John. 1975. *Domestic Slavery in Africa.* New York: Barnes and Noble.

Grant, Douglas. 1968. *The Fortunate Slave.* New York: Oxford University Press.

Guèye, Mbaye. 2001. "La tradition orale dans le domaine de la traite négrière." In Djibril Tamsir Niane, ed., *Tradition orale et archives de la traite négrière.* Paris: UNESCO.

Hazoumé, Paul. 1937. *Le pacte de sang au Dahomey.* Paris: Institut d'Ethnologie.

Herskovits, Melville J. 1938. *Dahomey: An Ancient West African Kingdom.* 2 vols. New York: J. J. Augustin.

Hurston, Zora Neale. 1942. *Dust Tracks on a Road: An Autobiography.* Philadelphia: J. B. Lippincott.

Isert, Paul Erdmann. 1992. *Letters on West Africa and the Slave Trade: Paul Erdmann Isert's Journey to Guinea and the Caribbean Islands in Columbia.* Trans. and ed. Selena Axelrod Winsnes. 1788. Reprint, Oxford: Oxford University Press.

Kane, Oumar. 1974. "Les Maures et le Futa-Toro au dix-huitième siècle." *Cahiers d'études africaines* 54 (14–2): 237–52.

Koelle, Sigismund Wilhelm. 1854. *Polyglotta Africana.* London: Church Missionary House.

Lambert, Sheila. 1975–76. *House of Commons Sessional Papers of the Eighteenth Century.* Vols. 68–73. Wilmington, Del.: Scholarly Resources.

Lamiral, Dominique. 1789. *L'Affrique et le peuple affriquain considérés sous tous leurs rapports avec notre commerce et nos colonies.* Paris: Dessene.

Law, Robin. 1991. "King Agaja of Dahomey, the Slave Trade, and the Question of West African Plantations: The Mission of Bulfinch Lambe and Adomo Tomo to England, 1726–32." *Journal of Imperial and Commonwealth History* 19:137–63.

Law, Robin, and Kristin Mann. 1999. "West Africa in the Atlantic Community: The Case of the Slave Coast." *William and Mary Quarterly* 56 (2): 318–20.

Lovejoy, Paul E., and David Richardson. 1999. "Trust, Pawnship, and Atlantic History: The Institutional Foundations of the Old Calabar Slave Trade." *American Historical Review* 104 (April): 333–55.

Malenfant, Colonel. 1814. *Des Colonies et particulièrement de celle de Saint-Domingue.* Paris: Audibert.

Mannix, Daniel P., and Malcolm Cowley. 1962. *Black Cargoes: A History of the Atlantic Slave Trade, 1518–1865.* New York: Viking Press.

Matthews, John. 1791. *A Voyage to the River Sierra Leone on the Coast of Africa.* London: White and Son.

Meillassoux, Claude. 1991. *The Anthropology of Slavery: The Womb of Iron and Gold.* Chicago: University of Chicago Press.

Miers, Suzanne, and Igor Kopytoff, eds. 1977. *Slavery in Africa: Historical and Anthropological Perspectives.* Madison: University of Wisconsin Press.

Moore, Francis. 1738. *Travels into the Inland Parts of Africa.* London: E. Cave.

Oldendorp, C. G. A. 1987. *History of the Mission of the Evangelical Brethren on the Caribbean Islands of St. Thomas, St. Croix, and St. John.* Ed. Johan Jakob Bossart. Trans. Arnold R. Highfield and Vladimir Barac. 1777. Reprint, Ann Arbor: Karoma Publishers.

Park, Mungo. 1971. *Travels in the Interior Districts of Africa, Performed in the Years 1795, 1796, and 1797.* 1799. Reprint, New York: Arno Press/New York Times.

Pruneau de Pommegorge, Antoine. 1789. *Description de la nigritie.* Amsterdam: Maradan.

Robertson, Claire C., and Martin A. Klein, eds. 1997. *Women and Slavery in Africa.* Portsmouth, N.H.: Heinemann.

Rodney, Walter. *A History of the Upper Guinea Coast, 1545–1800.* Oxford: Clarendon Press, 1970.

Roger, Baron. 1828. *Kélédor, histoire africaine.* Paris: Nepveu.

Rømer, Ludvig Ferdinand. 1989. *Le Golfe de Guinée, 1700–1750: Récit de L. F. Römer marchand d'esclaves sur la côte ouest-africaine.* Trans. Mette Dige-Hess. Paris: L'Harmattan.

The Royal African; or, Memoirs of the Young Prince of Annamaboe. 1720. London: W. Reeves.

Russwurm, John Brown. 1830. "Letter." *African Repository* 6 (April): 60–61.

Said, Nicholas. 1873. *The Autobiography of Nicholas Said, a Native of Bornu, Eastern Soudan, Central Africa.* Memphis: Shotwell.

Snelgrave, William. 1971. *A New Account of Some Parts of Guinea and the Slave-Trade.* 1734. Reprint, London: Frank Cass.

Truman, George. 1844. *Narrative of a Visit to the West Indies in 1840 and 1841.* Philadelphia: Merrihew and Thompson.

Verdun de la Crenne, Jean René Antoine. 1778. *Voyage fait par ordre du roi en 1771 et 1772, en diverses parties de l'Europe, de l'Afrique, et de l'Amérique.* Paris: Imprimerie Royale.

Villard, André. 1943. *Histoire du Sénégal.* Dakar: Maurice Viale.

Wadström, Carl Bernhard. 1790. "Observations sur la traite des nègres avec une description de quelques parties de la côte de Guinée durant un voyage fait en 1787 et 1788." In Robert Norris, *Voyage au pays de Dahomé.* Paris.

———. 1794. *An Essay on Colonization, Particularly Applied to the Western Coast of Africa with Some Free Thoughts on Cultivation and Commerce.* London: Darton and Harvey.

Windley, Lathan A. 1983. *Runaway Slave Advertisements: A Documentary History from the 1730s to 1790.* Vol. 2, *Maryland.* Westport, Conn.: Greenwood Press.

Chapter 7
Anglo-Efik Relations and Protection against Illegal Enslavement at Old Calabar, 1740–1807

Paul E. Lovejoy and David Richardson

Get Slaves honestly, if you can,
And if you cannot get them honestly,
Get them.

—Traditional saying

Resistance by enslaved Africans to their status has been an important theme in the literature on transatlantic slavery. Most attention has focused on rebellion and other forms of resistance by slaves in the Americas, where evidence of such activities is perhaps most readily found. Resistance by enslaved Africans onboard ship and within Africa itself is attracting increasing attention, too, as violent and nonviolent forms of resistance come to be recognized as common to each stage of transatlantic slavery.[1] Transatlantic slavery was shaped, however, by both African resistance to and participation in the processes that resulted in the shipment of up to twelve million Africans as slaves to the Americas. Africans were, in other words, both victims and suppliers of the Atlantic slave trade. While the resistance of the enslaved to their conditions on the African coast has been recognized, the ways in which the slave suppliers protected themselves against seizure and deportation has received scant attention. It is difficult to believe that in the absence of such forms of protection—and the security for suppliers that it created—the Atlantic slave trade could have reached the scale it did at its height, between 1750 and 1850. Understanding how certain groups were able to protect themselves from arbitrary enslavement also yields insights into the political economy of slave trading in Africa. In particular, it exposes not only how the risks of participation in the slave trade were managed but also how profits from that trade were distributed and how it influenced African economic development.

In focusing on those who directed the trade in Africa, we recognize that it is not always easy to see the mechanisms by which people tried to protect themselves against enslavement. Sometimes protection involved efforts to enslave others considered as enemies. Sometimes protective measures may have given the appearance of resistance to the slave trade, notably in safeguarding the status of privileged groups, which clearly was not a challenge to the institution of slavery itself. At some ports along the Atlantic coast it is possible, nevertheless, to disentangle those who were protected from enslavement from those who were not. Moreover, one may discern some of the mechanisms used to protect the status of "insiders"—that is, those protected from enslavement—from being seized and transported to the Americas and, sometimes, the conditions in which such mechanisms could fail, even if only temporarily. Our analysis focuses on the port of Old Calabar, which supplied over a quarter of a million persons for export to the Americas between 1740 and 1807, making it the second largest slave port in the Bight of Biafra after Bonny, and one of the principal ports in Atlantic Africa at this time.[2] Although the French shipped some slaves from the port, largely in the decade after 1783, the British dominated the shipments supplied by local Efik traders before 1807. Anglo-Efik relations were thus pivotal to Old Calabar's trade with the Atlantic world from 1740 to 1807 (see Lovejoy and Richardson 1999, 337–38). Relative to other ports in the Bight of Biafra, information on trading arrangements in this period at Old Calabar is substantial, allowing us to identify how and with what success local Efik dealers in slaves were able to protect themselves from enslavement and shipment to the Americas. Our study of Old Calabar focuses on how insiders were defined, or at least defined themselves, as being immune from enslavement. It also explores how local institutions were adapted to serve the interests of group protection. While such efforts were not always successful, as we shall see, it is perhaps surprising to discover how successful they could be.

Defining Insider Status

Old Calabar comprised by the mid-eighteenth century a number of settlements, or "wards," that had grown out of an original settlement of Ibibio-speaking people at Creek Town (Obio Oko) who had adopted a new ethnic label, Efik.[3] Creek Town dominated the trade of Old Calabar during the seventeenth century, when exports of slaves were modest, but other wards, or "towns," were later founded further down river. Of these the most important were Old Town (Obutong), Duke Town or New Town (Atakpa), and Henshaw Town, each of which was headed by a single family. By the end of the seventeenth century, Obutong, controlled by the Robin family, seems to have emerged as the principal commercial ward, a position it probably retained until the 1760s. Located on the Calabar River, Obutong was better placed than Obio Oko to serve slave ships but found itself under pressure by the mid-eighteenth century, when another group formerly resident at Obio Oko, the Duke family, founded Atakpa, just below Obutong, apparently in 1748. This new "town" quickly became a rival to Obutong as the scale of slave shipments from Old Calabar rose after 1750. By the 1780s it seems, as we shall see later, to have eclipsed Obutong as the leading commercial center. Thereafter, possibly with support from Obio Oko and Henshaw Town, and then by the 1810s on its own, the Duke family of Atakpa appears to have dominated the export slave trade from Old Calabar through to its close in 1841.

The slaves sold by Efik traders at Old Calabar were supplied from inland markets controlled by traders from Aro Chuku whose dispersed settlements in the interior came to command the trade in much of Igbo and Ibibio country in the eighteenth century.[4] In effect, Aro merchants accumulated captives at their fairs at Bende and Uburu before moving them down to the coast through other centers such as Ita on the Cross River, a major intermediate market on the way to Old Calabar. Merchants from Old Calabar also traded directly with Ibibio Country and with Cameroon. European traders gained access to Aro or other inland traders only indirectly through dealings with merchants at coastal trading centers such as Old Calabar, to whom they advanced goods on credit as a means of lubricating trade with the interior. As Aro traders traveled widely in the interior and

Efik traders of Old Calabar traveled to inland markets, their protection from illegal seizure during their travels inland was as important as Efik traders' protection from seizure by Europeans if the export trade from Old Calabar was to prosper.

How Aro traders were able to travel with security and thus expand their trade network in tandem with the growing export trade in slaves is not yet fully understood. Their control of the oracle of Aro Chuku, with its power to condemn those that offended it to slavery, was one important mechanism, as was the use of body markings in chalk—on the wrist for men and the neck for women—to guarantee safe passage.[5] Unlike scarification, which was permanent and thus helped to define outsiders as much as insiders, especially when individuals traveled far from home, chalk or similar markings might be erased but could nevertheless provide a code of recognition to other insiders. To these mechanisms of protection Aro traders almost certainly developed others, some of which were also used by their Efik partners to deter illegal seizure, whether by Africans or by Europeans.

Fundamental to the creation of distinctions between those who could and could not legally be enslaved at Old Calabar (and probably in its hinterland as well) were kinship structures and the perpetuation of such structures based on kinship. This is most clearly evidenced at Old Calabar, whose wards often became identified with particular Efik families and their lineage that had migrated from Obio Oko. These families—the Robins at Obutong, the Dukes at Atakpa, and the Henshaws at the town that shared their name—dominated the life of such wards, association with which afforded the families and their dependents protection against illegal enslavement except when protection was forfeited because of some misdemeanor. Protection through ward membership applied not only to close family but also to employees, retainers, and even domestic slaves. This did not, however, prevent such slaves from being sacrificed in a demonstration of families' wealth and power at funerals of leading ward members or on other occasions.

At Old Calabar distinctions based on language or dialect reinforced kinship in separating insiders from outsiders. The language of Old Calabar traders, Efik, was itself a dialect of Ibibio, the parent language spoken by at least a significant proportion of those dispatched from the port to the Americas. Most others deported from Old Calabar were Igbo speakers.[6] The extent to which development of the Efik dialect was a conscious policy of those who settled at Old Calabar is unknown, but if it was, it probably developed from the mid-seventeenth century, when Old Calabar was established. Moreover, its role in identifying insiders was underscored by the growing use of additional languages by the Efik. Of these the most important was English, or at least a pidgin version that became the lingua franca. Initially acquired though personal dealings with British traders—the most common visitors to Old Calabar before 1807—the skills of some leading Efik traders in spoken and written English were further honed through personal visits to England. Such visits probably occurred from as early as the 1750s and may have been supplemented later in the century by visits to other European states such as France. Some Efik became skilled, therefore, in both English and French. Such skills were exemplified in commercial correspondence between the Efik elite and their European trading partners and in a diary kept in English by Ntiero Edem Efiom (Antera Duke) in the 1780s (see Duke 1956; Asuquo 1978).[7] Furthermore, interaction with Europeans at the coast and visits to Europe helped the Efik to acquire new commercial practices and to instill in them tastes for European-style dress and even home furnishings.[8] Efik society assumed therefore an increasingly creole character, only in this instance creolization modified an African language, Ibibio, not a European language. In doing so, it extended the range of cultural markers that helped to distinguish the Efik from those they dealt in as slaves.

To suggest that kinship, ward membership, and trade-related cultural change were the only elements that defined Efik identity in Old Calabar and its hinterland would be misleading. Equally important were secret societies and related developments such as scripts to communicate decisions made by such societies among its members. Secret societies were common to both Efik and Aro ethnic groups, with common membership of societies existing in some cases, thereby facilitating movement by each of the groups throughout the hinterland of Old Calabar, specifically the interior of the Cross River and neighboring Cameroon. Among the societies known to have existed, the most closely studied has been the Ekpe society, which seems to have been introduced into Old Calabar from the interior in the mid-seventeenth century at the time of the founding of Obutong.[9] A society whose masquerade was associated with the leopard, Ekpe was not the only organization with a totem, but it emerged as the most powerful institution throughout Old Calabar and its hinterland during the eighteenth century. Although Ekpe was not confined to Old Calabar and its activities were not centrally controlled, the relationship between Efik identity and the development of Ekpe was central to facilitating expansion of slave-trading activities in the interior.

An exclusively male society, with females barred from entering or even approaching its premises, Ekpe expanded its membership during the eighteenth century, forcing men to purchase membership if they did not join willingly. Individuals who were not members but were on the streets when the Ekpe masquerade was being "run" could be punished, usually by whipping. Membership was divided into a series of grades under the leadership of the *eyamba,* or chief priest or official, entry to each grade costing progressively more as one rose through the ranks. The highest grades of Ekpe tended, therefore, to be restricted to the wealthiest families, the senior members of such families often purchasing entry for their more junior members. Because the society came to assume tax-collecting and even law-making and enforcement functions, competition for control of Ekpe, particularly the position of eyamba and the ruling council, sometimes became intense or even violent among the various ward leaders of the port. Among the powers of the society's council, a body comprising members of its highest grades, was that of "blowing *ekpe,*" or imposing summary justice on offenders. The penalties ranged from fines to sale into slavery or execution, even for kin.[10] Membership did not prevent individuals being punished for alleged wrongdoing, but it tended to confer insider status as the society's ability to impose sanctions and enforce its decrees was strengthened. Underpinning this was the reduction to writing of the *nsibidi* sign language (see Dayrell 1909, 1911; MacGregor 1909), which allowed the influence of Ekpe to be consolidated by providing it with a mechanism for displaying decrees. Together with nsibidi, Ekpe was thus adapted by Efik merchants to promote and protect their own interests in the slave trade, whether in the Ibibio region along the Cross River or into the Cameroons. As the Aro also maintained their own secret Ekpe association, an interlocking grid of secret societies developed throughout the hinterland of Old Calabar, collectively protecting members from arbitrary seizure and, by their exclusion, helping to define those who could be legally enslaved.

Protection from illegal enslavement within Old Calabar and its hinterland was ultimately related, therefore, to cultural and institutional factors. More specifically, it was afforded to those whose appearance, habits, family ties, language skills, and even knowledge identified them as insiders. The masquerade associated with Ekpe was not accessible to outsiders, but could be used to intimidate, punish, or coerce them, whether by "running ekpe" through the streets, by taking direct action against individuals, or by issuing decrees. Moreover, although individuals may have benefited from action by the society, all measures taken by Ekpe were secret in the sense that they reflected collective decisions of the society's grand council and were not attributable to any individual. Through Ekpe, therefore, the Efik of Old Calabar were able collectively to define and to monitor the enforcement of the boundaries between legal and illegal enslavement. In some instances, and in common with other mechanisms underlying slavery and the slave trade, the operation of Ekpe involved coercion. Similar functions were almost certainly performed by secret societies in the areas controlled by Aro and others that supplied slaves to the traders of Old Calabar.

To what extent did the processes that defined the status of those who controlled the slave trade of Old Calabar protect them from deportation to the Americas? How permeable, in other words, was the boundary between legal and illegal enslavement? The further one moves inland from Old Calabar, the more difficult it is to answer such questions. There is, however, firm evidence that at times kin or dependents of even the most prominent of Old Calabar's merchants were seized and carried away to the Americas. Such events provoked outrage as well as threats of retaliation by such merchants against offending shipmasters or other ships of the same nation or port. They also demand explanation if we are to evaluate the effectiveness of mechanisms to protect insiders from enslavement at Old Calabar. This, in turn, casts light on Afro-European trade relations and the efficiency with which slave trading was conducted at the port, thereby facilitating its integration into the transatlantic economy.

To evaluate the mechanisms to protect slave traders from illegal seizure, we shall focus on two crucial events in the history of the pre-1807 Old Calabar slave trade. The first is the so-called massacre of 1767, which resulted in the deaths of up to three hundred residents of Obutong and the deportation to the Americas of at least two sons as well as other kin and dependents of the ward's head. The second is the increased reliance from the 1760s, if not earlier, on human pawnship to secure advances of British credit to Efik traders, a development that, like the massacre of 1767, also eventuated in shipment to the Americas of relatives or dependents of such traders. Not all those taken away as pawns were illegally taken, as far as Efik and British traders were concerned, but pawnship arrangements could result in enslavement, thereby blurring the line between legal and illegal enslavement. Moreover, from both the perspective of Old Calabar merchants and the Europeans trading there, they might also be identified with *panyarring* (arbitrary seizure of a person in compensation for a debt or offense) and confused with kidnapping. Analysis of these events helps, therefore, to reveal the complexities of commercial relations arising from local legalisms on this frontier of the transatlantic economy. It also helps to expose the political constraints on the security of Efik traders and their kin as well as of British credit and thus on possibilities for the growth of slaving at Old Calabar from 1750 to 1807.

The Massacre of 1767

The massacre of 1767 was one of the most traumatic episodes in the history of the Old Calabar slave trade, at least until British withdrawal from the trade after 1807 (see Williams 1897, 536–48; Nair 1972, 24–25; Noah 1980, 17–19;

Paley 2001; Sparkes 2002). Although accounts of this event do not always agree, contemporaries were united in suggesting that the massacre arose from a conspiracy of captains of several British ships and leading residents of Atakpa or Duke Town, to entrap those of Obuong, or Old Town.[11] The roots of the massacre seem to have lain in interward rivalry for control of the slave trade at Old Calabar following the founding of Atakpa around 1748, and in growing tensions between Obutong traders and British traders in the 1760s over recovery of debts. As one commentator noted, however, a critical factor in the entrapment of Obutong traders seems to have been their trust in the British to mediate in the rivalry with Atakpa.[12] In the ensuing ambush, up to three hundred Obutong residents were slaughtered, according to contemporary reports. In addition, at least two sons of Robin John Ephraim, the head of Atkapa, were shipped, with an unknown number of others, as slaves to the Americas, while another son sought refuge with the captain of a British ship, who took him to Liverpool as a free man. With assistance from British merchants, all three sons subsequently returned to Obutong by 1773, six years after the massacre, each one having received some education in Britain (Williams 1897; Paley 2001; Sparkes 2002). Their return, however, could not prevent a decisive and permanent shift of control of the export slave trade from Obutong toward other wards, notably Atakpa. In this respect, the massacre of 1767 led to a palace revolution within the Efik elite that controlled the slave trade of Old Calabar.

Most discussions of the events of 1767–73 have centered on British involvement, but what is revealed about the protection from enslavement of Efik traders? The most obvious lesson was that such protection was more than a cultural or institutional issue; it was also a political issue. Thus, whatever the importance attaching to the various mechanisms identifying the Efik as insiders, interward rivalry or conflict could not only jeopardize but also actually undermine the protection that such mechanisms helped to create. British complicity in the massacre seems, indeed, to have depended on division within the Efik commercial elite as Atakpa vied with Obutong for control of trade at Old Calabar. At the same time, the willingness of the Duke family to conspire with the British may have reflected concerns about the damaging impact of Obutong's debts on wider Anglo-Efik trade relations. In this respect, it is conceivable that the British were unknowingly used by the Efik leaders of Atakpa as instruments of Ekpe to help punish Obutong for failings that threatened the wider community's interests. Be this as it may, the massacre seems to have shown that interward unity rather than disunity was essential to safeguard Efik traders from seizure and possible sale overseas.

It is unlikely that the slaughter and deportation of Obutong residents removed or even eased political conflict at Old Calabar, at least in the short term. Obutong may have become less important as a trading center at Old Calabar after 1767, but, in an effort perhaps to rebuild trust with Robin John Ephraim, British traders helped to repatriate his sons in 1772–73.[13] Ephraim in turn sought to use trade links with the British specifically to acquire arms, maybe to pursue revenge against Atakpa. Whether the resentment of Obutong against Atakpa erupted into further violence between the two wards is uncertain, but there is evidence of continuing violence at Old Calabar in the 1770s.[14] In particular, a letter of June 1780 to the merchants of Liverpool from the leaders of Obia Otu, Atakpa, and Henshaw wards reported that "we was [at] war again with one part our country [Obutong?]," though it went to note that "now we make peace again." The authors of the letter also claimed there was "one King for all Callabar and trad [*sic*] [in] one places," a "Great Law" having been approved to protect captains of ships from assaults ashore.[15] The last was perhaps a reference, among others things, to the imprisonment and poisoning in 1775, allegedly by residents of New Town (or Atakpa), of two Liverpool captains, Edmund Doyle and Thomas Fidler, though the precise reason for their killing is unknown.[16] In seeking to reassure Liverpool traders of their safety, the new leaders of Old Calabar seem by 1780 to have recognized the importance of political unity and stability to the security of all traders—British and Efik—and thus to the commercial future of the port. In short, after the massacre of 1767 and its aftershocks, political order, personal security, and trade came to be seen as inseparable companions. One possible byproduct of the search for order at Old Calabar after 1767 may have been the redefinition of Obutong ward as an outsider within the political and social structure of Old Calabar.[17] Significantly, the head of Obutong was not a signatory to the letter to Liverpool merchants from Old Calabar in June 1780.

Pawnship and Panyarring

If political disunity posed risks to the protection of Efik traders and their kin from illegal enslavement, so too did involvement in the conduct of slave trading at Old Calabar of a large number of such traders and their dependents. Cases are to be found where British traders appear simply to have seized and sailed away with relatives or employees of local merchants. In 1760 two boys of Duke Abashy of Obutong were taken away by a Liverpool trader, even though they were later acknowledged to be "Freemen & No Slaves."[18] Nearly thirty years later, in 1789, two canoemen of Duke Ephraim of Atakpa, named Abashey and Antegra and described as free men, were said to have been carried away "for nothing and Supposed Sold" by a Bristol trader.[19] In each case, the local merchant who suffered the loss was a senior figure, but this was clearly insufficient to deter the traders involved from committing what was seen as an illegal act. Both Duke Abashy and Duke Ephraim sought the return of those they had lost by writing to merchants they knew in Liverpool and Bristol, though whether these efforts were successful is unknown. How commonplace such events were is unclear, but those taken away in these two cases were seen as having been illegally enslaved. For Duke Ephraim at least, the appropriate response to such an action was to seek retribution by making "Bristal Ship pay," that is, to seize, or panyar, another Bristol ship or its crew.

Not all cases where ship captains sailed away with relatives, dependents, or employees of Efik traders were such obvious cases of illegal enslavement. Much confusion or uncertainty seems to have arisen as a result of advances of credit at Old Calabar by British traders and their insistence, in many cases, that local Efik merchants offer human pawns as collateral for security of loans. The use in the export slave trade of pawnship, an indigenous African institution of some antiquity, was an important institutional adaptation.[20] Although introduced into Afro-European trade elsewhere from the seventeenth century, the earliest known examples of human pawnship in Anglo-Efik trade are from the early 1760s.[21] Thereafter, references to pawnship proliferate, with one report from a trader who visited Old Calabar in 1772–73 indicating that the use of pawns as collateral was "the way trade is carried on there."[22] Thus pawnship as well as the credit it underpinned were commonplace at Old Calabar, at least in the years after the massacre of 1767, if not earlier.

Among the Efik, a distinction was made between pawns and slaves. This is most evident in the diary of Antera Duke in the 1780s, where he uses the term *slave* and distinguishes it from *pawn* (or *pown, paun,* or *prown*) (Duke 1956, 86, 95, 109–10). This distinction was apparently consistent with that made elsewhere in Africa, reflecting the fact that pawns could normally be redeemed whenever the debt was repaid, whereas slavery was for life and its status was inherited, unless the slave and offspring were manumitted. In practice, pawnship might bear some similarity to slavery when a debt remained unpaid across generations of the same family, but the person pawned could still ultimately be redeemed. When adapted to the export slave trade, however, contracts underpinning pawnship tended to be more time specific, at least in the eyes of British traders anxious to achieve as quick a turnaround time as possible in Africa. Moreover, should the trader fail to repay his debts by supplying slaves of satisfactory quality and in appropriate numbers within an allotted time, pawns became forfeit and could be carried away. The fact that pawns were usually held onboard ship rather than ashore facilitated their confiscation if necessary, although ships could not easily sail without warning. Among British traders, distinctions between pawns and slaves became blurred, with, in the words of one British captain, every pawn received being "considered a Slave, until he is redeemed."[23] Some Efik merchants also evidently understood that when giving pawns as collateral against the future delivery of slaves, the pawns could be taken away and sold if no offer to redeem them was made.[24] Foreclosing on pawns and selling them in the Americas did not necessarily amount to illegal enslavement in the eyes of Efik traders. It did, however, allow them to secure loans without exposing themselves to arbitrary seizure and sale into slavery.

Although in theory pawnship reconciled Efik traders' demands for credit with protection from enslavement, in practice reconciliation proved problematic, notably when pawns were relatives of the debtor. The ratio of slaves to pawns in transactions was evidently more than at par and could be as high as two or three slaves per pawn (see Lovejoy and Richardson 2001a), giving each pawn a premium of 50 percent or more over an equivalent slave. British willingness to accept a ratio of pawns to slaves of less than unity probably reflected their belief that Efik traders would wish to protect those given as pawns from enslavement. With this in mind, British captains seem to have insisted on the inclusion of relatives of Efik dealers among pawns. This may have proved difficult to ensure, but British traders seem to have had some success. Indeed, there is firm evidence that sons of some of the leading Efik traders were included among pawns held on British ships. Several sons of Robin John Ephraim of Obutong were held on British ships in the 1770s and there are indications that other prominent Efik pawned close family members to secure credit.[25] Pawnship thus was tied to kinship, a situation that British ship captains sought to exploit in their efforts to accelerate or at least ensure recovery of debts. As one British observer noted in 1790, relatives of pawns were "always particularly anxious" when they believed a ship "would sail away with the pawns."[26]

British traders may have seen kinship ties between Efik traders and their pawns as a lever to pressure the former to fulfill contracts, but how far did they exploit this? Perhaps because the pawns were related to local traders, captains were evidently reluctant at times to sail with them, even when the time agreed for their redemption had expired. A trade in pawns between ships seems to have existed, as some exchanged their pawns for the slaves of others, allowing the former to leave by selling their debts to the latter and to preserve good relations with local traders (Duke 1956, 49, 59). Moreover, even if pawns were taken to the Americas, captains were sometimes reluctant to sell them, maybe for fear of the repercussions of such actions on trade at Old Calabar. Family ties between Efik traders and their pawns were therefore two-edged, supplying a lever in debt recovery but also inducing caution in its use. Contracts between Efik and British traders were probably mainly oral, though there is evidence of written contracts, but whether oral or written, contracts were contestable, thus accentuating the need for caution on the part of shipmasters in foreclosing on pawns. Only when Efik traders acknowledged that debts were overdue and that pawns were thus forfeit was it probably safe for British ships to sail away with them without risking some form of retaliation.

Various avenues were open to Efik traders to protect pawns—kin or otherwise—from what they regarded as illegal seizure. Sometimes they sought to forestall ships close to completing their trade from sailing, perhaps because they still had pawns on board. The principal device used was to call on Ekpe to impose a collective boycott of trade with such a ship by "blowing ekpe" on it (Duke 1956, 59). This would impede taking on any additional slaves as well as the provisions and water needed for the Atlantic crossing. This ability to intercede was just one of the powers that the Ekpe society possessed to regulate trade. In this, as in other aspects of trade regulation, Ekpe functioned as a merchant guild, coordinating local action to regulate the treatment and protection of pawns and thus to safeguard the interests of the leading traders of Old Calabar who used pawns as collateral. In other cases, efforts to protect pawns involved panyarring, or the seizure of ships or crew, in order to force offending captains to return pawns illegally detained. In 1773, Robin John Ephraim, or "Grandy King George," of Obutong seems to have resorted to "stoping Sum of [the] people" and the boats of two ships in order to "get my Pawns from them." Two of Ephraim's sons seem to have been among those held in pawn on board the two ships in question. On this occasion, Ephraim's resort to panyarring to recover his sons may have been influenced by the fact that "the New town people" [i.e., Atakpa] had "blown abuncko [ekpe] for no ship to go from my water to them nor any to cum from them to me" (Lovejoy and Richardson 2001b, 104). Once the possibility of a collective response by all wards through Ekpe was removed by the action of Atakpa, panyarring was perhaps the only option left to Ephraim to recover his pawns.

Whether related or not to Efik traders, pawns were in an ambiguous position in late-eighteenth-century Old Calabar. To British ship captains, all pawns were potential slaves, whereas to the Efik, pawns that were family and kin, that is, insiders, could not be enslaved. Only pawns deemed outsiders, including those who had effectively been reduced to slavery in the interior, could be taken away and sold in the Americas, and then only when not redeemed within an agreed time period. Thus, for the Efik, protection of pawns from illegal enslavement revolved around ensuring that pawned relatives should not be deported and that, among pawns considered outsiders, only those that could not be redeemed were deported. The evidence suggests that on both counts Efik traders were, at best, only partly successful. The Anglo-Efik correspondence of the time contains complaints from Efik traders of the confiscation of pawned relatives by British ship captains as well as the taking away of relatives who may have been pawned. Though the evidence is not conclusive, traders of Obutong may have been particularly prone to lose relatives in this way, especially after the massacre of 1767. In addition, shipmasters reported the inclusion of pawns among the slaves on board as they cleared Old Calabar for the Americas. In 1788 the master of the Liverpool slaver *Gascoigne* claimed to have 120 "Pledges" [pawns] among the 540 slaves on board when he left Old Calabar.[27] He was not alone in doing so. As the master of the *Gascoigne* reported leaving behind debts amounting to a further hundred slaves, it is likely that most, if not all, the pawns he carried away were unredeemed victims of market failure at Old Calabar. Nevertheless, as in any case where oral and written contracts were involved, the contracts underpinning Anglo-Efik credit arrangements could give rise to disagreement between the parties over their interpretation, including the elasticity of deadlines. Thus, whereas Efik traders sometimes wished to extend time schedules for debt repayment because of slave supply problems, shipmasters anxious to leave African waters tended to be reluctant to do so. Ambiguity in interpreting deadlines created therefore much scope for differences of interpretation over the legality of the confiscation of pawns. The risk to pawns of being taken away by British ship captains was real, and, notwithstanding Efik efforts to protect them, some of those taken away were illegally enslaved. As a result, an unknown, though probably small, proportion of people of Efik origin or connection accompanied the Igbo- and Ibibio-speaking peoples, who comprised the vast majority of those deported from Old Calabar. Although the evidence is slender, it is possible too that they may have been joined by some related to traders of the Cross River interior.[28]

Like trade systems elsewhere, the development of the slave trade at Old Calabar relied on the creation of conditions of security for all the parties who dealt in slaves. As control of supply remained in African hands, protection of local traders from the risk of enslavement, whether by others in the trading hinterland or by shippers of slaves at the coast, was especially important if the trade of the port was to grow. Central to control of the slave trade at Old Calabar were the Efik, who relied on ethnicity to underpin protection from enslavement internally and on local institutions such as the Ekpe society to do likewise when trading with Europeans. Various factors ensured, however, that Efik traders and their kin continued to face the risk of enslavement, at least by Europeans, in the second half of the eighteenth century. One factor was political conflict within the wards of Old Calabar, which culminated in civil war between at least two wards in 1767 and probably further violence thereafter. One result of such events was the massacre of many residents of the previously dominant commercial ward of Obutong and the deportation of some others to the Americas. To the risks of enslavement arising from political conflict were added other threats arising from the pawning of relatives and others in order to secure British credit. Although human pawnship as a means of providing collateral for credit was not confined to Old Calabar, the indications are that use of pawns as collateral for loans largely reflected the lack of a local political authority capable of underwriting or enforcing private order credit arrangements.[29] In this respect, pawnship—and, at Old Calabar, the resultant exposure of Efik to enslavement in the event that pawns were unredeemed—was itself an indicator of political instability and division at the port. The story of the eighteenth-century slave trade at Old Calabar suggests, therefore, that protection against illegal enslavement was at least as much a political question as an ethnic or institutional one and that after the massacre of 1767 few, if any, of the Efik had reason to feel totally secure.

NOTES

This chapter is part of an ongoing study of the Bight of Biafra and the Atlantic slave trade in the eighteenth and early nineteenth centuries. We thank the Social Sciences and Humanities Research Council of Canada, through its Major Collaborative Research Program, for its generous support in funding the York/UNESCO Nigerian Hinterland Project and the research upon which it is based. We also thank Jordan Goodman, Jean-Marc Masseaut, Nathalie Sannier, and Silke Strickrodt for advice and research assistance. The usual disclaimer applies.

1. For resistance onboard ship, see Richardson, this volume; Behrendt, Eltis, and Richardson 2001 and the literature cited therein.
2. For data on slave shipments see Eltis et al. 1999.

3. For the history of Old Calabar see Aye 1967; Latham 1973; Noah 1980; Akak 1986; Oku 1989.

4. On the Aro, see Dike and Ekejiuba 1990; Nwauwa 1990; Ijoma and Njoku 1991; Nwokeji 1999.

5. On the importance of the oracle, see Northrup 1978, 114–16.

6. There is much debate about the ethnicity of the slaves taken from the Bight of Biafra; see Northrup 2000 and the literature cited therein. While acknowledging that ethnic labels had "imprecise, shifting and overlapping meanings during the era of the Atlantic slave-trade," Northrup estimates, nevertheless, that by the late eighteenth century "Old Calabar's slave exports may have been well over half Igbo" (14).

7. On letters from Efik traders to British merchants, see Lovejoy and Richardson 2001.

8. On commercial practices, see Lovejoy and Richardson 1999, 342.

9. References to Ekpe (or Egbo) are to be found from the early eighteenth century onward (e.g., Snelgrave [1734] 1971, 7–12, which refers to voyages made by Snelgrave up to thirty years earlier) and were commonplace by the early nineteenth century. For more modern discussions see Talbot 1926; Noah 1980, 27–32, 48, 71–72; Simmons 1956; Jones 1956.

10. For an instance of fines imposed by the society, see Duke 1956, entry for 18 January 1785. For descriptions of Ekpe sanctions, see Jones 1956, 142; Holman 1959, 1:393.

11. For contemporary evidence on the massacre, see Public Record Office, KB 1/19 Michaelmas 1773, affidavit of William Floyd, 5 October 1773, and affidavits of Thomas Jones, 18 September, 21 October, and 15 November 1773; Minutes of Evidence of John Ashley Hall, 1–2 March 1790, and of Ambrose Lace, 12 March 1790, in Lambert 1977, 72:515–60, 633–36.

12. Minutes of Evidence of John Ashley Hall, 1–2 March 1790, in Lambert 1977, 72:516.

13. The involvement of British traders and others in the repatriation of Robin John Ephraim's sons is discussed in Paley 2001 and Sparkes 2002.

14. For correspondence from Robin John Ephraim and his sons to British traders in the 1770s, see Lovejoy and Richardson 2001b.

15. The letter was published in *Liverpool General Advertiser,* 21 February 1788, and is reprinted in Lovejoy and Richardson 2001b, 109–10.

16. On the poisonings, see the Minutes of Evidence of John Ashley Hall in 1790, in Lambert 1977, 72:538–39. The minutes imply that the poisonings took place in 1775, though the voyage records suggest they more likely occurred in 1774 (see Eltis et al. 1999, voyage nos. 91575 and 91764). Hall insisted the murders were committed by New Town, not Old Town. Among the owners of Doyle's ship was Ambrose Lace, who helped one of Ephraim Robin John's sons to escape Old Calabar after the massacre of 1767 and, after educating him in Liverpool, assisted him to return to Obutong in 1773. At this time the feud between Atakpa (New Town) and Obutong (Old Town) was still going on, with Atakpa seeking to prevent trade with and from Obutong. Whether Doyle and Fidler traded at Obutong is unclear, but it is possible that, at least in Doyle's case, his links with Lace made him a target of New Town. If this was so, then he was a

victim of the ongoing political conflict between the two wards, a conflict that in 1780 the signatories to the letter to Liverpool merchants implied had ended.

17. In a long letter apparently written in 1773 to Ambrose Lace of Liverpool, Grandy King George (Robin John Ephraim) of Obutong observed that New Town had sought to prevent commercial intercourse between the two wards (Lovejoy and Richardson 2001b, 106–7).

18. William Earle to Duke Abashy, Merseyside Maritime Museum, Letter Book of William Earle 1760–61, 10 February 1761.

19. Duke Ephraim to Rogers & LRoach [Laroche], Public Record Office, C 107/12, 16 October 1789.

20. For a discussion of human pawnship generally in Africa, see Falola and Lovejoy 1994.

21. On pawnship in Afro-European trade elsewhere in Africa, see Lovejoy and Richardson 2001a.

22. Minutes of Evidence of John Ashley Hall, who traded at Old Calabar in 1772–73, in Lambert 1977, 72:227.

23. Minutes of Evidence of James Fraser in Lambert 1977, 71:15. The comments of Fraser, who operated on the African coast for twenty years, applied to "Angola," by which he presumably meant the Loango coast, but also to the Upper Guinea Coast and to "other parts."

24. See the deposition signed by Robin John Otto Ephraim and others of Obutong in 1776 in Williams 1897, 541.

25. For the 1770s, see Lovejoy and Richardson 2001b. In 1787 a trader named King Ambo was required to give one of his sons as a pawn in place of another pawn that had absconded (Duke 1956, 59).

26. Evidence of John Ashley Hall, 1–2 March 1790, in Lambert 1977, 72:227.

27. Richard Rogers to James Rogers, Public Record Office, C 107/12, April 1788. See also the letter from Robin John Ephraim to Thomas Jones, 11 November 1773, where the head of Obutong complained that four of his sons whom he had pawned had been taken away (Lovejoy and Richardson 2001b).

28. Evidence presented recently by Northrup (2000, 9) suggests that Efik speakers may have comprised up to 15 percent of the exported slaves obtained in a hundred-mile radius of Old Calabar in the later eighteenth century. The percentage was even higher among peoples taken within a fifty-mile radius of the port.

29. This issue is discussed more fully in Lovejoy and Richardson, forthcoming. See also Lovejoy and Richardson 2001a, where variations among West African trading centers in relying on pawnship to underwrite credit are described.

BIBLIOGRAPHY

Akak, E. O. 1986. *The Palestine Origins of the Efiks.* 3 vols. Calabar: Akak and Sons.

Asuquo, Ukorebi U. 1978. "The Diary of Antera Duke of Old Calabar, 1785–1788." *Calabar Historical Journal* 5:32–42.

Aye, E. U. 1967. *Old Calabar through the Ages.* Calabar: Hope Waddell Press.

Behrendt, Stephen D., David Eltis, and David Richardson. 2001. "The Costs of Coercion: African Agency in the Pre-Modern Atlantic World." *Economic History Review* 54:454–76.

Dayrell, Elphistone. 1909. "Some Nsibidi Signs." *Man* 10:113–14.

———. 1911. "Further Notes on Nsbidi Signs and Their Meaning from the Ikom District, Southern Nigeria." *Journal of the Royal Anthropological Institute of Great Britain and Ireland* 41: 521–40.

Dike, K. O., and Felicia Ekejiuba. 1990. *The Aro of South-Eastern Nigeria, 1650–1980.* Ibadan: University Press.

[Genuine] "Dicky Sam." 1884. *Liverpool and Slavery: An Historical Account of the Liverpool-African Slave Trade.* Liverpool: A. Bowker and Son.

Duke, Antera [Ntiero Edem Efiom]. 1956. "The Diary of Antera Duke." In Cyril Daryll Forde, ed., *Efik Traders of Old Calabar.* London: International African Institute.

Eltis, David, Stephen D. Behrendt, David Richardson, and Herbert S. Klein, eds. 1999. *The Trans-Atlantic Slave Trade: A Database on CD-ROM.* Cambridge: Cambridge University Press.

Falola, Toyin, and Paul E. Lovejoy, eds. 1994. *Pawnship in Africa: Debt Bondage in Historical Perspective.* Boulder: Westview Press.

Holman, James. 1959. *Holman's Voyage to Old Calabar.* 1834. Reprint, Calabar: American Association for African Research.

Ijoma, J. O., and O. N. Njoku. 1991. "Highpoints of Igbo Civilization: The Arochukwu Period." In A. E. Afigbo, ed., *Groundwork of Igbo History.* Lagos: Vista Books.

Jones, G. I. 1956 . "The Political Organization of Old Calabar." In Cyril Daryll Forde, ed., *Efik Traders of Old Calabar,* 116–60. London: International African Institute.

Lambert, Sheila, ed., *House of Commons Sessional Papers of the Eighteenth Century.* 147 vols. Wilmington, Del.: Scholarly Resources, 1977.

Latham, A. J. H. 1973. *Old Calabar, 1600–1891: The Impact of the International Economy upon a Traditional Society.* Oxford: Clarendon Press.

Lovejoy, Paul E., and David Richardson. 1999. "Trust, Pawnship, and Atlantic History: The Institutional Foundations of the Old Calabar Slave Trade." *American Historical Review* 104:333–55.

———. 2001a. "The Business of Slaving: Pawnship in Western Africa, c. 1600–1810." *Journal of African History* 42:67–90.

———. 2001b. "Letters of the Old Calabar Slave Trade." In Vincent Carretta, ed., *Genius in Bondage,* 89–115. Louisville: University Press of Kentucky.

———. "'This Horrid Hole': Commerce and Credit at Bonny, 1690–1840." Forthcoming.

MacGregor, J. K. 1909. "Some Notes on *Nsibidi.*" *Journal of the Royal Anthropological Institute of Great Britain and Ireland* 39:209–19.

Nair, Kannan K. 1972. *Politics and Society in South Eastern Nigeria, 1841–1906.* London: Frank Cass.

Noah, Monday Efiong. 1980. *Old Calabar: The City States and the Europeans, 1800–1885.* Uyo, Nigeria: Scholars Press.

Northrup, David. 1978. *Trade without Rulers: Pre-colonial Economic Development in South-Eastern Nigeria.* Oxford: Clarendon Press.

———. 2000. "Igbo and Igbo Myth: Culture and Ethnicity in the Atlantic World, 1600–1850." *Slavery and Abolition* 21:1–20.

Nwauwa, A. O. 1990. "The Dating of the Aro Chiefdom: A Synthesis of Correlated Genealogies." *History in Africa* 17:227–45.

Nwokeji, G. Ugo. 1999. "The Biafran Frontier: Trade, Slaves, and Aro Society, c. 1750–1905." Ph.D. diss., University of Toronto.

Oku, Ekei Essien. 1989. *The Kings and Chiefs of Old Calabar, 1785–1925.* Calabar: Glad Tidings Press.

Paley, Ruth. 2001. "After Somerset: Mansfield, Slavery, and the Law in England, 1772–1830." In Norma Landau and Donna Andrews, eds., *Crime, Law, and Society.* Cambridge: Cambridge University Press.

Simmons, Donald C. 1956. "An Ethnographic Sketch of the Efik People." In Cyril Daryll Forde, ed., *Efik Traders of Old Calabar,* 1–26. London: International African Institute.

Snelgrave, William. 1971. *A New Account of Some Parts of Guinea and the Slave-Trade.* 1734. Reprint, London: Frank Cass.

Sparkes, Randy J. 2002. "The Two Princes of Calabar: An Atlantic Odyssey from Slavery to Freedom." *William and Mary Quarterly* 59:555–84.

Talbot, Percy Amaury. 1926. *The Peoples of Southern Nigeria: A Sketch of Their History, Ethnology, and Languages.* 4 vols. London: Oxford University Press.

Williams, Gomer. 1897. *History of the Liverpool Privateers and Letters of Marque, with an Account of the Liverpool Slave Trade.* London: W. Heinemann.

Part 3

Offensive Strategies

Chapter 8

Igboland, Slavery, and the Drums of War and Heroism

John N. Oriji

IGBOLAND IS AMONG THE AREAS of West Africa that experienced the most intensive slave-trading activities during the seventeenth and nineteenth centuries. Although the total number of Africans enslaved remains unknown, available estimates suggest that about 637,500 Igbo slaves, amounting to 75 percent of the total shipments from the Biafran hinterland, landed in the Americas between 1640 and 1800 (see Oriji 1986). Furthermore, ex-slaves of Igbo ancestry constitute a majority of the population in Bonny, Okirika, and many other eastern delta states that served as depots and exchange centers for European merchants.

Much is already known about how the slave trade was organized in the Igbo hinterland and its impact on local communities (Oriji 1986; see also Oriji 1982; Dike 1956; Ekejiuba 1972; Northrup 1978). But the growing literature on the slave trade provides little insight into the responses it elicited in the hinterland. My research uses oral traditions and other sources to examine how individuals, families, and communities responded to the slave trade and enslavement.

Igbo response differed from one area to the other, and it is necessary to distinguish between the various ecological zones of the region, and explain the degree to which they were either involved in slave trading or subjected to slave raids and the other forms of social violence they engendered. The major ecological zones relevant to this study are

- western Igbo communities, which offer us some of the earliest evidence of slavery in Igboland;
- northern Igboland, including Okigwe, the Enugu-Nsukka area, and the Awka-Onitsha axis, which experienced the most intensive raids and provided the most diverse forms of resistance;
- riverine and coastal towns, whose middlemen sold captives to European traders;
- southeastern Igbo communities, including the homeland of the Aro slave traders and their Abam warriors, who were the main slave dealers in the hinterland;
- southern Igbo communities of Owerri, Mbaise, Ngwa, Asa-Ndokki, Ikwere-Etche, and other places, which were occasionally raided by Abam warriors.

WESTERN IGBOLAND

Cult Slaves, Exiles, and Escapees

Cult slavery is probably one of the most ancient forms of enslavement in Igboland. Its genesis lies in the holistic cosmology of agrarian Igbo societies dominated by the earth deity (Ala/Ana), in which there was no separation between religious power and the judicial and other arms of government. Major laws that were of common interest to a society were then ritualized with the earth force to transform them into the sacerdotal realm. Thus, individuals who violated the sacred laws of Ala involving homicide, incest, and stealing of farm crops were accused of committing acts of sacrilege (Iru Ala) and held liable and responsible for their actions (Meek 1937, 5; Oriji 1989). The Igbo system of jurisprudence was similar to the Mosaic law in that it did not provide much leeway for those found guilty. An individual, who committed homicide for example, might be killed or sold into slavery, unless he/she paid adequate compensation to the injured family, and carried out a protracted and expensive ritual cleansing ceremony in Ala shrine (Isa Ihu, or washing one's face) (Oriji 1989). The tragic fate of Okonkwo in Chinua Achebe's *Things Fall Apart* (1984) after he had committed manslaughter, clearly illustrates how rigidly the laws of Ala were enforced. In spite of the towering heights he had attained in the Umuofia clan, Okonkwo had to go into exile with his family to his maternal home, undergo ritual cleansing, and pay painful penalties, including the destruction of his yams and his compound (31–33, 113–18).

Individuals who wanted neither to take refuge in Ala shrine and become Osu (cult slaves) nor to go into exile had an option left for them to save their lives. They might escape say at night to a distant place to found new homes, and continue to live as free citizens. The escapees are associated with the origins of many communities like the Ogwashi-Ukwu and Ibusa of western Igboland, the Ugboko of Udi, the Osu clan of Mbano, and the Umuru and Umogba of the Ikwerre-Etche axis (Oriji 1992, 1994, 33–34).

Strategies against the Slave Trade

The earliest documented account of slave raids and kidnapping in the Igbo area comes from the memoir of Olaudah Equiano, which happens also to be the first "slave narrative" in the New World (Edwards 1969, 9). Although Vincent Carretta has, in a recent study (1999), raised issues about Equiano's nationality and date of birth, he affirmed the historicity of some of the events he recorded. In addition, Equiano's account of his capture and enslavement in his homeland did not differ remarkably from the nineteenth-century oral accounts of the slave trade collected in parts of the Igbo hinterland by G. I. Jones (1995) and other ethnohistorians. The memoir provides some insight on the diverse measures the Igbo were taking to prevent the depredations of the slave raiders. According to Equiano, he had undergone some military training, including shooting and throwing javelins. Presumably, he and other young boys, after their training, were expected during their adolescent years to become members of the local militia responsible for defending their community against the incursions of slave raiders and other agents of violence. The militia was equipped with "fire-arms, bows and arrows, broad two-edged swords and javelins" (Edwards 1969, 9). Equiano also revealed that some children acted as scouts, helping in the absence of their parents to reconnoiter the movement of the slave raiders (Jones 1967, 84–85).

Admittedly, we do not know if the slave raiders Equiano discussed were from communities in his homeland, which some believe lies in western Igboland (Jones 1967, 61). The notorious Ekumeku society—if it existed by then—is known to have carried out intensive raids in the area during the nineteenth century. It is also likely that the raiders were the Abam, whom the Aro used in recruiting slaves in parts of the Biafran hinterland. Equiano did affirm that his people were already linked with long-distance traders he called "Stout Mahogany-colored men," or Oye-Ebo ("Red Men"), who sold commodities like firearms and gunpowder, probably in exchange for slaves (85).

Jones has hypothesized that the red men, who probably rubbed themselves with camwood as a disguise, were Igbo traders (65). Presumably, they were the

Aro, who in fact used camwood and sold it in the hinterland with other commodities Equiano mentioned in his memoir.

NORTHERN IGBOLAND

The organization of the Aro trade network and the symbiotic relationship that existed between Aro traders and their Abam warriors have been examined by many researchers (e.g., Oriji 1980; Ekejiuba 1972; Dike 1956). It is necessary, however, to point out that the Aro adopted diverse methods in recruiting slaves, including their oracle (Ibini Ukpabi), and the Okonko (Ekpe) society, which served as major judicial institutions in the hinterland. But recent historiography confirms that the Abam constituted the primary organ of violence the Aro used in dominating the slave trade during the eighteenth and nineteenth centuries. A majority of the slaves they recruited were obtained by raids, kidnapping, and at times, slave wars involving the Abam.[1] The success the Abam achieved in warfare lies primarily with the skillful guerilla tactics they adopted during an incursion, and is not due to their superior weapons. Lightning raids were often conducted at night against an unsuspecting community, enabling the Abam to return safely to their base. As this study will show, there were some cases when vigilant communities that caught Abam spies or had inklings of an impending invasion routed the invaders.

As I have argued elsewhere (1986), Abam raids were not evenly spread in Igboland. They were largely concentrated in the northern section, which was distant from the Arochuku (the homeland of the Aro), lacking the Okonko society and other networks of trade the Aro had helped in spreading in parts of southern Igboland. The semisavanna environment of the north also helped in facilitating the movement of the Abam in the area. Each community the Abam invaded, however, devised its own methods of responding to the raids, as evidenced by the following examples.

According to oral tradition, Enwelana, the priestly king of the Nri (Eze Nri), was so deeply touched by the loss of human lives and the socioeconomic dislocations caused by the Abam that he appealed to Okolie Ijoma of Ndikelionwu, the leading Aro slave dealer, who engaged the Abam's services to end the slave trade. But as Okolie Ijoma failed to heed the warning, the Eze Nri is said to have pronounced a ritual curse on him and the Abam, declaring them unwanted persons in his domain (Osuala 2000, 10–11). The curse may not have stopped the raids, but it put the Aro and Abam in greater physical jeopardy, since anyone in Nri was free to attack and even kill them without being accused of committing murder and forced to carry out a ritual cleansing ceremony in the shrine of the earth goddess. In addition, if a variant of the tradition is correct, the curse may have had some psychological effect, since Okolie Ijoma was said to have been so troubled by the calamities that might befall him that he had to apologize to the Eze Nri for his nefarious activities (ibid.).

Like the Nri, the people of Enugu-Ukwu town were constantly exposed to Abam raids. Their response was to adopt the strategy of the fox and wage a cold war against the Abam by avoiding direct military confrontations with them. The strategy involved dropping poisoned food, water, and wine for the Abam in strategic routes and other places they often used to invade the town. This strategy terrified the Abam, who mysteriously died in large numbers before an invasion, and in consequence, they excluded the town from future military operations (Isichei 1977, 84–85; Oriji 1992).

Abam incursions into Awka elicited a different response from its inhabitants. They mobilized themselves, forming a local vigilante group armed with Snider rifles to repulse the incursions. The sound of the guns alerted the local population to an invasion and thus helped in aborting Abam raids. The Awka also built high walls around their houses to foil kidnappers. During slavery the walls not only had perforations for firing guns but towers for monitoring the movement of intruders (Oriji 1992).

Some communities, however, reasoned that due to their limited manpower and material resources they could not effectively defend themselves against the Abam. Such communities allied with their neighbors for their mutual defense. Typical examples are the Umuchu, consisting of Ihite, Ogwugwu, and Okpu-na-Achala—autonomous communities that are said to have collectively hired the services of a native doctor, not only to cement their unity but to prevent Abam incursions with his medicine, called Ichu (lit., prevention, driving away). It was from the medicine that the community derived its present common name, Umuchu (children of Ichu). The native doctor, the tradition further claims, buried symbols of Ichu in strategic places like the central Nkwo market and Odere Lake, which are currently called Nkwo Ichu and Odere Ichu, respectively (Oriji 1994, 47). Similarly, the Isuochi and Nneato of Okigwe formed confederations that helped them in warding off Abam invasions (Isichei 1976, 85).

Riverine and Coastal Towns

Unlike northern Igboland, the slave trade in the riverine and coastal towns was dominated by their middlemen, who purchased slaves primarily from the Aro and other hinterland traders. The Aro, however, refrained from raiding the towns because they were landlubbers, unskilled in canoe warfare. In addition, the Aro realized that it would be suicidal to mount military operations against the towns fortified with cannons and other imported weapons that were unavailable in the hinterland. Slavery in the area was thus conducted by riverine towns like Aboh, which took advantage of its superior weapons to raid nearby towns on the Niger, such as Onitsha, forcing its king to transfer the central market to a more secure place near the Anambra River in the middle of the nineteenth century (Henderson 1972, 86).

SOUTHEASTERN IGBOLAND

Abam raids in southeastern Igboland are relatively few because the Aro discouraged military incursions in their homeland to avoid the disruption of trade and the large number of pilgrims and others who were visiting Arochukwu to consult their oracle. In addition, the Abam and other communities in the so-called Aro confederacy are said to have formed a pact not to raid one another. They also used the Ekpe/Okonko society associated with the Aro to promote their commercial interests. According to Jones, Ekpe evolved during the eighteenth century among the trading elite of the Ekoi and the Efik-Ibibio of the Cross River region. Ekpe later diffused into nearby Arochukwu communities, whose leading traders were the first Igbo people to be initiated into the society. The Aro then began to propagate Ekpe (Okonko in Igbo) during their expansion, seeking out leading people in strategic exchange centers who served as their commercial agents and founders of Okonko in their localities (Eze Ngbara). Local leaders of Okonko, for example, provided security and hospitality to itinerant Aro traders and also sold slaves to them, in exchange for firearms, gin, and other imported goods. Okonko helped the Aro to trade and at times settle in communities where they would have encountered some stiff resistance (Jones 1964, 19).[2]

In spite of the peaceful method the Aro adopted in their expansion, the Igbere example suggests that they and their Abam warriors engaged in kidnapping and raids in some southeastern Igbo communities. Igbere traditions claim that their community, originally called Ebiri, after their eponymous ancestor, was targeted on two occasions for enslavement by the Aro, known in local parlance as Aro Oke Igbo (Ukaegbu 1974, 13; Oriji 1992, 181).

During the first wave of the incursions, the Aro deployed the Abam to kidnap Ebiri people, forcing them to flee from their original homeland in Oroni to a new location presently called Eke-Igbere. The flight of the Ebiri might have helped them become more vigilant in safeguarding their new settlement. They mobilized and armed their warriors, who patrolled their community regularly. It is then not surprising that when the Abam mounted their second raid against the Ebiri, which took the form of a full-scale military invasion, they were routed and forced to retreat. The heroism the Ebiri displayed during the invasion is remembered in local folklore, and they have continued to proudly preserve their collective identity by calling their town Igbo Erughi ("the town the Aro could not reach/capture"), which was anglicized as Igbere during the colonial period (Ukaegbu 1974, 13; Oriji 1992, 181).

Abam raids in southern Igboland were, for a variety of reasons, relatively less widespread than in the northern section. The dense tropical rainforest presented logistic problems for the Abam, deterring their movement from one place to the other. As already mentioned, the Okonko society, which served as an arm of the Aro trade network, was well established among many communities stretching from the Owerri-Orlu and Mbano-Mbaise axis to the Ngwa-Ikwerre area and elsewhere. Moreover, some of the communities were known for their martial culture and vigilance in warding off invaders. The Ikoro war gong, located either in their common cultural center or in a compound of the traditional holder of authority, was an important institution in the area. The martial music of Ikoro alerted a community of an impending Abam invasion. Its secret messages, which could be decoded only by elders and warriors, helped them mobilize for civil defense and informed them of routes the invaders might take. The defeat of the invaders was celebrated with much fanfare, and warriors and others who had distinguished themselves in battle danced joyously to the lighter music of Ikoro played for their entertainment.[3]

Southern Igboland

Oral traditions collected from Mbieri and Egbu indicate that the arrival of the Aro aroused much alarm and hostility from their inhabitants. Ikoro music was played and warriors armed themselves and quickly moved to the town square, where the Aro hoped to negotiate with the traditional authorities and elders for a place to settle. Their request was denied by the communities, who suspected that they were spies of the Abam, who would soon embark on kidnapping and enslaving people for the immigrants. Warriors were then ordered to expel the Aro from the two communities, forcing them to flee the Owerri axis.[4]

As in other parts of southern Igboland, Abam raids in the Aba-Ngwa axis were largely sporadic, excepting the invasions of Umuajuju and Ohia-Ukwu, the densely populated cultural and commercial centers of the Ntigha-Uzo and Ohanze communities. The magnitude of the raids and the massive population movements they engendered suggest that the Aro probably hoped to settle and colonize the two strategic market centers. Some Umuajuju people, for example, are said to have fled to nearby communities like Ngwa-Obi, Amaise, Amavo, and Amasa, while those of Ohia-Ukwu dispersed to Ibeme, Ndiakata, and as far north as Ngboko-Amiri (Oriji 1998, 43–45).

The invasion of the two communities and the horrifying stories refugees told about their experiences spread to various parts of the Ngwa region, arousing in their remembered history an unparalleled degree of vigilance and military preparedness among the people. For example, women carried out economic activities like farming in groups (Oru Ogbo), and those who attended distant markets were accompanied by their husbands or armed male escorts. As in other places, Ikoro was used to alert people of an impending Abam incursion. The increasing militarization of Ngwa society during the Atlantic slave trade is further evidenced by the consecration of war gods like Ike-Oha (lit., the power of the community), and the initiation of young men into its cult to protect them from bullet wounds. The young men, after their initiation, were given military training and drafted as warriors to defend their community against external aggression. Also consecrated was Udu-Agha (lit., war pot) carried by the head warrior, who alerted people of an invasion and led other warriors to attack the invaders. Warriors were also involved in other civil defense activities, including the policing of their communities. They mounted roadblocks to fend off Abam infiltrators, and in places like Ikem Elu village of the Nvosi community, stones and other deadly weapons were used to chase off Aro traders crossing the area. Interestingly, the Aro, who avoided the Ikem Elu route, nicknamed the village Ndi Olu Mbe (those who throw stones at us), a popular name the village continues to bear.[5]

Some communities also deployed their young men and professional hunters armed with Dane guns (also called flintlocks, these were the main guns imported to West Africa during the slave trade), machetes, and other deadly weapons to help in searching possible hideouts of the Abam in the forests. Young men who, for example, killed the Abam during the search or an invasion were entitled to dance and recount their heroic exploits while responding to the drum signals of Ese-Ike (lit., drum of men of prowess) played during the burial ceremony of distinguished elders and titled men (Oriji 1998, 43–45).[6]

The alertness of the Ngwa and the weapons they used in defending their communities are affirmed by Major A. Leonard, an adventurous British military officer who had penetrated the Ngwa region by the late nineteenth century: "Although the people [Ngwa] who enroute turned out in thousands to look at us appeared to be very friendly and peacefully disposed, not a man apparently moved a step without carrying a naked sword in one hand and a rifle at full lock in the other. Even the boys, some of them not higher than an ordinary man's knee . . . walked out armed with bows and pointed arrows" (1898, 190).

The harassment of the Abam and Aro posed a threat to their lives and undermined long-distance trade. It is then understandable why Aro informants told F. Ekejiuba (1972, 26) that the trade routes crossing the Ngwa region were among the most dangerous in southeastern Nigeria. The increasing hostility and insecurity the Aro experienced in Ngwaland are also helpful in understanding why they later adopted a more peaceful method of trade in the area.

There were many factors that helped in determining how and why the Aro and their Abam warriors invaded Igbo communities. Among them was their location, alertness, and ability in defending themselves. The Abam certainly were a source of terror in many places, but as the Igbere and other examples show, they were not invincible. Their human losses, however, recede into insignificance if compared with those of communities they invaded such as Nri, Umuajuju, Ohia-Ukwu and other places.

The findings of the study are also helpful in raising fundamental issues on slavery at two levels of human dimension. The first one, dealing with the individual level, shows that slaves or would-be slaves who had an opportunity to escape to freedom, did so without hesitation even if it meant leaving their family members and other close relatives behind. The Osu and others provide a typical example of these escapees. At the second level associated with communities, responses to slavery varied ranging from "passive resistance," to mass mobilization, involving a local militia, scouts and others who were actively engaged in civil defense. The study questions the views of David Northrup (1978, 65) and others who argue that the slave trade was a normal commercial transaction which was conducted largely in the hinterland by peaceful methods. The Igbo example clearly shows that slavery and the slave trade were the primary cause of violence in the West African sub-region for over three centuries. It is also clear that without the stiff resistance mounted by many individuals and communities, slavery would have had a more devastating impact in the hinterland.

NOTES

1. For a discussion of the debate that has raged over the methods the Aro used in expanding in the Igbo hinterland, see Oriji 1986.

2. For details of the relationship between the Aro and Okonko leaders, see Oriji 1982.

3. *Ikoro* is the title of a journal published during the 1970s by the Institute of African Studies, University of Nigeria, Nsukka. The underlying functions of the Ikoro gong are stated in the journal.

4. I obtained information regarding the expulsion of the Aro in Mbieri and Egbu respectively in interviews with Eze H. M. Aguta, the traditional ruler of Mbieri, 26 February 1981, and F. Orisakwe, a schoolmaster at Egbu, 7 July 1980.

5. The village originally known as Ikem Elu has been called Ndiolumbe since its encounter with the Aro.

6. Details of Abam invasions of the two communities are also found at the Nigerian National Archives, Enugu, EP 7021, no. 68, J. G. C. Allen, *Intelligence Reports on the Ngwa Clan* (1933), 2:4–5.

BIBLIOGRAPHY

Achebe, Chinua. 1996. *Things Fall Apart.* Portsmouth: Heinemann.

Allen, J. G. C. 1933. "Intelligence Report on the Ngwa Clan." Nigerian National Archives, Enugu, Eastern Provinces, 7021, no. 68, vols. 1–2.

Allison, Robert J., ed. 1995. *The Interesting Narrative of the Life of Olaudah Equiano Written by Himself.* Boston: Bedford/St. Martin's.

Carretta, Vincent. 1999. "Olaudah Equiano or Gustavus Vassa? New Light on an Eighteenth-Century Question of Identity." *Slavery and Abolition* 20 (3): 96–105.

Dike, Kenneth O. 1956. *Trade and Politics in the Niger Delta 1830–1885: An Introduction to the Economic and Political History of Nigeria.* London: Oxford University Press.

Edwards, Paul, ed. 1969. *Equiano's Travels: The Interesting Narrative of the Life of Olaudah Equiano or Gustavus Vassa the African.* London: Heinemann.

Ekejiuba, Felicia. 1972. "The Aro Trade System in the Nineteenth Century." *Ikenga: Journal of African Studies* 1 (1): 11–26.

Henderson, R. 1972. *The King in Every Man: Evolutionary Trends in Onitsha Ibo Society and Culture.* New Haven: Yale University Press.

Isichei, Elizabeth. 1976. *A History of the Igbo People.* London: Macmillan.

Jones, G. I. 1964. *The Trading States of the Oil Rivers: A Study of Political Development in Eastern Nigeria.* London: Oxford University Press.

———. 1967. "Olaudah Equiano of the Niger Ibo." In Philip Curtin, ed., *Africa Remembered: Narratives by West Africans from the Era of the Slave Trade.* Madison: University of Wisconsin Press.

Leonard, A. 1898. "Notes of a Journey to Bende." *Journal of the Manchester Geographical Society* 14:190–207.

Meek, C. K. 1937. *Law and Authority in a Nigerian Tribe.* London: Oxford University Press.

Northrup, David. 1978. *Trade without Rulers: Pre-colonial Economic Development in Southeastern Nigeria.* Oxford: Oxford University Press.

Oriji, John N. 1980. "Evolution of Oracular Trade amongst the Ngwa-Igbo of Southeastern Nigeria." *Transactions of the Historical Society of Ghana* 18:7–17.

———. 1982. "A Re-Assessment of the Organization and Benefits of the Slave and Palm Oil Trade amongst the Ngwa-Igbo." *Canadian Journal of African Studies* 16 (3): 523–48.

———. 1986. "Slave Trade, Warfare, and Aro Expansion in the Igbo Hinterland." *Genève-Afrique* 34 (2): 108–18.

———. 1989. "Sacred Authority in Igbo Society." *Archives de Sciences Sociales des Religions* (Paris) 1:113–23.

———. 1992. "Ethical Ideals of Peace and the Concept of War in Igbo Society." In T. Falola and R. Law, eds., *Warfare and Diplomacy in Precolonial Nigeria,* 176–84. Madison: African Studies Program, University of Wisconsin.

———. 1994. *Traditions of Igbo Origin.* New York: Peter Lang.

———. 1998. *Ngwa History: A Study of Social and Economic Changes in Igbo Mini-States in Time Perspective.* New York: Peter Lang.

Osuala, J. 2000. *The Original History of Aba Township: The Making of the Japan of Africa.* Aba: Monarch Communications.

Ukaegbu, E. 1974. *History of Igbere.* Aba: Span Publishing Company.

CHAPTER 9

"A Devotion to the Idea of Liberty at Any Price"

Rebellion and Antislavery in the Upper Guinea Coast in the Eighteenth and Nineteenth Centuries

Ismail Rashid

CONTEMPORARY EUROPEAN OBSERVERS AND regional oral traditions allude to large-scale slave revolts and numerous fugitive enclaves in the Upper Guinea Coast in the eighteenth and nineteenth centuries. These escapes and uprisings disrupted politics, the economy, and society. Though scholars have started paying attention to African resistance to enslavement in the continent, studies of the slave revolts and communities in West Africa have been limited (Lovejoy 1986; Lovejoy and Hogendorn 1990; Glassman 1995; Klein 1988; Miers and Roberts 1988). Exaggerations, if not misperceptions, about Africans' complicity in the Atlantic slave trade and about their acceptance of servitude persist (Thornton 1992). Indeed, many scholars refuse to acknowledge the acts of resistance by enslaved Africans as part of a continuous thread of antislavery in the continent and still insist on seeing antislavery as emanating solely from the religious, economic, and philosophical ideas of the eighteenth-century European Enlightenment (Miers and Roberts 1988; Sanneh 1999).

Knowing the precise nature of the ideas and the forms of social consciousness that animated enslaved Africans is difficult since most of the historical evidence is refracted through the lens of European travelers, abolitionists, and colonial administrators. Nonetheless, these records point to the opposition to enslavement by Africans that were manifested in rebellious actions, the existence of free communities, and in some cases the appropriations and creative reinterpretations of hegemonic ideas. This chapter will show that, in the case of the Upper Guinea Coast, enslaved Africans routinely affirmed their freedom, not by absorption into the slaveholding societies or by renegotiations of dependent relationships—as argued by some scholars—but by outright rejection and opposition to servitude. The two rebellions in the region (the main focus here)—the Mandingo Rebellion in the eighteenth century and the Bilali Rebellion in the nineteenth—attest to the tenacity of the enslaved in resisting slavery and asserting their freedom.

This chapter conceives of resistance as a plethora of spontaneous, organized covert or overt actions designed to thwart the intentions of kidnappers, slave traders, and slaveholders. On a continuum, these actions encompass the quotidian forms of resistance amplified by James Scott (1985) as well as the more violent contestations, which underline the works of C. L. R. James (1963, 1969). At the point of capture and the early stages of enslavement, the enslaved resisted primarily to reassert sovereign control over what John Stuart Mill defines as one's "self," "mind," and "body" and to reestablish a sense of personal dignity. At the points of the commercial exchange—holding pens and transportation—resistance took on an added layer, as captives fought against the processes that attempted to regularize and legitimize the theft of their persons and fix the badge of bondage on them more securely. Within slaveholding societies, where the weight of the hegemonic institutional and ideological forces and relationships were being manipulated to reinforce the subjugation of the enslaved, they fought to break the hold of these forces and relationships. This chapter pays considerable attention to violent resistance because violence was integral to the Atlantic slave trade. Also, violent actions sometimes provide texts not readily available from quotidian actions and hence give historians wider scope to study the ideas and actions of the enslaved. By the eighteenth century, military violence had become the dominant means by which major elite groups acquired and reproduced political and social power in the Upper Guinea Coast (Rodney 1970; Barry 1998).

The Historical Context of Resistance

Centuries of migration, Islamic expansion, and trade shaped the political and cultural landscape of the Upper Guinea Coast region, drained by the Kouleté,

Scarcies, and Sierra Leone River basins, and bordered by the Futa Jallon highlands and the Atlantic coast. Limba, Bullom, Temne, Baga, Loko, Soso, Mandingo, Kuranko, and Fula both shared and competed for control of the terrain. By the mid-eighteenth century, the Fula dominated the highlands of the Futa Jallon while the Mandingo, Soso, Bullom, and Temne controlled various stretches of the Atlantic coastline. Though many of these groups shared close cultural, linguistic, and religious affinities, Islam became the dominant force in their religious, social, and political differentiation (Fyfe 1964, 30–35; Clarke 1966, 39; Finnegan 1965).[1]

Three interrelated historical developments shaped the political and social context of enslavement and resistance to enslavement in the eighteenth and nineteenth centuries. The first was the rise of relatively powerful polities like Futa Jallon and Moriah. Moriah was one of several small Mande states whose ruling lineages tried to expand their territorial, economic, and religious reach (Skinner 1980, 58–59). Futa Jallon was the most successful polity in this direction, mainly because its Fula elite decided to launch a jihad in the 1720s after the lead of Futa Toro and Futa Bundu in Senegal. Even though it was successful in converting many people to Islam, the jihad also became a justification for the enslavement of the non-Islamic peoples in the area (Rodney 1968, 274–76; Klein 1992, 35; Barry 1998, 95–102). Within the African landscape, Islam provided a coherent and clearly enunciated discourse for enslavement. As the Imam of Futa Jallon put it in a letter to the governor of Sierra Leone in 1810:

> They are the Kafirs, and they are like ass [*sic*] or like cattle; they know not the rights of God, and still less the rights of men. And in our parts you are not sold any man who knows the God of truth. . . . The people whom men used to sell into your hands do not acknowledge the religion of Moses (peace be upon him) nor the religion of Mohammed nor is one of the prophets (May God send blessing on him and peace).[2]

The second historical development was the dramatic shift in the Atlantic slave trading system, which reached its height in the mid-eighteenth century in terms of organization, the number of enslaved Africans transported, and the prices paid for them. By the late 1790s the trade had contracted and demand and prices fell. The number of people transported went from 108,100 in the 1760s to 47,200 in the 1780s (Lovejoy 1983, 50–51; Manning 1990, 19). Flooding of the slave marts, the disruption in the trade occasioned by the American and French Revolutions, an embargo by Futa Jallon rulers to force up prices, and intermittent regional conflicts all contributed to the decline in the trade.

The third, and perhaps most crucial, development in the turning of the tide against slavery was the rise of abolitionism and the founding of the Freetown settlement in 1787. In spite of its inauspicious beginnings, the colony grew to become a symbol of antislavery; some of its more committed and scrupulous residents took the task of antislavery seriously and worked to wean the surrounding African chiefs and peoples from their slaving ways. After the British Crown took over in 1808, they provided the military and institutional muscle—the Naval Squadron and the Mixed Commissions—necessary to stem the flow of slavery in the region. In one of the most profound ironies of history, Britain, the very country that had helped facilitate the dramatic expansion of slavery in the eighteenth century, was trying to curtail it in the nineteenth century. The Freetown settlement provided occasional refuge for escapees from enslavement but the state's enforcement capacity was initially felt more on the high seas than on land. However, between the diplomatic expeditions of Watts in 1794 and that of Blyden in 1872 to Timbo, the capital of Futa Jallon, the capacity of the colonial power to intervene in regional affairs expanded considerably.[3]

Transformations in Internal Slavery

Rodney (1970), Lovejoy (1983), and Manning (1990) have demonstrated that the Atlantic trade in Africans radically transformed not only the character of servitude but of societies in the continent. These changes were felt in the general tenor of life, the lack of security, and the perversions of institutions and local beliefs. Kidnappings and wars proliferated, and accusations of witchcraft, adultery and several other frivolous crimes multiplied (Matthews 1788; Wadström 1968). African chiefs and resident European traders usually picked on the powerless and unprotected. Whole families were sold for the crimes committed by one relative. Enslavement for debts also became widespread. Traders enslaved children, wives, kinsmen, and subjects to offset debts accrued by parents, husbands, kinsmen, and rulers. Few survived the "red water" ordeal prevalent in the Sierra Leone area to try witchcraft (Fyfe 1964, 75). By the eighteenth century, justice for the accused frequently meant their enslavement and sale to a passing ship. For example, to atone for their bad behavior, one chief sold his subjects to European traders; another pawned his brothers for liquor; a woman was sold for being "saucy to the queen" of a town. In another instance, a European slave trader sold his workers on suspicion of a liaison with his African "wife." Free men and women who happened to be in the wrong European boat at the wrong time got carried off to slavery. Kidnappers and slave traders used all kinds of tricks—they would cajole, lie, and even get their victims drunk—to sell them (Wadström 1968, 80–84).

Demographically, the change in internal servitude effected by the Atlantic slave trade was evident in the number of captives held by elites of the different polities. One observer estimated that enslaved persons constituted about three-fourths of the region's population. Kings, headmen, and traders held from hundreds to thousands of men and women in captivity. Fula, Mandingo, and Soso societies were heavily dependent on the slave trade and enslaved labor for local food production (Matthews 1788, 149; Newton 1962, 17; Blyden to J. Pope Hennessy, in Blyden 1978, 103). Colonial data on slavery in Sierra Leone in the early twentieth century still showed high rates of slaveholding among these groups. Nearly 35 percent of Mandingo and Soso society and 20 percent of Temne society were estimated to be enslaved.[4]

This proliferation of enslaved people led to further differentiation in the social structure of the Upper Guinea Coast societies as the slaveholding elite separated their bonded population into recently enslaved and house enslaved. Ordinary or plantation slaves were newly bought or captured males and females.[5] Used in mostly agricultural and transport tasks, they were outsiders with no affinity or attachment to their slaveholder's family and community, and could be sold easily. By the late eighteenth century, as the Atlantic slave trade declined, the slaveholders in the Upper Guinea Coast created a spatial separation between the free population and ordinary slaves. They placed the latter in separate villages called *runde* in Fula, *dakha* in Soso, and *jong kunda* in Mandingo.[6]

The second group, domestic slaves, or *rimaibe, olisos,* or *wolisos* (Fula, Temne, and Soso), were born in servitude or had been enslaved for a fairly long period. They were "in some respect considered as a branch of the family" (Matthews 1788, 150). They performed mainly domestic work and could not be sold, unless they committed serious crimes. In the late eighteenth and early nineteenth centuries, frequent accusations of witchcraft meant they remained vulnerable to sale (153).

Islamic law, indigenous rules, and elite paternalism sought to minimize wanton murder, excessive abuse, and cruelty against the enslaved. The children of male slaveholders and enslaved women could expect freedom both under Qur'anic and African customs. *Olisos* or *rimaibe,* socialized within the slaveholders' communities, received the most protection and "privileges" (Thomas 1916, 159). Ordinary slaves acquired more protection and rights through their acceptance of their enslavement and good behavior. In the short run, however, the newly enslaved had to be broken and subjugated by their holders through branding, flogging, hard work, poor living conditions, and liability to sale (Matthews 1788, 180).

A Continuum of Resistance: From Capture to Slave Caravel and Slave Village

> Africans are not bereft of finer feelings, but have a strong sense of attachment to their native country, together with a just sense of the value of liberty.
>
> —Alexander Falconbridge, *An Account of the Slave Trade on the Coast of Africa*

African resistance to enslavement began from the moment of captivity and continued in the barracoons on the coast and the holds of the slave caravels (Wax 1966; Piersen 1977; Rathbone 1985; McGowan 1990). Africans countered the dehumanization that accompanied each stage of the enslavement process with covert and overt strategies that included escape, mutiny, marronage, and suicide. Contemporary observers also noted the Africans' instinctive and more reflexive acts of resistance to their sudden loss of freedom. Some screamed to attract attention to their kidnappers, and if they were fortunate, their abductors could be frightened off. Once on the slave ships, others became melancholic and, even with coaxing or force, refused food and medicine and starved themselves to death. Many committed suicide by jumping overboard or hanging themselves (Wadström 1968, 84; Falconbridge 2000, 215). According to an account from the son of Naimbanna, an eighteenth-century ruler in Sierra Leone, retold by Wadström: "Unless secured, they will strike or stab any person who approaches them. It is common for them to cut their own throats, or otherwise destroy themselves. He is persuaded, he has known above an hundred commit suicide before they could be got to the ships" (1968, 14–15).

Eighteenth-century European accounts of the Upper Guinea Coast are littered with vignettes of violent resistance by enslaved Africans. In 1720, Tamba, a chief on the Rio Nunez, organized his people against the African and European slave traders. He obstructed their trade and executed the middlemen he captured. He was caught, sold, and enslaved but organized a revolt among the captives on the ship. It was brutally put down; Tamba was killed and his liver fed to his supporters, who were subsequently executed (Barry 1998, 121).

Around 1750 about one hundred captives led by a Fula named Old Mano rebelled on board a Danish slave ship, the *Claire B. Williams.* Aided by a local headman, they fled and established a free settlement in the mountains off the Sierra Leone coast. The community became a target for slave raiders, and the residents and the escapees were said to be "so jealous . . . of strangers, that they permit them not to approach, and even watch the avenues of their town" (Wadström 1968, 79). Yet when the French attacked the newly established settlement for freed slaves in 1794, they provided refuge for some of the settlers.

Others were equally determined though not as fortunate, and they had to pay the supreme price for resistance: death. Around 1789 a group of enslaved people revolted aboard an American brig. A man began the attack; he rushed into the cabin and "laid open the captain's face and breast with an axe, and severely wounded a passenger." (Wadström 1968, 79; Fyfe 1962, 24). The captain subsequently died. The captives released the wounded, and the seamen who put up no resistance. In another case, a military chief, who had been defeated and sold off by a rival, coordinated the rebellion:

> No sooner had the captain and his friends sat down to dinner than a signal was given. The slaves rose to a man, knocked off each other's fetter, and headed by the chief, attacked the barricade. But they failed. The guns were pointed at them, some were killed, many leaped into the sea, and the insurrection was quelled. The captain enquiring for the ringleader, the chief came out boldly and avowed that he was the man; that he wished *to give liberty* to all slaves on board; that he regretted his defeat on their account, but that, as to himself, he was satisfy [*sic*] with the prospect immediately, obtaining what he termed his own liberty. The captain hung him instantly to the yard-arm. (transcribed by Wadström 1968, 86; emphasis mine)

In another account, forty enslaved people revolted on a Boston slave ship. They loosened their iron manacles and killed the captain and the crew, despite their plea that they were willing to surrender and let the enslaved escape. They kept some seamen to steer them to safety but the ship eventually ran aground. Three of the seamen they had spared went ashore and mobilized a slave trader and an armed party against the rebels. A battle ensued between the rebels and the slave trader. Out of ammunition, and having lost some of their numbers, the rebels attempted to escape on a raft. They were caught and resold into slavery (Wadström 1968, 87).

Resistance was not only directed at the trade but also at internal enslavement. From mid- to late eighteenth century, many revolts broke out on the Upper Guinea Coast as the enslaved fought against African and European slave traders and holders. In 1756 the enslaved population in Futa Jallon rose against the slave-owning class, declared themselves free, and migrated northwest toward Futa Bundu. They built a well-fortified settlement called Kondeah, which was repeatedly attacked by the Fula and their allies (Laing 1825, 400–412). James Watt, a British emissary to the *almamy,* cites two other rebellions against the Futa Jallon elite during his visit to Timbo in 1794. He noted the extensive destruction caused by the revolt, its brutal repression, and the execution of thirty men among the leaders.[7] Other slaveholding polities in the region also experienced rebellions. In many instances, the formerly enslaved peoples established liberated communities, which became magnets for other fugitive and rebellious slaves (Barry 1998, 122). The free communities should be seen as counter to the runde. Like the maroons in the Caribbean and the Americas, the enslaved Africans consciously created these communities to assert their freedom, separate themselves from their slaveholders, and gain autonomy over their lives (Schwartz 1969–70; Heuman 1986).

The Mandingo Rebellion, 1785–96

> negro slaves are not always so happy with their negro masters as European apologists for slavery at the present day would have everybody believe.
>
> —F. W. H. Migeod, *A View of Sierra Leone*

As a consequence of the frequent rebellions, the slaveholding elite vigorously policed the enslaved people; in Futa Jallon they banned them from carrying firearms. However, the restrictive measures could not prevent the slave uprising, which broke out in 1785. It was one of the largest and most protracted antislavery rebellions and it affected the entire Upper Guinea Coast. It involved a group of Temne, Baga, and Bullom people and was directed against the Mandingo ruling and slave-owning elite in Moriah, a state founded around the 1720s. The Moriah elite, made up of warriors, traders, and Islamic missionaries, considerably extended their influence and their power over the economy and politics of the northern rivers region between the 1720s and 1760s. This expansion led to their encroachment on neighboring Bullom, Baga, and Temne territories. The ensuing conflicts provided a reservoir of captives for trade to Europeans on the coast and for local agricultural production. Moriah became not only a major slaveholding society but also an important commercial center connecting interior and coastal trades. The enslaved represented 70 to 80 percent of Moriah's population by the 1770s, and produced most of the rice, the state's major commodity (Skinner 1980, 52–58).

The Moriah elite held their plantation slaves in villages that rapidly multiplied within fifty years. One ruler, Fenda Modu Dumbuya, owned up to nine villages reportedly producing about a hundred tons of rice and a hundred tons of salt annually. The slaveholders usually worked new captives on their rice plantation before selling off some of them to the Europeans on the coast. However, the excess and "rejects" from the trade provided a more permanent stratum of population for the slave villages. It was primarily the harshness of servitude and the tyranny of the slaveholders that led to the revolt (Matthews 1788, 154–55). The elite also kept a smaller number of household slaves. These included long-serving and trusted people as well as slave wives and concubines, whose children inherited their master's free status.

The enslaved Baga, Temne, and Bullom carefully planned and timed the revolt. They seized the opportunity presented by an outbreak of war between Moriah and neighboring Soso polities over a fugitive Baga "murderer" to assert their freedom. On the cause, timing, and course of the revolt, Matthews wrote:

> The Mandingoes, who are extremely cruel in the treatment of their slaves, had carried this practice [witchcraft trials] to such excess that in 1785, there was a general insurrection. The slaves took an opportunity, when the principal part of their fighting men were out upon an expedition, to attack their masters; several of whom they put to death, and had their heads carried before them on poles, as ensigns of victory and liberty; they then set fire to the rice which was ready to be cut, which reduced the Mandingoes to distress, who afterwards retreated to their towns, which were fortified in such a manner, and so effectually stopped every avenue that led into the country from whence the Mandingoes could receive assistance, that their late masters were under the necessity of suing for peace. (1788, 154–55)

The rebels had a number of leaders but only two, Mambee and Dansage, are identified in the available sources. The rebellion, which affected the entire northern rivers region, involved from six to eight hundred people residing in the slave villages. They torched the rice fields, the state's economic mainstay. Many rebels took refuge at Yangiakuri, Kani, and Funkoo, in Soso country. Located on the foothills of the mountain ranges from where the Kolenten (Great

Scarcies) River rises, Yangiakuri was easily defensible. The insurgents further fortified the town with twelve-foot-high mud walls and three large security towers. They increased their numbers by recruiting and providing refuge for other enslaved men and women and also attracted Soso freemen. These were most likely commoners whose socioeconomic condition would not have been radically different from that of the rebels. Within a decade, additional smaller settlements had sprung up around Yangiakuri, Kani, and Funkoo (154–55). When the conflict between the Moriah rulers and the Soso abated, the slaveholding classes resumed their offensive against Yangiakuri and the other maroon communities. They waylaid, raided, captured, and sold into slavery all the fugitives they could. In response, the rebels organized themselves and attacked Moriah, Melakori, Berriera, Kissy, and other Mandingo polities. They also captured and sold several members of the ruling elite of these territories (Mendez 1975, 10).

The tide turned against the insurgents when the Soso and the Mandingo reached a truce. Before 1795 the slaveholding Soso ruling elite had tolerated—and even tacitly supported—the rebels against the Mandingo, especially since it complemented their own war effort. But when the enslaved masses among them became restive and increasingly joined the ranks of the insurgents, the Soso elites became alarmed and allied with their Mandingo counterparts since the revolt now threatened the entire socioeconomic foundations of the region.

The Soso-Mandingo alliance, supported by a European mercenary, Thomas Rand, attacked the rebel settlements with heavy armaments in the rainy season of 1795. They destroyed the smaller ones, killed most of their inhabitants, and sold the rest into slavery. Yangiakuri proved more difficult to capture and, as the alliance suffered heavy casualties in its repeated attempts to breach its walls, it shifted tactics. The Soso and Mandingo encircled and blockaded the town in an attempt to starve its approximately nine hundred inhabitants into submission. They then built high palisades and platforms from which they sniped at the residents and shot flaming arrows into their thatch-roofed houses (Winterbottom 1803, 154–58). The tactics reduced the town's population to about five hundred.

The enslaved and the free Soso who had joined them fought courageously for a common cause. They refused to surrender and chose to "starve themselves to death, [rather] than come living to the enemy" (Afzelius 1967, 123). Under the leadership of Dansage, Mambee, and others, they inflicted heavy casualties on the Soso-Mandingo alliance. According to one estimate, the coalition was decreased from twenty-five hundred to less than a thousand fighters (119). The rebels were eventually defeated when Dansage was betrayed and captured in an attempt to replenish the rebels' military supplies. Dalla Mohammed (Dala Modu), son of Fenda Modu, head of a powerful Mandingo family from Wonkafong (Fyfe 1962, 89, 96) provided an interesting insight to the defeat of the rebels at Yangiakuri. Modu was a headman, imam, and trader who settled in Freetown with fifty followers. The government accused him of slave trading and deported him. In his trial he claimed he had been made an imam and a headman for his role in defeating the Yangiakuri insurgents: "five kings were gathered against Yangiakuri and they promised me that if I could take the place I should be made an Imam, and I fought against it for five months and half and took it, and burnt it down, and threw down the walls. And I brought all the captives before kings, and put them on side."[8]

Implicit in Dala Mohammed's testimony was that it took more than military might to defeat the rebels, who had been accused of practicing "witchcraft." It is difficult to verify his version of the events, but there was no doubt that the Modu family was embroiled in slavery activities in the region. Other contemporary observers state that the majority of the residents of the maroon villages were killed or sold into slavery (Afzelius 1967, 123; Kup 1961, 167–68). A small number led by Mambee escaped and were able to found a settlement in Bena, a Soso polity on the upper reaches of the Great Scarcies River.

The attitude of the Mandingo elite to their captives in the aftermath of the rebellion is not known due to a lack of appropriate records. However, two observations in the nineteenth and early twentieth century provide clues that it did change over time. Blyden, traveling through Moriah and its surrounding areas in 1873, indicated that some slaveholders took a more active interest in the conversion of their captives to Islam. He stated that the King of Tasin built a large mosque in Fansiggah, one of his slave towns. While conversion was optional for adults, the children of the enslaved were instructed in the Qur'an. He maintained that the "slave who embraces Islam is free."[9] Colonial officials, who commented on domestic slavery in the early twentieth century stated that though the Mandingo considered the enslaved as "distinctly inferior," they treated them with "exceptional liberality and consideration." They allowed three personal farming days, gave them "decent clothes" on Fridays and holidays, and ensured the men were married at a suitable age.[10] The Mandingo Rebellion did play a role, no matter how obliquely, in kindling this "exceptional liberality" on the part of slaveholders.

Slave Revolts in the Nineteenth Century

Unlike the revolts of the late eighteenth century, the nineteenth century slave rebellions occurred in a transformed international and local context. The ability of slaveholders to dispose of the enslaved in large numbers to European slavers for transportation overseas diminished by the decade. Yet the resistance of the enslaved demonstrated some elements of continuity and some elements of change. Some continued to escape, kill slave owners, and set up separate communities. For example, in 1825–26, enslaved Kuranko and Kono led by Tamba slaughtered their Soso owners, as well as freemen and their families in Yana and then sought refuge in Tambakka (Migeod 1926, 49–50).

In other instances, even though the elements of social separation and rebellion were evident, the context of their execution was dissimilar because the spread of Islam made a significant difference. In penetrating the lives of the enslaved, either through their own voluntary conversion or the agency of their masters, Islam established a shared religious language in which master and slave could partake, albeit from different vantage points. Whatever the perspective, it offered new possibilities of freedom and resistance for the enslaved. That shift in the relationship between Islam and antislavery became clearer in the Hubbu Rebellion against the Futa Jallon state in the 1850s. Led by a reformist Muslim cleric, Mamadu Juhe, and his son Abal, it was motivated by popular disaffection against the political and social excesses of the Futa Jallon ruling aristocracy. The rebels, consisting of slaves, peasants, and other social outcasts, separated themselves from the state and established autonomous theocratic communities on its outskirts. According to Blyden, "They are called Hooboos or Hubus because on leaving their homes they chanted a verse from the Koran in which the word Hubu appears twice. The verse says: 'Nuhibu Rusul Allahi huban Wahidan,' meaning 'Those possessed of the love of God's messenger.'"[11]

The very source of their name contained their delegitimation of their masters' religious claims and the legitimation of their own. By asserting to possess the "love of God's messenger" the rebels appropriated the mantle of jihad and its accompanying *baraka* (grace) which was the religious foundation of Futa Jallon's aristocratic hegemony. To rub salt in the wound, an 1873 circular noted that the "republic, led by Abal, son of Juhe, had liberated itself from all obligations towards the *Almami,* that it had no intention whatsoever of recognizing his authority, that it had abolished slavery, and that it welcomed all who freed themselves from their masters" (Barry 1998, 155).

The Futa Jallon elite, the heirs of a great Islamic revolution, roundly denounced Mamadu's "pretensions as a sacred teacher." They attacked and destroyed the Hubbu's capital, Lamiah, setting in motion the movement's gradual disintegration into banditry.[12] In its use of violence, flight, and social separation, the Hubbu Rebellion demonstrates a number of important lessons on slavery in the region. It highlighted the persistence of patterns of resistance adopted by earlier generations of rebels. It showed the new ways in which the enslaved turned to Islamic discourse to contest the legitimacy of their oppressors. It also revealed the contradictory logic, if not outright inadequacy of the absorptionist paradigm; for if Islam was supposed to ensure the de-marginalization of the enslaved outsiders, why did they choose to violently reject the dominant society of their enslavement?

The Bilali Rebellion, ca. 1838–72

> He [Bilali] succeeded in forming a large powerful party, and in rousing among a large portion of servile population not only a devotion to the idea of liberty at any price, but a strong attachment to himself and a hatred for all those who hold slaves; and he is by no means scrupulous as the price he pays for their support.
>
> —Edward Blyden to Governor Arthur Kennedy, 10 January 1872

This contradictory logic of absorption was more glaring in the Bilali Rebellion, one of the most violent and prolonged instances of resistance of the internally enslaved. The uprising was directed mainly against the Soso ruling elite of Kukuna. Bilali, the leader of the revolt, was the son of Almamy Namina Sheka Dumbuya (r. ?–1837), the Soso king of Kukuna, and of an enslaved Kuranko woman. The qualities Bilali displayed were profoundly evocative of the follower of the Prophet Muhammad, whose name he bore. The original Bilali, an enslaved African, had attained his freedom by becoming one of the first converts of the fledgling faith. Muhammad rewarded his fortitude and devotion by appointing him the religion's first muezzin, the official caller to prayer. Almamy Dumbuya, a Muslim, must have recognized the symbolism of the name when he gave it to his son by his enslaved concubine. Though the king never publicly acknowledged Bilali as his child, he ensured that he received extensive Qur'anic and military training. He also indicated, as was customary, that the young man should be freed after his death. When Almamy Dumbuya died in 1838, however, the family failed to respect his wishes. Instead his successors, Almamy Terena (r. 1837–50?) and Almamy Arafan Mumini (r. 1850–74), sought to prolong Bilali's servitude.

Bilali then fled with his family and supporters. They went first to Dentege, a small village not far from Kukuna, and then, harassed by the Kukuna slaveholders, he went to the Tonko Limba country in 1838 (Skinner 1980, 217; Fyfe 1962, 283–84).[13] The Limba, who had been historically victimized by the different slave-raiding and slave-owning aristocracies in the region, gave him refuge and land to establish a settlement. Throughout the history of slave trading and holding in the region, the Limba remained on its margins. Colonial officials in the early twentieth century noted they only had a 5 percent rate of slaveholding and suggested that the slaveholders were those who had had long association with the Temne and had been Islamized, like the Sella and Tonko Limba (correspondence on slavery). Bilali' s settlement, Laminyah, became a refuge for fugitives from the surrounding Soso and Temne country. He remained a devoted Muslim and his reputation for opposition to slavery and his steadfastness in protecting and defending the liberty of his followers grew. In return, the fugitives gave him their unflinching loyalty and committed themselves to defending Laminyah and other free settlements that cropped up around it.[14]

Bilali's escape from slavery and his establishment of a safe haven for fugitives incensed not only his former master, Almamy Mumini, but also other major slaveholders in the region. They regarded them derisively as *murtah* (runaways, in Soso).[15] His actions, especially the provision of refuge for escapees, potentially threatened the entire slaveholding complex in the region. His free community and its rigidly antislavery posture truly represented a break from the vicious, predatory culture of slavery. His opponents saw Laminyah as a second Freetown in the heart of their region and spared no effort in trying to uproot it.[16]

For more than three decades this New Spartacus, as the British described him, resisted different Soso, Mandingo, and Temne kings who tried to curtail his growing power and support. Repeated attempts to destroy Laminyah failed. The revolt subsequently became intertwined with dynastic conflicts in Moriah and commercial rivalry over the strategic town of Kambia, which had retained its centrality in the Atlantic economy even when the emphasis shifted from slaves to agricultural commodities. The conflict drew in military forces from nearly all the major polities in the region (including Tonko Limba, Kukuna, Bena, Moriah, Sumbuya, Samu, Magbema, Kawlah, Mambolo, and Kasseh and from Temne and Mende territories south of the Rokel River).[17] The slaveholding elite was so desperate to defeat Bilali that Kandeh Bukhari, one of the kings of Moriah resorted to recruiting soldiers from his slave villages. He promised the enslaved people their freedom in exchange for military support. Blyden succinctly described Bukhari's strategy and the apprehensions it generated among the slaveholding elite in the region:

> Thus, by a sort of *simili similibus* process he hopes to extinguish Bilali's power—*servi contra servas.* The arming of slaves—an expedient always

> dreaded in slave-holding countries—is looked up as even more serious than the war which has just been averted. The thinking portion of the community are justly alarmed at the gigantic dimensions of which the conflict must assumed if it be made to assume an anti-slavery struggle—a situation for which they are certain [*sic*] not prepared.[18]

The British colonial government in Freetown also became concerned about the conflict, especially since it disrupted trade.[19] In response to petitions from its subjects, the government tried to end the conflict with a combination of violence and diplomacy. In 1857 the government attacked and occupied Kambia. In 1861 it signed treaties with the warring parties in which they promised to keep the peace and open the trade routes.[20] In 1870 the Soso and Temne leaders finally agreed to end their crusade against Bilali on the condition that he would stop granting asylum to fugitive slaves. Bilali agreed. The animosity against Bilali dissipated with the outbreak of civil war in Moriah.[21]

The dynastic competition and commercial rivalry provide only part of the reason why the regional elite arranged themselves into contentious factions during the Bilali's rebellion. At the heart of his revolt was the failure or inadequacies of the developing mechanisms of absorption within the society. As a Muslim and the son of a freeman, Bilali could rightfully claim his freedom, especially after the death of his father/slaveholder. Furthermore, being an oliso, it was culturally improper, if not impolitic, for his relatives to seek to accentuate rather then attenuate his servile status. So both in terms of customary and Islamic usages, his relatives and their supporters violated accepted practices. Blyden indicated that even some of Bilali's enemies conceded his entitlement and right to defend his freedom. What they did not accept was his right to foster antislavery by recruiting and providing refuge for the enslaved. The divisions reflect the differences over interpretation of the evolving practices of slavery and their rates of adjustment to the changing historical reality.

The intervention of Blyden, and indeed the Freetown colonial administration, is crucial to understanding the contradictory logic of the antislavery struggle of late-nineteenth-century Sierra Leone. On one hand, Blyden's mission and intervention in Bilali's rebellion positively linked the evolving indigenous tradition of antislavery with the Enlightenment abolitionism of the Freetown colony. He provided the language for the colonial bureaucrats in Freetown and London to understand the essence of Bilali's struggle and intervene favorably on his behalf. As an Islamophile, he praised the capacity of the religion to fully realize its antislavery and civilizing potential in the region. On the other hand, the intervention revealed the contradictions in British commitment to antislavery. Blyden gave eloquent testimony of the devastating consequences of slavery and of the impoverished condition of the enslaved.[22] Yet the accommodation with the slaveholders that he proposed was accepted and implemented by the British. Long before the debates of the 1920s, the antislavery element in the abolitionist ethos of Freetown had become subservient to its commercial element. Until 1928, when the government legally abolished the system, the fear of financial injury to the colony's interest was deemed far more important than the eradication of internal slavery (Rashid 1999).

Between the eighteenth and nineteenth centuries, the character of servitude changed greatly in the Upper Guinea Coast. Those who were in the process of being enslaved, as well as those who were enslaved, used different methods to counter the different manifestations of servitude. From the point of capture to the ships or to the slave villages, they utilized escape, violence, and marronage to try to restore a sense of self-dignity and autonomy over their bodies. The outcomes of their actions were mixed, and success was never guaranteed. The social consciousness and the manner in which the enslaved articulated their quest for freedom beyond visible actions are difficult to retrieve historically. The eloquent testimonies of lettered African and European interlocutors give us tantalizing insights into that consciousness but we can neither ignore the accompanying biases nor forget that they are not the voices of the enslaved.

Yet there is no doubt that the rebellions, and free communities created by those who resisted slavery, provided focal points for combating servile oppression and creating local memories of antislavery. Slaveholders and slave traders regarded the rebellions and the fugitive communities as potentially destructive of the whole regional complex of slaveholding and they spared no efforts in crushing the rebellions or eradicating the communities. Despite the mixed fortunes of the enslaved as they struck out for freedom and reclamation of control over their personhood, it was the slaveholders, in and out of Africa, who were ultimately on the losing side of history. The same historical forces that had given them leverage over their fellow humans were increasingly being used against them.

Notes

1. See also PRO CO 879/25/332, Particulars Relating to the Tribes and Districts of Sierra Leone and its Vicinity, compiled by J. C. Parkes of the Aborigines

Department from information furnished by T. G. Lawson, Government Interpreter; Parkes 1894.

2. PRO CO 268/8, Three Letters from the Imam of Foota Jaloo and the Negro Chiefs in the neighbourhood of Sierra Leone, 1810, Letter the First.

3. For accounts of these missions see Reade 1873, vol. 2; Laing 1825; PRO CO 267/316, E. W. Blyden, "Report on Expedition to Falaba."

4. Sierra Leone National Archive (hereafter SLNA), CMD 3020, Correspondence Relating to End of Slavery, 1928.

5. The Fula made a further distinction among the newly enslaved, *rakeek,* those who are considered objects of commerce, and *abeed,* those who are held as property by the enslavers. PRO CO 268/8, Three Letters, Letter the First.

6. These villages still exist today in parts of Soso, Bullom, and Mandingo countries. Members of the former slaveholding families can still point them out, even though they are quick to concede that slavery is a thing of the past and that descendants of formerly enslaved people owe them no special obligations.

7. Rhodes House Library, Journal of James Watt, 1794.

8. See addendum to PRO CO 268/8, Three Letters, 1810. Letter the First.

9. Edward Blyden to Alexander Bravo, Report of the Expedition to Timbo in Hollis Lynch, *Selected Letters of Edward Wilmot Blyden* (New York: KTO Press, 1978), 121.

10. SLNA, CMD 3020, Correspondence Relating to End of Slavery, 1928.

11. PRO CO 267/320, Blyden's Report in Kennedy to Granville, 10 March 1873

12. Edward Blyden to Alexander Bravo, *Letters of Blyden,* 126–7.

13. Sheikh Gibrill Dumbuya (regent chief) and Abdul Koroma (farmer), interview by author, Kukuna, Sierra Leone 18 July 2002.

14. CMS Archives, CA1/024/25. See Blyden to Governor Arthur Kennedy, 10 January 1872; Blyden to Kendall, 12 January 1872; Sheikh Gibrill Dumbuya and Abdul Koroma, interview by author, Kukuna, Sierra Leone 18 July 2002.

15. Interview with Sheikh Gibrill Dumbuya and Abdul Koroma.

16. SLNA, Governor's Despatches to the Secretary of State, 1872–74, Kendall to Earl Kimberly, 14 February 1872.

17. PRO CO 267/316, "Report on Expedition to Falaba"; PRO CO 879/25/332, "Particulars relating to the Tribes and Districts of Sierra Leone and its Vicinity," compiled by J. C. Parkes and T. G. Lawson.

18. Blyden to Major Alexander Bravo, Acting Governor of Sierra Leone, 1873, Report of expedition to Timbo, January to March 1873, in Blyden 1978, 119.

19. SLNA, Governor's Despatches to the Secretary of State, 1872–1874, Petition from Traders of Scarcies River to Pope Hennessy, 27 August 1872.

20. PRO CO 267/260/3, Governor Hill to the Secretary of State, 13 February 1858; PRO CO 267/263/63, Governor Hill to the Secretary of State, 18 April 1859.

21. PRO CO 267/316, "Report on Expedition to Falaba"; SLNA, Governor's Despatches to the Secretary of State, 1872–1874, no. 20, Pope Hennessy to Earl of Kimberley, 10 February 1873.

22. Blyden to Pope Hennessy, Report of Falaba Expedition, 26 March 1872, in Blyden 1978, 103.

Bibliography

Afzelius, Adam. 1967. *Sierra Leone Journal, 1795–1796.* Trans. and ed. Peter Kup. Uppsala: Inst. för Allm. och Jämförande Etnografi.

Atkins, John. 1735. *A Voyage to Guinea, Brasil, and the West Indies.* London: C. Ward and R. Chandler.

Barry, Boubacar. 1998. *Senegambia and the Atlantic Slave Trade.* Cambridge: Cambridge University Press.

Blyden, Edward Wilmot. 1978. *Selected Letters of Edward Wilmot Blyden.* New York: KTO Press.

Brooks, George E. 1993. *Landlords and Strangers: Ecology, Society, and Trade in West Africa, 1000–1630.* Boulder: Westview.

Butt-Thompson, F. W. 1926. *Sierra Leone in History and Tradition.* London: H. F. and G. Witherby.

Clarke, J. I. 1966. *Sierra Leone in Maps.* London: University of London Press.

Cooper, Frederick. 1979. "The Problem of Slavery in African Studies." *Journal of African History* 20:103–25.

Fage, J. D. 1969. "Slavery and the Slave Trade in the Context of West African History." *Journal of African History* 10:393–404.

Falconbridge, Anna Maria, Isaac DuBois, and Alexander Falconbridge. 2000. *Narrative of Two Voyages to the River Sierra Leone during the years 1791, 1792, 1793, with Alexander Falconbridge: An account of the Slave Trade on the Coast of Africa.* Ed. Christopher Fyfe. Liverpool: Liverpool University Press.

Fanon, Frantz. 1963. *The Wretched of the Earth.* New York: Random House.

Finnegan, Ruth. 1965. *A Survey of the Limba of Northern Sierra Leone.* London: HMSO.

Fyfe, Christopher. 1962. *History of Sierra Leone.* London: Oxford University Press.

———. 1964. *Sierra Leone Inheritance.* London: Oxford University Press.

Fyle, C. Magbaily. 1979. *The Solima Yalunka Kingdom: Pre-colonial Politics, Economics, and Society.* Freetown: Nyakon Publishers.

Genovese, Eugene. 1972. *Roll Jordan Roll: The World the Slaves Made.* New York: Vintage Books.

Glassman, J. 1995. *Feasts and Riot: Revelry, Rebellion, and Popular Consciousness on the Swahili Coast, 1856–1888.* London: James Currey.

Heuman, Gad, ed. 1986. *Out of the House of Bondage: Runaways, Resistance, and Marronage in Africa and the New World.* London: Frank Cass.

Hoare, Prince. 1828. *Memoirs of Granville Sharp, Esq.* London: Henry Colburn.

James, C. L. R. 1963. *The Black Jacobins: Toussaint L' Ouverture and the San Domingo Revolution.* New York: Vintage Books.

———. 1969. *A History of Negro Revolt.* 1938. Reprint, New York: Haskell House.

Klein, Martin. 1988. "Slave Resistance and Emancipation in Coastal Guinea." In Suzanne Miers and Richard Roberts, eds., *The End of Slavery in Africa,* 203–19. Madison: University of Wisconsin Press.

———. 1992. "The Impact of the Atlantic Slave Trade on the Societies of the Western Sudan." In Joseph E. Inikori and Stanley L. Engerman, eds., *The Atlantic Slave*

Trade: Effects on Economies, Societies, and Peoples in Africa, the Americas, and Europe. Durham: Duke University Press.

———. 1998. *Slavery and Colonial Rule in French West Africa.* Cambridge: Cambridge University Press.

Kup, Peter. 1961. *History of Sierra Leone, 1400–1787.* London: Cambridge University Press.

Laing, Alexander Gordon. 1825. *Travels in Timannee, Kooranko, and Soolima Countries, in Western Africa.* London: J. Murray.

Lovejoy, Paul E. 1981. *The Ideology of Slavery in Africa.* London: Sage Publications.

———. 1983. *Transformation in Slavery.* Cambridge: Cambridge University Press.

———. 1986. "Fugitive Slaves: Resistance to Slavery in the Sokoto Caliphate." In Gary Okihiro, ed., *In Resistance: Studies in African, Caribbean, and Afro-American History.* Amherst: University of Massachusetts Press.

Lovejoy, Paul E., and Jan S. Hogendorn. 1990. "Revolutionary Mahdism and Resistance to Colonial Rule in the Sokoto Caliphate, 1905–6." *Journal of African History* 31:217–44.

Lynch, Hollis Ralph. 1967. *Edward Wilmot Blyden: Pan-Negro Patriot, 1832–1912.* New York: Oxford University Press.

Manning, Patrick. 1990. *Slavery and African Life.* Cambridge: Cambridge University Press.

Matthews, John. 1788. *A Voyage to the River Sierra Leone.* London.

McGowan, Winston. 1990. "African Resistance to the Slave Trade in West Africa." *Slavery and Abolition* (May): 5–29.

Mendez, Ivan. 1975. "Resistance to Slavery in West Africa." Paper presented at the School of Oriental and African Studies (SOAS), University of London.

Miers, Suzanne, and Igor Kopytoff, eds. 1977. *Slavery in Africa: Historical and Anthropological Perspectives.* Madison: University of Wisconsin Press.

Miers, Suzanne, and Richard Roberts, eds. 1988. *The End of Slavery in Africa.* Madison: University of Wisconsin Press.

Migeod, F. W. H. 1926. *A View of Sierra Leone.* London: K. Paul, Trench, Trubner.

Newton, John. 1962. *The Journal of a Slave Trader, 1750–1754.* Ed. B. Martin and M. Spurrell. London: Epworth Press.

Nowak, Bronsilaw. 1986. "The Mandingo Slave Revolt of 1785–1796." *Hemispheres* (Wrocław) 3:150–69.

Okihiro, Gary Y., ed. 1986. *In Resistance: Studies in African, Caribbean, and Afro-American History.* Amherst: University of Massachusetts Press.

Parkes, J. C. Ernest. 1894. *Elementary Geography of the Colony of Sierra Leone and Its Hinterland.* Freetown: J. T. Sawyer Excelsior Printing Works.

Piersen, William. 1977. "White Cannibals, Black Martyrs: Fear, Depression, and Religious Faith as Causes of Suicide among Slaves." *Journal of Negro History* 62 (2): 147–59.

Rankin, F. Harrison. 1836. *The White Man's Grave: A Visit to Sierra Leone in 1834.* 2 vols. London: Richard Bentley.

Rashid, Ismail O. D. 1999. "'Do daddy nor lef Make dem carry me': Slave Resistance and Emancipation in Sierra Leone, 1894–1928." In Suzanne Miers and Martin A. Klein, eds., *Slavery and Colonial Rule in Africa.* London: Frank Cass.

Rathbone, R. J. A. R. 1985. "Some Thoughts on Resistance to Enslavement in West Africa." *Slavery and Abolition,* December, 147–59.

Reade, Winwoode. 1873. *The African Sketch Book.* 2 vols. London: Smith, Elder and Co.

Rodney, Walter. 1966. "Slavery and Other Forms of Social Oppression in the Context of the Atlantic Slave Trade." *Journal of African History* 7:431–43.

———. 1968. "Jihad and Social Revolution in Futa Jallon in the Eighteenth Century." *Journal of the Historical Society of Nigeria* 4 (2): 269–84.

———. 1970. *A History of the Upper Guinea Coast 1545–1800.* Oxford: Clarendon Press.

Sanneh, Lamin. 1999. *Abolitionists Abroad: American Blacks and the Making of Modern West Africa.* Cambridge, Mass.: Harvard University Press.

Schwartz, Stuart B. 1969–70. "The *Mocambo:* Slave Resistance in Colonial Bahia." *Journal of Social History* 3:313–33.

Scott, James C. 1985. *Weapons of the Weak: Everyday Forms of Peasant Resistance.* New Haven: Yale University Press.

Skinner, David E. 1980. *Thomas George Lawson: African Historian and Administration in Sierra Leone.* Stanford: Hoover Institution.

Thayer, James Steel. 1981. "Religion and Social Organization among a West African Muslim People: The Susu of Sierra Leone." Ph.D. diss., University of Michigan.

Thomas, Northcote W. 1916. *Anthropological Report on Sierra Leone.* Part 1, *Law and Customs of the Timne and Other Tribes.* London: Harrison and Sons.

Thornton, John. 1998. *Africa and Africans in the Making of the Atlantic World, 1400–1800.* Cambridge: Cambridge University Press.

Wadström, C. B. 1968. *An Essay on Colonization Particularly Applied to the Western Coast of Africa with Some Free Thoughts on Cultivation and Commerce.* 1794. Reprint, New York: Augustus Kelley.

Wax, D. 1966. "Negro Resistance to the Early American Slave Trade." *Journal of Negro History* 51 (1): 1–15.

Willis, John Ralph. 1985. "The Ideology of Enslavement in Islam." In John Ralph Willis, ed., *Slaves and Slavery in Muslim Africa.* Vol. 1, *Islam and the Ideology of Enslavement.* Totowa, N.J.: Frank Cass.

Winterbottom, Thomas. 1803. *An Account of the Native Africans in the Neighbourhood of Sierra Leone.* London: C. Whittingham.

Wylie, K. 1977. *The Political Kingdoms of the Temne: Temne Government in Sierra Leone, 1825–1910.* New York: Africana Publishing.

Chapter 10

Strategies of the Decentralized

Defending Communities from Slave Raiders in Coastal Guinea-Bissau, 1450–1815

Walter Hawthorne

> The Balantas are fairly savage blacks. They have trade with Beafares and Buramos, and meet them at their fairs. The adults can only bring themselves to see our people reluctantly, and they refuse to be slaves of ours: [if enslaved] they die from their obstinancy.
>
> —André Alvares Almada, *Tratado breve dos rios de Guiné*, 1594

Historians have been much more concerned with explaining questions surrounding how Africans produced, transported, and sold captives than with exploring African strategies against the slave trade.[1] In some instances, strong groups generated captives through kidnapping, raiding, and sentencing criminals (see esp. Larson 2000, 12–16; Hawthorne 1999; Walvin 1992, 26; Rawley 1981, 272). In others, states harvested them through large-scale warfare conducted beyond their borders on "slaving frontiers."[2] Onto these frontiers, elites sent armies that entered like powerful waves, dragging some victims away to the sea and turning those who remained into "human flotsam" (Miller 1988, 149).

Those affected by these invasions were often members of less militarily powerful, politically decentralized societies. Indeed, historians have generally agreed that "[o]n the whole it is probably true to say that the operation of the slave trade may have tended to integrate, strengthen and develop unitary territorial authority, but to weaken or destroy more segmentary societies" (Fage 1969, 402; see also Boahen 1989, 61; Manning 1990, 132; Klein 1992, 40–41). This is largely because states had a greater ability to organize people for large-scale projects such as defending communities against attack, conducting raids, and moving captives over long distances (esp. Lovejoy and Hogendorn 1979).[3]

But what happened to the people Joseph Miller dubbed flotsam—individuals who comprised the decentralized societies that remained outside the control of states but on their slaving frontiers? Were they simply passive victims? Did they do little more than struggle to keep their heads above water as they were tossed in the turbulence of "wildly swirling currents of political and economic change" (Miller 1988, 149)? Were they unable to respond to the challenges of a new era? Or did they fight back, adopt strategies to defend their communities against the slave trade?

With a focus on the Guinea-Bissau region of the Upper Guinea Coast, an area that sat on the slaving frontiers of the powerful interior state of Kaabu and the smaller coastal state of Casamance, this chapter will begin to answer these questions. The compilation of historical studies focused on the coast between West Africa's Saloum River and northern Liberia remains, Boubacar Barry recently noted, "an unfulfilled task" (1998, 317). The region possesses a wide array of ethnic groups that speak myriad languages, and its inhabitants crafted a great variety of decentralized political configurations, many relying on local—village or household—control. Though a small number of studies provide the broad outlines of the area's history, they have generally depicted the relatively homogenous populations of the great states that controlled the savanna-woodland interior as the forces determining the direction of historical change. In other words, historians have typically described decentralized societies as passive recipients of large historical processes, as flotsam washed along by waves radiating from states (e.g., Lopes 1999; Rodney 1970; Brooks 1993; Barry 1998).

However, a focus on Guinea-Bissau's decentralized coastal zone can teach us two important things about African responses to the pressures brought to bear by the Atlantic slave trade. First, by turning our attention directly to those living on the frontiers of great slaving states, we can see that these individuals should not be dismissed as helpless victims. Indeed, decentralized communities adopted a number of strategies against the slave trade (esp. Hawthorne 2001). Second, a focus on those living on the frontiers of great slaving states demonstrates that decisions about whether or not to produce and sell captives to regional and Atlantic merchants were based on calculations made at the most local of levels—in households and villages. That is, in placing our analytical lens squarely on the decentralized societies of coastal Guinea-Bissau, it becomes evident that the "most important effect of the slave trade" may not have been "the way it shaped the nature of the state" (Klein 1992, 40–41). The slave trade's impact on states was important, but its impact on local communities was also important and is a topic we have only begun to understand. As I have demonstrated elsewhere (1999), slave raiding as a process was chaotic, attracting myriad participants from a variety of types of political configurations. Powerful states certainly harvested slaves, but some decentralized societies chose to produce and trade captives as well. When small-scale communities entered the slave trade, elevated elites—kings or other state leaders—were not the decision makers; common people—village chiefs, age grade members, committees of elders, and others who controlled the most local of power structures—were. Their entrance into the trade followed careful examinations and lengthy debates about local needs and about the options available on the dangerous slaving frontiers of powerful regional states. Thus, in Guinea-Bissau some communities determined that their best strategy for survival was to produce and to trade captives so that they could have access to valuable imports, especially iron, which was needed to forge strong weapons for defense and to reinforce digging and cutting tools to increase agricultural productivity (ibid.). For some then, the best way to resist enslavement was to become slavers.

THE ORIGINS OF THE CAPTIVES EXPORTED FROM THE GUINEA-BISSAU REGION

Whether or not particular communities in coastal Guinea-Bissau produced and traded captives, their members certainly bore the brunt of the wave of violence that swept over the Upper Guinea Coast and Senegambia from the sixteenth through the nineteenth centuries. This wave dragged many thousands of people off into the sea as Guinea-Bissau became a focal point of the Atlantic demand for slave laborers (Hawthorne 1999, 101). Surveys of New World slave populations make clear that many of those captured and sold to merchants at Guinea-Bissau's ports had their origins in coastal zones occupied by decentralized societies. For example, drawing on Peruvian censuses from 1548 to 1560, James Lockhart (1968, 173) shows that 34 percent of the 207 slaves whose identities are discernable came from coastal Guinea-Bissau; they hailed from the Banhun, Brâme, and Beafada ethnic groups. Philip Curtin (1969, 98–99) also finds that significant portions of Afro-Mexicans whose identities are revealed in a 1549 census had originated in coastal Guinea-Bissau and Senegambia: Cassanga, Banhun, Beafada, and Brâme captives being accounted for. Finally, Frederick Bowser's study (1974) of data from Peruvian records indicates that the Upper Guinea Coast supplied an astonishing 56 percent of the captives reaching that colony between 1560 and 1650. The majority came from the coastal reaches of Guinea-Bissau, more than twenty-four hundred having Brâme, Banhun, Cassanga, Diola, Balanta, Bijago, Beafada, or Nalu origins (1974, 39–41). These figures dovetail nicely with one ship captain's late-sixteenth-century comment that the Guinea-Bissau region produced "more slaves than the rest of Guinea" (Almada 1984, 86).

Captives continued to be exported from the region in significant numbers in the seventeenth and eighteenth centuries, when Kaabu reached the apex of its power. To be sure, many were taken from coastal Guinea-Bissau.[4] However, the later part of the eighteenth century witnessed a shift in origins of the slaves exported from the region. After mid-century—by which time a jihad that was started by Fulbe in Futa Jallon had spread—slaves who hailed from the interior could be found in increasing numbers at Guinea-Bissau's ports. They were shipped over long-distance trade routes, some of which led to Geba, on the upper Rio Geba, and then to waiting ships at Bissau and Cacheu (Hawthorne 1999, 103). Eventually, this jihad would affect Kaabu and become what Walter Rodney called "the greatest recruiter of slaves in the latter part of the eighteenth century" (1970, 236; see also Rodney 1968, 281). Nonetheless, people whose origins were in coastal Guinea-Bissau continued to be sold, often in large numbers (Hawthorne 1999, 103–5). As in the centuries that preceded, many of these captives were produced by states such as Kaabu and Casamance. However, people were also snatched from their villages by raiding parties sent out by many of the countless small communities that sat on the slaving frontiers of these powerful states. As I recently argued, "The Atlantic slave trade was insidious because . . . [it] opened up the possibility for people holding power at all levels of society—and on the margins of society—to direct that power toward seizing captives" (118).

Settlement Patterns and Defensive Fortifications

However, not all decentralized societies chose to produce and trade captives. By pursuing a number of defensive strategies, many resisted the incursions of powerful state-based armies and the threats of neighboring communities. One of the most important strategies was abandoning places that were easily accessible and therefore vulnerable to attack. Africans in the Guinea-Bissau region, then, moved from difficult-to-defend savanna-woodland zones and coastal upland territories to areas in which natural barriers provided protection and inhibited the maneuvering of armies. As interior states began to form before the fifteenth century and to harvest captives for sale to Atlantic merchants in the late fifteenth and sixteenth centuries, many groups saw migration as the best way to avoid enslavement and subjugation. Hence, as Barry argues, when the Mandinka founded Kaabu, they displaced "indigenous populations from the Bajar group, together with Jola, Beafada, Papel, Balante, Bainuk, Baga, Nalu, Landuma, and others, whose descendants today live in the southern Rivers area between Gambia and Sierra Leone" (1998, 7).[5] These groups, Rodney tells us, were *refoulés;* that is, they were driven from the hinterlands to the coast probably as the result of expansions and aggression by the Mandinka and other Mande speakers (Rodney 1970; Lopes 1999).

Such observations dovetail nicely with the oral traditions of one group of coastal refoulés. The Balanta claim that the region between the Rios Mansoa and Geba—an area they call Nhacra, which is part of the broader region of Oio—is their homeland. The Balanta say that they migrated there "in times long past" from somewhere in the east. In addition, Balanta migration myths have two other common threads: the Balanta left the east because of conflicts with either state-based Mandinka or Fula, and these conflicts resulted from a Balanta propensity for stealing from their more prosperous neighbors or desire to avoid enslavement. For example, elder Estanislau Correia Landim told me, "The origin of the Balanta was in Mali. For reasons involving Balanta thefts, Malianos revolted against the Balanta. For this reason, Balanta left there. That is, some Balanta were stealing some things. When a thief was discovered, he resolved to kill the person who had discovered him. For this reason, Malianos chased after the Balanta. . . . When the Balanta left Mali, they went to Nhacra and then to Mansoa."[6]

Speaking of early conflicts and the reasons Balanta occupy the shores of the Rios Geba and Mansoa, Fô Kidum told a similar story: "Balanta and other ethnic groups did not have good relations. There were always wars with other ethnic groups over land and theft. I can say that B'minde [Muslims in the east] always emerged victorious and pushed the Balanta to littoral regions that the Balanta discovered later were good for agriculture."[7]

Other evidence for Balanta resistance to Mandinka raids and attempts at establishing suzerainty can be found in the Mandinka word *balanto.* In the language of the Mandinka, this word means "those who resist," indicating that Balanta were not easy to seize or to incorporate into an expanding state (Carreira 1947, 4). That is, when Mandinka struck at coastal communities, enslaving some and incorporating others into their state, at least one group, that which became known as the Balanta, must have remained recalcitrant.

In part, the Balanta and other coastal groups resisted enslavement by exploiting the advantages offered by the region in which they lived. Put simply, the coast offered more defenses and opportunities for counterattack against slave-raiding armies and other enemies than did the savanna-woodland interior. In the early twentieth century, Portuguese administrator Alberto Gomes Pimentel explained how the Balanta utilized the natural protection of mangrove-covered areas—*terrafe* in Guinean creole—when they were confronted with an attack from a well-organized and well-armed enemy seeking captives or booty: "Armed with guns and large swords, the Balanta, who did not generally employ any resistance on these occasions . . . , pretended to flee (it was and is their tactic), suffering a withdrawal and going to hide in the 'terrafe' on the margins on the rivers and lagoons, spreading out in the flats some distance so as not to be shot by their enemies. The attackers . . . then began to return for their lands with all of the spoils of war" (1927, 4). Organizing rapidly and allying themselves with others in the area, the Balanta typically followed their enemies through the densely forested coastal region. At times, the Balanta waited until their attackers had almost reached their homelands before giving "a few shots and making considerable noise so as to cause a panic." The Balanta then engaged their enemies in combat, "many times corpo a corpo" (ibid.).

The lowlands close to the sea offered other advantages. Large armies relying on horse warriors could not operate effectively along the riverine, marshy, and tsetse-fly infested coast. The parasite *Trypanosoma brucei rhodesiense*, which is carried by tsetse flies, took a toll on horses, and the area's many rivers presented effective barriers even to the movement of large numbers of foot soldiers (Hawthorne 1999, 107). Indeed, in a sixteenth-century battle between an army of the powerful coastal state of the Cassanga and the followers of "King Bambara," ruler of a Banhun chieftaincy, the Rio Cacheu played a key role. The Cassanga chief had to call upon Portuguese allies, who hoped to purchase slaves after the battle, to assist in the transportation of his troops across the river. Moreover, upon being surprised in a Banhun ambush, the Cassanga were massacred as they returned to the river in retreat. Almada said that as the Cassanga tried in haste to board their boats "many were drowned, for the numbers were so great that those of our men who were assisting the king [of the Cassanga to escape] had to kill many Cassangas, cutting their hands off as they clung to boats" (1984, 67).

Further, by assuming a defensive-household or fortified-village posture in the era of the Atlantic slave trade, decentralized coastal groups erected barriers to invaders. Almada (1984, 67) described this strategy, in the battle he observed. The forces of "King Bambara" appeared braced for an invasion since they "were in fortified positions" near the Rio Cacheu. Almada also noted that in coastal Guinea-Bissau the houses "are large and well built, and have so many doors and rooms that they are more like labyrinths than houses." They made them that way, he said, because slave raiders caused the people "so much trouble" (90). Many groups further defended themselves by agglomerating their homes into very tight and fortified village formations. In 1606, Baltasar Barreira (1989, 24) noted that across coastal Guinea-Bissau, households were scattered about the coastal zone in a dispersed pattern. That is, farmers constructed households close to the lands that family members cultivated.

Yet beginning in about this period and more often in the centuries to come, observers noted that people were concentrating their houses into very tight village units. These descriptions become especially prevalent in the period when the slave trade from the region was at its peak. Indeed, as armies and smaller bands of slave raiders increasingly attacked decentralized coastal farmers at the end of the sixteenth and start of the seventeenth centuries, people responded by abandoning difficult-to-defend locations, for isolated and marshy regions near rivers where they concentrated into fortified villages. In villages, they could combine forces to put up a unified front against attackers (Hawthorne 2001).

Robin Horton speculates that among precolonial decentralized societies "the dispersed settlement pattern was characteristic of peoples who were expanding or maintaining themselves territorially against negligible or relatively uncoordinated resistance." On the other hand, "the compact village pattern was characteristic of peoples who were defending themselves and their lives against formidable opponents intent on annexing the one and extinguishing the other" (1976, 91–92). Clearly, in the era of the Atlantic slave trade, the people of the Upper Guinea Coast needed to defend themselves against any number of very powerful opponents.

Indeed, in his study of Guinea-Bissau, Avelino Teixeira da Mota noted, "Wars between coastal groups (wars to which European action gave a new stimulus to hunt slaves to sell) gave rise to a type of settlement characterized by concentrations of isolated populations between which were depopulated areas. This facilitated defense." The rise of the Atlantic slave trade, then, saw the creation of *terras de ninguém,* or no-man's-lands, as dispersed populations abandoned difficult-to-defend areas and concentrated themselves in places relatively safe from attack (1954, 1:205–8). One such area was João Landim, north of Bissau, on the opposite side of the Rio Mansoa. It protected "the Brames de Bula from the incursions of neighbors, above all Balanta and Papel" (1:218). The Balanta also say that this area possessed no people before the nineteenth century, when they began to migrate there.[8] The name that the Brâme gave an island in the Mansoa to the southwest of João Landim is also testament to its position as a dangerous terra de ninguém. They called the island Baducô, which means "one who stays." In the era of the Atlantic slave trade, whoever was daring enough to venture that far risked the possibility of being forced to stay, that is, risked being captured (1:218).

Linguistic analysis also points to the conclusion that the rise of the Atlantic slave trade compelled coastal farmers to abandon dispersed settlement patterns in favor of defensive villages. When discussing the Upper Guinea Coast, André Donelha wrote, "Their villages are walled around with very large timbers, firmly fixed in the ground, in three or four circling fences, and surrounded outside the ditches. And on these walls, which are here called tabancas, there are very high towers and guard-posts, made of very tall timbers, with wooden walks . . . from which old men shoot their arrows so as not to be useless" (102–3). In the region of Guinea-Bissau, Coelho said that the settlement of Cacheu was "surrounded by a stockade formed of pointed stakes with sharp tips, fastened together with cross-bars, and it has two gates which are closed at night. The fence is called the tabanca" (1985, chapter 3, 12). As late as 1888 people in the Guinea-Bissau region were protecting their villages with such walls. That year one observer noted, "The most important populations are protected by strong tabancas. . . . The houses or huts are arranged in a circle. Around them is constructed a type of wall, with tall and thick trunks of trees" (Oliveira 1888–89, 307).

The words *atabanca* and *tabanca* were Mane in origin (Almada 1984). In the era of the Atlantic slave trade, *tabanca* was incorporated into the local creole language of trade. There, it took on a slightly different meaning. The Mane word for fortification came to mean village, which is the meaning of *tabanca* in Guinea-Bissau's widely spoken creole today. This association supports the conclusion that compact settlements served one purpose—defense.

Oral narratives that I collected among coastal Balanta farmers are further evidence of the concentrating of dispersed households as a defensive strategy against slave raiding. For example, Adelino Bidenga Sanha stated,

> As for the tabanca of Quinhaque, the founder was Nthomba Dhata, and after him the others came because of the good agricultural conditions in the zone.

> Little by little the tabanca grew to the point where it is today. The people who came did not all come from the same blood. Some were simply friends who came to procure land. On the other hand, the tabanca grew rapidly because of the wars of the Fula. Because of these wars, the Balanta liked to agglomerate so as to make groups for war or to counter attacks of Fula and Mandinga, who at times attacked Balanta. After agglomerating, Balanta began to marry among themselves. This contributed to the enlargement of this and other tabancas.[9]

Similarly, Fona Benuma told me, "In times long past, Balanta mistreated their fellow Balanta. They did not have a chief who could reprimand anyone who abused others. Thus, no one had the courage to build a house far from the houses of others since it could be attacked in the night and the people killed."[10]

Acquiring Guns and Iron for Fashioning Weapons

Before attempting to gauge the success of coastal refoulés, let us examine other ways decentralized communities in coastal Guinea-Bissau defended themselves against slave raiders. One of the most important challenges that tabanca residents faced was acquiring iron that could be used to fashion strong weapons. Arms—strong arms—were needed to ward off attacks by small groups of kidnappers who sought to snatch an unsuspecting victim, larger bands of men sent out by neighboring communities to seize a few captives, and powerful armies from Kaabu or Casamance who could destroy entire villages and drag away great numbers of people.

It was perhaps the fear of coming into contact with slavers that compelled many people in Guinea-Bissau to carry arms wherever they went. At the end of the eighteenth century, Philip Beaver noted the ubiquity of weapons in the region: "These people are always armed either with a gun, a sword, or an assagaye or spear, or all of them together, according to the wealth of the individual. . . . They all invariably wear a long knife stuck in the cloth which goes round their middle" (1968, 327). In the same vein, N'Sar N'Tchala, speaking of "times long past," told me, "Whenever people went to the *bolanha* [lowland field] to farm, each carried an arm—a machete or knife or some instrument for fighting. No one could stay in the bolanha alone and work without running the risk of being killed."[11]

But how did coastal communities obtain these arms or the materials needed to forge them? Elsewhere, I argue that the need to defend themselves against attack compelled some decentralized groups to participate in slave raids. They "had to produce captives and had to trade them so that they could get arms to deter slave raiders or kidnappers" (1999, 108). In other words, some communities chose to participate in the slave trade because of very immediate and local concerns. In some ways this argument harks back to "gun-slave cycle" theories (Inikori 1982; Lovejoy 1983, 66–68). Historians supporting this explanation for why Africans harvested and sold slaves argue that to defend their people from attacks by neighboring states' slaving armies that were armed with European guns, African leaders were forced to produce and to trade captives in order to obtain guns for their own armies. However, John Thornton (1992, 98–116) forcefully refutes the notion that European arms were a significant factor in African warfare. Imported guns, he points out, were cumbersome, inaccurate, unreliable, difficult to repair, and provided only one shot before they had to be reloaded. Hence, they gave little or no real advantage to those possessing them.

The problem with both gun-slave cycle arguments and Thornton's critique of them is that they focus exclusively on guns. In Guinea-Bissau, warriors used few guns when staging attacks. Iron weapons and iron-reinforced weapons—swords, knives, spears, and arrows—were ubiquitous. However, iron, and the ore from which it was produced, could not be found in abundance in the region. Before the arrival of Atlantic merchants, coastal communities tapped into interregional trade routes to garner small quantities of the precious metal, offering salt, mollusks, and other items produced in the area in exchange. Beafada merchants who traded with interior smiths dominated these routes until the late fifteenth and early sixteenth centuries, when Luso-African competitors with superior sailing vessels prevailed. At this point, coastal communities were forced to deal with new trading partners—partners whose orientation was to the Atlantic. These merchants did not have as great an interest in salt and mollusks. They demanded slaves, ivory, and beeswax. Thus, some coastal communities harvested these things and, in return, received iron and a variety of luxury goods.

In calculating how they would survive on the slaving frontiers of powerful states, some of the many decentralized societies in Guinea-Bissau decided that the best way to obtain the iron they needed to forge powerful weapons was to produce and market captives. European sources and African oral traditions make clear that many Balanta, Beafada, Papel, Bijago, Brâme, Banhun, and Diola decided to do just this. Most did not make slaving the cornerstone of their economies. They harvested and traded slaves when iron was needed. Nonetheless, many thought participating in the slave trade was the only way they could fight back. Hence, one of the cruel ironies of the era was that producing slaves was often seen as the best defense against enslavement (Hawthorne 1999).

However, not all coastal communities produced slaves. Many found that they could garner iron in two other ways. One strategy was to seize captives and to ransom them back to the villages from which they had come. Myriad Balanta communities that were reluctant to have direct trade contacts with Europeans pursued this strategy (Almada 1984, 92 [see epigraph, this ch.]). Indeed, oral narratives and travelers' accounts are rife with descriptions of how captives were ransomed. For example, in 1927, Alberto Gomes Pimentel wrote that when the Balanta seized people they were often held until "relatives" paid some price for the freedom of their kin (1927, 15–16). Cattle, he said, were often demanded as payment, but other items were also requested. Oral narratives also give us a picture of what might have been a typical transaction. Speaking of Balanta raids, one informant said that "prisoners were tied to the branch or trunk of a *cabeceira* tree for some time. Those of strength communicated to the families of the prisoners that they should pay a ransom for the prisoners if they were to be freed."[12] Others also spoke of the exchange of captives for a ransom.[13] Through ransoming, some Balanta communities avoided entry into the regional trade in slaves but managed to increase the wealth of their communities and to gain valuable items, such as iron, that they needed for defense against slave raiders.

A second strategy was to garner weapons and the materials from which to forge them by visiting regional markets or by tapping into regional trade networks and offering nonslave items for exchange. Cattle, salt, and a variety of agricultural products were in demand in regional and long-distance markets. Though these goods were not as valuable as captives, they could be and were traded for weapons, iron, and a variety of other commodities. Rich in goods because of connections to the Mandinka-dominated state of Kaabu, Beafada attracted large numbers of people to their markets. In the later part of the sixteenth century, the largest Beafada market was held at Bijorrei and may have drawn an astounding twelve thousand people (Almada 1984, 110; Rodney 1970, 32). Markets of varying sizes appear to have been held in many locations in coastal Guinea-Bissau. They were staged periodically, according to a schedule that varied from place to place. Brâme markets, for example, were held on a six-day rotation; Beafada markets occurred once every eight days; and, on other parts of the coast, markets were staged on "fixed days which are not changed, and the days are Wednesdays and Fridays" (Almada 1984, 87; see also 110). On the island of Bissau, Papel also hosted markets. Before the Luso-African takeover of regional trade routes, Bissau served as an important link between southern Beafada-Sapi and northern Banyun-Bak trade networks. Hence, it attracted a great number of merchants, area farmers, and products. Further, in later periods Papel rulers encouraged relations with Europeans and hosted a large European merchant population. "On the island," Manuel Álvares wrote in 1616, "they have many markets to which the Balantas come with cows, goats, varieties of food crops, which the Papels here buy from them for iron, cloths from the Island of Santiago and palm oil" (1974, 60). Clearly, Balanta and other groups could garner highly prized iron not only by producing and trading captives but also by breeding and trading livestock and by cultivating crops.

Coastal Africans could also obtain iron by trading nonslave items with merchants who plied regional and long-distance trade routes. From coastal villages, goods such as hides, salt, and other agricultural products were transported along trade network dominated by Luso-Africans and *lançados* who were connected to the broader Atlantic system. Lançados were Portuguese men who "threw themselves" onto Africa's shores, integrating into local societies and becoming important links in Atlantic coastal trade. To facilitate exchange in an area that lacked the broad-based institutions that policed markets, protected trade routes, and regulated exchange within states' borders, lançados forged kinship ties with people in coastal communities. That is, they worked within the predominant mode of social interaction—the extended family—to intensify relations between themselves and coastal peoples. Such ties were not established quickly or easily. Indeed, many lançados lived for decades in coastal villages. They participated in ceremonies and rites of passage, married area women, and established households. Lançado-African marriages produced a new group of intermediaries—Luso-Africans—who had close ties to both African communities and Atlantic merchants at the ports of Bissau and Cacheu.

Through their connections with lançados and Luso-Africans, coastal groups were able to obtain small quantities of guns and, more important, the iron they needed to craft other weapons. With these they not only defended their communities but, as Joshua Forrest demonstrates, at times attempted to stop the slave trade from the region. Indeed, in the 1730s in the area around Bissau, villagers, provoked by "opposition to Portuguese involvement in slave trading," obtained weapons through "illegal trade" with Luso-Africans and used them against soldiers guarding a local fort. Similar attacks occurred at other slave entrepôts (Forrest, in progress). Further, well-armed coastal groups frequently raided slaving vessels. Describing Balanta attacks, French slave trader Jean Barbot noted in the 1730s that the reason so little was known about the course of the Rio Geba was

> its being inhabited on both sides by wild, savage Blacks, little acquainted with trade, who have often insulted such as have been forced to put in there,

> either for want of provisions, or some such accident. Besides, the tide runs out extremely rapid, and the entrance is much incumber'd with sand and shoals; and there is reason to believe that some ships have perish'd there, and others been assaulted by the natives, who wear long collars of old ropes about their necks, which it is likely they have had from such vessels as have been cast away, or they have plunder'd. (in Hair, Jones, and Law 1992, 170)

In 1777, Portuguese commander Ignacio Bayao reported from Bissau that he was furious that Balanta had been adversely affecting the regional flow of slaves and other goods carried by boats along Guinea-Bissau's rivers. It was "not possible," he wrote, "to navigate boats for those [Balanta] parts without some fear of the continuous robbing that they have done, making captive those who navigate in the aforementioned boats." In response, Bayao sent infantrymen in two vessels "armed for war" into Balanta territories. After these men had anchored, disembarked, and ventured some distance inland, they "destroyed some men, burning nine villages" and then made a hasty retreat back to the river. Finding their vessels rendered "disorderly," the infantrymen were quickly surrounded by well-armed Balanta. Bayao lamented that "twenty men from two infantry companies" were taken captive or killed.[14] Having sent out more patrols to subdue the "savage Balanta" and having attempted a "war" against this decentralized people, the Portuguese found that conditions on Guinea-Bissau's rivers did not improve.[15]

Viewing the regional slave trade as a threat to their communities, the Balanta continued their raids on merchant vessels transporting captives and other goods.[16] Such raids would tax Portuguese patience throughout the nineteenth and well into the twentieth century, when resentment about Portuguese colonization of the coast brought renewed attacks (Correia e Lança 1890, 50–51). Thus, by garnering weapons and iron in regional markets and from Luso-African merchants, many Balanta communities, like those of other decentralized coastal societies, were not only able to stand up to threats posed by the slaving armies of Kaabu and Casamance, they were also able to withstand assaults by Portuguese who were attempting to profit by insuring the smooth running of the coastal trade routes that moved captives to area ports.

In the politically decentralized Guinea-Bissau region, communities pursued a number of strategies against the slave trade. They migrated to easily defended coastal locations, adopted new architectural style, concentrated their houses into tabancas, and found ways to purchase weapons and the iron from which to forge them. But just how successful were these strategies? If nineteenth-century population estimates are any indication, at least one decentralized society on the slaving frontier of one of West Africa's most important producers of slave exports—Kaabu—was extremely successful in defending its members and providing sustenance for them. From Guinea-Bissau, slave exports continued until well into the nineteenth century. Yet in 1890 the governor of what had by then become a Portuguese colony was able to write, "The margins of the Rios Mansoa and Geba constitute the center of radiation of the rice culture in Guiné Portuguesa and possess the greatest densities of population of the Colony" (Correia e Lança 1890, 16). Balanta comprised the bulk of this population, living along the rivers of central Guinea-Bissau in such numbers that many found it necessary to begin to migrate. In the decades that followed, they would move to underutilized lands in the south, around the Rios Tombali and Cacine, and in the north, around the Rio Casamance. Other decentralized coastal societies seem to have been equally successful in defending their members. Throughout the era of the Atlantic slave trade they perfected agricultural techniques, tailoring them to the harsh environment of the coastal zone to which their ancestors had migrated. As Rodney notes, the accomplishments of decentralized coastal groups in the age of enslavement "make the surrounding [politically centralized] Mandinga work appear shoddy by comparison. Even the much-lauded Fula animal husbandry is far less scientific and efficient than that of many of the littoral peoples. That peoples who were far superior producers of food than the Mande and Fula are consistently dubbed 'Primitives' is due solely to the contention that they did not erect a superstructure of states" (1970, 25). The simple fact that Guinea-Bissau is today home to a diverse and vibrant mélange of decentralized societies is testament to the fact that the individuals who comprised these societies between the sixteenth and nineteenth centuries were not simply "human flotsam" that was tossed in the turbulence of "wildly swirling currents of political and economic change" (Miller 1988, 149). They adopted a variety of successful strategies to fight back. As slave trader André Álvares Almada (1984, 92) emphasized, they refused to be slaves.

Notes

1. Some works have focused on the ways in which states resisted the slave trade. See esp. McGowan 1990, 5–29; Rathbone 1985, 11–33.

2. On slaving frontiers, see Lovejoy 1983, 80, 83–87; Miller 1988, 140–53; Feierman 1995, 358–59; Davidson 1961, 197; Hawthorne 1998, 171–76. On warfare and the production of slaves, see Larson 2000, 12–13; Boubacar Barry 1998; Thornton 1992, 99; Miller 1988, 115–22, 122–59; Roberts 1987; Lovejoy 1983, 66–78, 135–58.

3. For a counterargument, see Hawthorne 1998, 106–78; 1999; 2001.

4. See, for example, the figures presented in Mettas 1975 (353). Twenty-three of thirty-two slaves purchased by a ship's captain in 1718 were of coastal origin. Historian Abdoulaye Ly estimates that Kaabu sold between twelve and fifteen thousand captives per year to Atlantic merchants in the seventeenth century, and Mamadou Mané figures that it had the potential to sell six hundred slaves annually to the Portuguese alone in the late 1730s. Cited in Forrest, in progress.

5. Mandinka is the linguistically correct spelling of an ethnic group sometimes referred to as Malinke (the Francophone version), Mandingo (Anglophone), or Mandingo (Lusophone).

6. Estanislau Correia Landim, interview by author, João Landim, 2 February 1995.

7. Fô Kidum, interview by author, Quinhaque, 7 January 1995.

8. Interview C10.

9. Adelino Bidenga Sanha, interview by author, Quinhaque, 7 January 1995.

10. Fona Benuma, interview by author, Encheia, 13 January 1995.

11. N'Sar N'Tchala, interview by author, Bera, 5 April 1995.

12. Cabi Na Tambá, interview by author, Mato-Farroba, 6 December 1996; also interviews with Mam NamBatcha, Cufar, 3 March 1995; Tona Na Isna and Suna Na Isna, Cantoné, 5 March 1995.

13. Mam NamBatcha, interview by author, Cufar, 3 March 1995; also interviews with Tona Na Isna and Suna Na Isna, Cantoné, 5 March 1995; Alfrede Neves, Chiguna Clusse, and Bcolof Sukna, Patche Ialá, 31 January 1995; Basca Fonre, Pam Bighate, Bwasat Basca, and Bian Bekle, Nhacra, 1 January 1995.

14. Archivo Histórico Ultramarino (Lisbon) Guiné, caixa 11, doc. 30.

15. Archivo Histórico, caixa 11, doc. 7; caixa 12, doc. 3

16. Archivo Histórico, caixa 14, doc. 62.

BIBLIOGRAPHY

Almada, André Álvares de. 1984. "Tratado breve dos rios de Guiné." Trans. P. E. H. Hair. Issued personally, for the use of scholars, Dept. of History, University of Liverpool.

Almeida, Januário Correia de . 1859. *Uma mez na Guiné.* Lisbon: Typ. Universal..

Alvares, Manuel. 1974. "Da ilha do Bissau, natural e qualidade do gentio que a povoa." In Avelino Teixeira da Mota, ed., *As viagens do bispo D. Frei Vitoriano Portuense à Guiné e a cristianização dos reis de Bissau.* Lisbon: Junta de Investigações Científicas do Ultramar.

Barreira, Baltasar. 1989. "Description of the Islands of Cape Verde and Guinea." In P. E. H. Hair, trans., "Jesuit Documents on the Guinea of Cape Verde and the Cape Verde Islands: 1585–1617," doc. 13, issued for the use of scholars, Dept. of History, University of Liverpool.

Barry, Boubacar. 1998. *Senegambia and the Atlantic Slave Trade.* Cambridge: Cambridge University Press.

Beaver, Philip. 1968. *African Memoranda.* London: Dawsons of Pall Mall.

Boahen, A. A. 1989. "New Trends and Processes in Africa in the Nineteenth Century." In J. F. A. Ajayi, ed., *Africa in the Nineteenth Century until the 1880s.* Oxford: Heinemann.

Bowser, Frederick P. 1974. *The African Slave in Colonial Peru, 1524–1650.* Stanford: Stanford University Press.

Brooks, George E. 1993. *Landlords and Strangers: Ecology, Society, and Trade in Western Africa, 1000–1630.* Boulder: Westview.

Carreira, A. 1947. *Vida social dos Manjacos.* Bissau: Centro de Estudos da Guiné Portuguesa.

Coelho, Francisco de Lemos. 1985. "Description of the Coast of Guinea (1684)." Trans. P. E. H. Hair. Issued for the use of scholars, Dept. of History, University of Liverpool.

Correia e Lança, Joaquim da Graça. *Relatorio da provincia da Guiné Portugueza: Referido ao anno economico de 1888–1889.* Lisbon: Imprensa Nacional 1890.

Curtin, Philip. 1969. *The Atlantic Slave Trade: A Census.* Madison: University of Wisconsin Press.

———. 1995. *African History.* London: Longman.

Davidson, Basil. 1961. *Black Mother: The Years of the African Slave Trade.* Boston: Little, Brown.

Donelha, André. 1977. *An Account of Sierra Leone and the Rivers of Guinea of Cape Verde (1625).* Ed. A. Teixeira da Mota. Trans. P. E. H. Hair. Lisbon: Junta de Investigações Científicas do Ultramar.

Fage, J. D. 1969. "Slavery and the Slave Trade in the Context of West African History." *Journal of African History* 10:393–403.

Feierman, Steven. 1995. "A Century of Ironies in East Africa." In Philip Curtin et al., eds., *African History.* London: Longman.

Forrest, Joshua B. "The Lineage of a Soft State in Africa: State and Civil Society in Guinea-Bissau." Work in progress.

Hair, P. E. H., Adam Jones, and Robin Law, ed. 1992. *Barbot on Guinea: The Writing of Jean Barbot on West Africa, 1678–1712.* London: Hakluyt Society.

Harms, R. 1981. *River of Wealth, River of Sorrow: The Central Zaire Basin in the Era of the Slave and Ivory Trade.* New Haven: Yale University Press.

Hawthorne, Walter. 1998. "The Interior Past of an Acephalous Society: Institutional Change among the Balanta of Guinea-Bissau, 1450–1950." Ph.D. diss., Stanford University.

———. 1999. "The Production of Slaves Where There Was No State: The Guinea-Bissau Region, 1450–1815." *Slavery and Abolition* (August): 97–124.

———. 2001. "Nourishing a Stateless Society during the Slave Trade: The Rise of Balanta Paddy-Rice Production in Guinea-Bissau." *Journal of African History* 42:1–24.

Horton, R. 1976. "Stateless Societies in the History of West Africa." In J. F. A. Ajayi and M. Crowder, eds., *History of West Africa,* 2d ed., 2 vols. London: Longman.

Inikori, Joseph E., ed. 1982. *Forced Migration: The Impact of the Export Slave Trade on African Societies.* London: Hutchison University Press.

Klein, Martin A. 1992. "The Impact of the Atlantic Slave Trade on the Societies of the Western Sudan." In Joseph E. Inikori and Stanley L. Engerman, eds., *The Atlantic Slave Trade: Effects on Economies, Societies, and Peoples in Africa, the Americas, and Europe.* Durham: Duke University Press.

Lamphear, J. 1976. *The Traditional History of the Jie of Uganda.* Oxford: Clarendon Press.

Larson, Pier. 2000. *History and Memory in the Age of Enslavement: Becoming Merina in Highland Madagascar.* Portsmouth: Heinemann.

Law, Robin. 1989. "Slave-Raiders and Middlemen, Monopolists and Free-Traders: The Supply of Slaves for the Atlantic Trade in Dahomey c. 1715–1850." *Journal of African History* 30:45–68.

Lockhart, James. 1968. *Spanish Peru, 1532–1560: A Colonial Society.* Madison: University of Wisconsin Press.

Lopes, Carlos. 1999. *Kaabunké, espaço, território, e poder na Guiné-Bissau, Gâmbia e Casamance pré-colonias.* Lisbon: Comissão Nacional para as Comemorações dos Descobrimentos Portugueses.

Lovejoy, Paul. 1983. *Transformations in Slavery: A History of Slavery in Africa.* Cambridge: Cambridge University Press.

Lovejoy, Paul E., and Jan S. Hogendorn. 1979. "Slave Marketing in West Africa." In Henry A. Gemery and Jan S. Hogendorn, eds., *The Uncommon Market: Essays in the Economic History of the Atlantic Slave Trade.* New York: Academic Press.

Manning, Patrick. 1990. *Slavery and African Life: Occidental, Oriental, and African Slave Trades.* Cambridge: Cambridge University Press.

Mettas, Jean. 1975. "La Traite Portugaise en Haute Guinée." *Journal of African History* 16:343–63.

Miller, Joseph C. 1988. *Way of Death, Merchant Capitalism, and the Angolan Slave Trade, 1730–1830.* Madison: University of Wisconsin Press.

Mota, Avelino Teixeira da. 1954. *Guiné Portuguesa.* 2 vols. Lisbon: Agência Geral do Ultramar.

Northrup, D. 1978. *Trade without Rulers: Pre-colonial Economic Development in Southeastern Nigeria.* Oxford: Clarendon Press.

Olivera, E. J. da Costa. 1888–89. "Viagem á Guiné." *BSGL* 8 a ser, no. 11–12.

Pimentel, Alberto Gomes. 1927. "Circumscrição civil de Mansôa: Etnografia." *BOGP* 50 (10 December): 1–26.

Rawley, James. 1981. *The Transatlantic Slave Trade.* New York: Norton.

Roberts, Richard. 1987. *Warriors, Merchants, and Slaves.* Stanford: Stanford University Press.

Rodney, Walter. 1968. "Jihad and Social Revolution in Futa Djalon in the Eighteenth Century." *Journal of the Historical Society of Nigeria* 4 (June): 269–84.

———. 1970. *A History of the Upper Guinea Coast, 1545 to 1800.* New York: Monthly Review Press.

Spear, T., and R. Waller, eds. 1993. *Being Maasai: Ethnicity and Identity in East Africa.* Athens: Ohio University Press.

Thomas, Hugh. 1997. *The Slave Trade: The Story of the Atlantic Slave Trade, 1440–1870.* New York: Simon and Schuster.

Thornton, John. 1992. *Africa and Africans in the Making of the Atlantic World.* Cambridge: Cambridge University Press.

Tosh, J. 1978. *Clan Leaders and Colonial Chiefs: The Political History of an East African Stateless Society.* Oxford: Clarendon Press.

Vansina, Jan. 1990. *Paths in the Rainforests: Towards a History of Political Tradition in Equatorial Africa.* Madison: University of Wisconsin Press.

Walvin, James. 1992. *Black Ivory: A History of British Slavery.* Washington, D.C.: Howard University Press.

CHAPTER 11

The Struggle against the Transatlantic Slave Trade

The Role of the State

Joseph E. Inikori

THE FIRST RECORDED SHIPMENT of captives from western Africa over the Atlantic by Europeans occurred in 1441 (Blake 1977, 5). These were victims of raids by the Portuguese in the small coastal communities of Senegambia.[1] Subsequently, persistent Portuguese demand for captives stimulated supply, on the basis of which trade in captives developed and the Portuguese gave up forceful capture, to be resumed later in west-central Africa after the establishment of their colony of Angola in the late sixteenth and early seventeenth centuries (Vansina 1992, 558–59). The Portuguese chronicler Azurara records that by 1448 nearly one thousand captives had been shipped to Portugal from western Africa (Blake 1977, 16–17). The colonization of the Americas by European powers in the early sixteenth century and the concomitant phenomenal growth of demand for slave labor there catapulted the trade to heights that completely dwarfed all trade in humans ever recorded in history, especially during the plantation revolution in the Americas, between 1650 and 1850. From the 1440s to the 1860s, millions of people, variously estimated by recent research at between

12 million and 20 million (Inikori and Engerman 1992; Inikori 1998; H. Klein 1999; Eltis 2000), were shipped against their will by Europeans and European colonists.

Why was demand for slave labor in the Americas exclusively focused on Africa? Why did the export of captives from Europe come to an end just as the demand for slave labor was about to explode? What conditions in Africa sustained the supply of so many export captives for so long a period of time? What did the individuals and communities do to protect themselves from capture and sale for export? What did the governments in Africa do to protect their subjects? What role did the shift of European demand from the predominance of African products to the predominance of captives play in the evolution of state institutions and the direction of foreign policy in the states of Africa? What factors explain state involvement in the export trade in captives?

Despite the impressive research of the past three decades these overlapping questions are not adequately addressed in the literature.[2] They help to define the focus of this chapter, which specifically addresses the role of the state in the struggle of communities and individuals in Africa against the Atlantic slave trade.

Conceptual Framework

Trade in humans is essentially a trade in stolen "goods," because individuals do not willingly offer themselves to be sold into chattel slavery nor do parents knowingly sell their children for enslavement. This means that in general the people sold are acquired by one form of force or another: kidnapping, organized raids, wars, and so on. Hence, no commercial transaction takes place between communities which lose their members to enslavement and those who take possession over them in the first instance. For the families and communities whose loved ones are lost forever, the loss is traumatic. It is similar to loss by murder, for which revenge is always sought. In all societies known to historians one of the primary responsibilities of government is to protect the lives and property of citizens. Families that lose members to murderers, kidnappers, raiders, or even in wars hold their governments responsible. Prolonged widespread losses spell political crisis and loss of legitimacy for rulers. It is thus a matter of self-interest rather than morality that rulers go to considerable lengths to protect their subjects against such losses. This is even reflected in the conduct of war between more or less equally matched states. The realization that both states stand to lose large numbers of their subjects, with the attendant political costs at home, acts as a major constraint on the decision by both parties to go to war, in the first place. If war does break out, the same considerations impose on both parties the need to treat war captives well and ultimately exchange them to avoid the wrath of their families.

However, it is totally a different matter where politico-military organizations capable of protecting communities against these losses are nonexistent. Kidnappers and raiders meet little resistance. A relatively strong state can impose its will and take away people for sale into export without fear of retaliation. Economic and political logic thus informs us that the development of a large-scale trade in captives for sale into chattel slavery depends on two critical conditions: the existence of a market for slaves and a developed transportation system capable of transporting them relatively cheaply; and the existence of weakly organized communities whose members can be captured and sold at little cost to the captors. For communities to avoid capture and enslavement, first, they must have governments strong enough to prevent internal breakdown of law and order under the pressure of large-scale export demand for captives. Without effective control of overseas exporters and complete elimination of local kidnapping for export sale, the internal stealing of humans engenders a cycle of intracommunity conflicts that expose members to capture and export. Second, they must have governments strong enough to inflict considerable punishment on external aggressors who may be tempted to capture and sell their subjects to profit from the market demand. It cannot be overemphasized that as long as there is market demand for captives at relative price levels that justify supply efforts, somebody is going to do what it takes to meet the demand. To hold back supply response in the face of market demand for captives, politico-military and economic conditions have to raise the cost of procuring captives for sale above the benefits from meeting the demand. As stated above, these politico-military conditions will also encourage equally matched strong states to exchange war prisoners rather than sell them for export.

Rise and Demise of Captive Exports in Medieval and Early Modern Europe

A brief examination of the rise and demise of captive exports in medieval and early modern Europe may help us understand the circumstances which sustained the transatlantic trade in captives for centuries. For obvious reasons Rome has to be at the center of the story. Imperial Rome developed the first major slave system to involve largely Europeans. While the initial captives enslaved came from the imperial wars of expansion, the empire subsequently developed a major market for captives. People from all the European territories that became part of the empire were enslaved during the process of conquest. But once those territories were incorporated, their people became Roman subjects and were protected by the imperial state against capture and enslavement. As the expansion reached its limits, therefore, the imperial slave market was fed with imports from outside the empire. The imports from Europe were supplied by the politically fragmented Germanic peoples, including the Anglo-Saxons in the Danish peninsula and the coastlands of northern Germany and Holland, who began trading captives with the Romans in the first two hundred years of the Christian era (Pelteret 1981, 100).

For as long as the Roman Empire remained strong, all European communities within it were protected by *pax romana* (Roman peace) against capture and sale. The British Isles and the Balkans were among those so protected. As Daniel Evans (1985, 42) pointed out, "However scant the pastures of the Dinaric highlands, however formidable the problems of communications, so long as Roman power remained firmly established on either side of this region, in the Danubian basin as well as on the Adriatic coast, so long were held in check the banditry, the feuds, all the tendencies toward social disintegration and slave catching that could easily arise in a land with such structrual features."

As the empire weakened and collapsed, effective centralized authority gave way to political fragmentation in Europe. Effective imperial control over Britain ended as the Roman legions were withdrawn in 407 (Pelteret 1981, 100). Roman authority in the Balkans collapsed in the late sixth century (D. Evans 1985, 43). From the fifth to the eighth centuries German leaders broke up western Europe into successor German kingdoms (Phillips 1985, 43). The disappearance of effective centralized authority and the proliferation of small political entities presented a potential environment for social conflict and enslavement. However, this did not happen on any significant scale immediately. The collapse of the Roman Empire was accompanied by the decline of the large urban markets for the products of slave labor in Europe. Without flourishing urban markets, the high cost of supervision involved in chattel slavery was uneconomic. A form of servitude that required little supervision was found in serfdom. Rather than new captives being demanded, the slaves of the Roman period were transformed over time into serfs, as were most previous free peasants (Phillips 1985, 43, 50–52; D. Evans 1985, 42–43). It was only after the establishment of a major slave market in the Mediterranean and the Muslim Middle East, with the rise of the Arab Islamic empire from the seventh century, that political fragmentation in Europe facilitated raids and social conflicts in response to export demand for captives (D. Evans 1985, 43).[3]

Britain was one of the victimized areas. Lacking a relatively strong centralized state to protect its communities, local bandits and external raiders responding to market demand raided Britain and took captives. Anglo-Saxons from the Danish peninsula and the coastlands of northern Germany and Holland were the main external raiders. Internal raids were conducted by the Irish and the Scots. Political conflicts engendered by these raids and other causes led to frequent wars whose prisoners were sold for export (Pelteret 1981, 100–101; D. Evans 1985, 43; Strickland 1996, 313–17). After the Anglo-Saxons successfully invaded and settled in Britain many of the indigenous people, the Celts, were captured and sold for export. Because the Anglo-Saxon invasion did not produce a strong centralized state, the British Isles remained a source of captives as the various immigrant groups preyed on each other, making war endemic (Pelteret 1981, 102).

On the continent, Frankish merchants were the early major slave traders following the disappearance of Pax Romana. In the eighth century the imperial wars of expansion by the Frankish kingdom provided them with numerous captives, many of whom were Saxons (Phillips 1985, 61). In the late Middle Ages and the early modern era Venetian merchants expanded the slave trade from the Balkans. In this politically fragmented region export demand for captives helped to fuel intergroup feuds.

Because the trade in European captives depended on two essential conditions —the prevalence of political fragmentation and the growth of markets for slaves—the emergence of relatively strong centralized states all over Europe brought it to an end. Between 786 and 814, the Frankish state expanded its control over much of western Europe, excluding only Scandinavia, the British Isles, the Iberian Peninsula, and southern Italy (Phillips 1985, 43, 52). Once the Saxons and others were conquered and incorporated into the empire, the Frankish state protected all its subjects against capture and sale (D. Evans, 1985, 43; Phillips 1985, 61). The successor states to the Frankish Empire in the late Middle Ages continued the protection with their sophisticated military organizations (W. Evans 1980, 28). Communities in parts of Europe incorporated into Dar al-Islam (the lands under the peace of Islam) were similarly protected (D. Evans 1985, 43).

In what is now the United Kingdom and the Republic of Ireland, the emergence of a relatively strong centralized state began with the Norman conquest of England in 1066. Subsequently, the rest of Britain and Ireland were brought under Norman control in the twelfth century, after the Normans gained control of the seas along the coast of England and extended their hegemony over the Scots,

Welsh, and Irish. As the imposition of the centralized authority of the Norman state ended political fragmentation, so also did it end the export slave trade from Britain and Ireland, which was outlawed at the Westminster Council of 1102.

Henceforth, trade in European captives was limited virtually to the Balkans, where political fragmentation was prolonged for centuries more. However, from 1389 the Ottomans began their conquest of the region. From 1463 to the end of the fifteenth century, the Ottoman Empire in the Balkans was slowly extended to its geographical limit, the "last ridge that separates the coastal region from the hinterland," beyond which Venice and its allies were in control (D. Evans 1985, 51). This prolonged period of conquest increased the supply of white slaves to the western Mediterranean, where demand expanded in the fourteenth and fifteenth centuries as sugar plantations developed in Cyprus, Crete, and Sicily. Italian merchants supplied the planters white slaves from the Black Sea region (W. Evans 1980, 34, 37–38; D. Evans 1985, 51–52, n54, 58). However, once the process of conquest was completed and the conquered Balkan territories were incorporated into the empire, the flood of captives generated by the Ottomans stopped.

At the same time, the export slave trade from Russia, "the largest single source of white slaves in the mid-fifteenth century," was also halted by the rise of the Russian Empire. With the accession of Ivan the Great as the grand duke of Moscow in 1462, a long period of political fragmentation came to an end and a relatively strong centralized state was established in the decades that followed. Like its neighboring Ottoman Empire, the Russian state was strong enough to protect its subjects from capture and export. Thus, as the Portuguese were completing their exploration of the coast of western Africa, the last sources of export captives in Europe were closed off (W. Evans 1980, 37–39).

The foregoing narrative of the rise and demise of the export trade in European captives shows a clear pattern that is pertinent to the subject of this chapter. The principal cause of slave raids and the sale of war prisoners was the existence of export demand to feed slave markets in the Mediterranean and the Muslim Middle East. Political fragmentation was only a permissive factor, not a cause. Given export demand for captives, the prevalence of politically fragmented communities, whose members could be captured and exported at little cost to the captors, facilitated self-reinforcing sociopolitical processes that placed captives on the market. The European evidence shows that the formation of strong centralized states was the most effective device used by weakly organized communities struggling to avoid capture and export. Ironically, the communities had to be conquered and forced into centralized states in order to be saved from capture and export. It is important to note that it was the rulers of territorial states who stopped the slave trade in their individual states in Europe: The trade in European slaves ended because the rulers of each European state were strong enough to protect their subjects. It was not the collective action of Europeans that stopped the trade. By the sixteenth century, the spread over all Europe of relatively strong centralized states with sophisticated military organizations restrained European powers from capturing and selling each other's subjects, which caused domestic sociopolitical problems for all. This development encouraged states to exchange war prisoners instead of selling them for export. It was this political expediency, rather than the ideological unwillingness of Europeans to enslave other Europeans (Eltis 1993, 2000), that prevented the export of European captives for enslavement in the Americas. There was no common European identity in the sixteenth and seventeenth centuries strong enough to psychologically restrain all Europeans from enslaving other Europeans if the politicoeconomic cost-benefit equations were right.

Socioeconomic and Political Organization in Atlantic Africa before the Large-Scale European Demand for Captives

The societies that the Portuguese encountered on the African Atlantic coast in the fifteenth century—referred to here as Atlantic Africa—together with their immediate hinterlands, were organized sociopolitically in a manner very different from those in the African interior, in particular the savanna societies of the western and central Sudan. It was these Atlantic African societies and their hinterlands that were directly impacted by European trade, in its changing forms, for decades before others farther in the interior were drawn in. To properly understand how European export demand for captives affected the historical process in Africa, these two broad regions of western Africa must be distinguished.[4] The tendency in the recent literature on the Atlantic slave trade to refer to Africa in general (Thornton 1992; H. Klein 1999) creates confusion in the analysis of causes and effects.

Before examining the differing sociopolitical organizations of Atlantic Africa and the savanna interior, a brief exposition of the military and commercial power elements, which defined the character of relations between European traders and African communities from the mid-fifteenth to the mid-nineteenth century, is pertinent. These power elements derived from the relative levels of commercial and political development in western Europe and western Africa in the fifteenth and sixteenth centuries. As shown earlier, by that time Europe was characterized by the prevalence of relatively strong centralized states with sophisticated military organizations. This phenomenon was, in the main, a product of two interrelated factors—population expansion and the growth of trade. The two regions experienced radically different population densities and participated in world trade to widely differing degrees: western Europe was by far more intensively involved in world trade centered in the Mediterranean from the eleventh to the fourteenth century, thanks in part to the desiccation of the Sahara region, which limited the participation of Africa south of the Sahara (Abu-Lughod 1989, 36, 55–77, 120–25).[5] These two factors (interacting with some lesser ones) combined to bring about over time differing levels of commercial and political development in western Europe and western Africa.[6] Thus, at the time seaborne trade began to develop between western Europe and western Africa, the former had a significant politico-military and commercial advantage. For this reason the European traders were clearly in control and the communities in Atlantic Africa responded to the changing needs of the economies of western Europe.

This latter point is reflected in the changes in what Atlantic Africa produced and sold to the European traders. Initially the latter demanded mainly gold, the central driving force behind the exploration of the African coast. Other products in demand included ivory, pepper, hides, and wood. As yet, the economies of western Europe had little need for slave labor, apart from the limited numbers employed in Portugal, Spain, Madeira, Cape Verde, and Saint Thomas. In response to this demand, Atlantic Africa produced and sold these products. The colonization of the Americas in the sixteenth century led to radical changes and by the mid-seventeenth century slave labor for the exploitation of the vast natural resources of the Americas began to take center stage. Again, Atlantic Africa responded to the changes in European demand. Then, the needs of western European economies changed once again, back to African products, the so-called legitimate commerce of the late nineteenth century. Atlantic Africa and the hinterlands responded as previously, and raw cotton, palm produce, cocoa, woods, gold, diamonds, and other products were produced and sold to European traders in rapidly expanding quantities. The pace of growth was such that in the early twentieth century one writer thought there was an "economic revolution in British West Africa" (McPhee 1926).

To say that the European traders were in control and that Atlantic Africa and the hinterlands responded to the changing needs of western European economies, as the preceding evidence makes clear, does not imply that the individuals and communities that responded were not trying to serve their own self-interests. All it means is that those self-interests could be served in several ways, but the realistic choices that could be made at the time were dictated by the conditions created by changing European demand: a common phenomenon in trade relations between societies at significantly different levels of politico-military and commercial development. As the British historian K. G. Davies pointed out several decades ago:

> The Europeans were opposed in the seventeenth century . . . But in the Caribbean and North America resistance was ineffectual, and in West Africa, where the Europeans had limited objectives, it was not of the strongest. Nothing stopped the establishment of white communities on the western shores of the Atlantic and nothing stopped the growth of a slave trade out of Africa. The tide of European manufactures washed away most of the opposition. European daring and European acquisitiveness did the rest. Like it or not, the Atlantic Ocean, north of the equator, was transformed in the course of the seventeenth century into a European lake. (1974, xi)

Returning to socioeconomic and political organization in Atlantic Africa and the savannah interior, it should be noted that in the centuries preceding the arrival of the Europeans the savanna interior was the center of socioeconomic and political development in western Africa. The open savanna lowlands encouraged regular interaction among its diverse populations. It was at the center of commercial and cultural relations between sub-Saharan Africa and the Mediterranean and Arab worlds. Following from all this, the most complex and sophisticated socioeconomic and political organizations in precontact western Africa were located in the savanna interior: Ghana (capital, Koumbi Saleh), Mali (capital, Niani), Songhay (capital, Gao). Other major centers of commerce and learning (Timbuktu, Jenné, Kano, etc.) were all located there. Logically these economies were penetrated by market activities to a much greater extent, and the societies experienced much greater class differentiation. What is particularly important to note is the numerically small annual export of captives from western Africa to the Mediterranean and Arab worlds, together with the limited socioeconomic impact, was virtually limited to the savanna interior. When scholars make the general point that African societies were involved in the sale of humans before the arrival of Europeans, the point is valid only for the societies of the savanna interior and not the predominantly kin-based societies of Atlantic Africa and their immediate hinterlands. Similarly, the existence in this early period of servile populations, closer to serfs than to chattel slaves, was also a phenomenon of the savanna interior and not Atlantic Africa.

When they came into contact with the Portuguese in the middle decades of the fifteenth century, the people of Atlantic Africa from Senegambia to the Kalahari Desert lived in small political units organized around lineage groups. As Wondji points out,

> By comparison with the big ethnic masses of the Sudan, where state-type societies predominate, the area [from the Casamance River to the Republic of Côte d'Ivoire, inclusive] is characterized by many small socio-cultural units organized on the basis of lineages, clans, and villages. From the River Casamance to the River Tanoe, between the northern savannah and southern coastline and the mountain ranges of Futa Jallon and the Guinea Spine and the western and southeastern coastline, there are more than a hundred ethnic groups and sub-groups. (1992, 368)

In Senegambia (comprising the basins of the Senegal and Gambia Rivers) these small political units were loosely connected as provinces to the states of the savanna interior (Barry 1992; Wondji 1992). With the disintegration of the Songhay Empire following the Moroccan invasion of 1591, the western Sudan became also politically fragmented just as European demand for captives began to intensify. From the upper Niger to the upper Voltas (including the Niger Bend or the inland delta of the Niger) centralized political authority disappeared and power became localized. All this development occurred, as Izard and Ki-Zerbo observe, "against a back-cloth of numerous ethnic groups with non-centralized authority" (1992, 327).

From the Gold Coast (now Ghana) to west-central Africa, political fragmentation was also the norm, even though the kingdoms of Benin (in southwestern Nigeria) and Kongo were in their process of territorial expansion and the consolidation of centralized political power in the fifteenth and sixteenth centuries. On the Gold Coast the Akan in the forest, according to Kwame Daaku, "lived in a group of small chiefdoms, which were organized on kinship lines" (1970, 4). Even as late as the seventeenth century, a map of the Gold Coast drawn by the Dutch in December 1629 shows forty-three independent political units (Daaku 1970, 144–45, 199).[7] From the river Volta to the Niger delta, in Nigeria, the largest political units in the fifteenth and sixteenth centuries were the kingdoms of Ife and Benin. In the area later covered by the Kingdom of Dahomey, the first state structure was that of Allada, founded in about 1575 (Akinjogbin 1967, 11). Before the Dahomean conquest in the early eighteenth century, this small area had five autonomous kingdoms: Allada, Whydah, Popo, Jakin, and Dahomey (ibid.). In neighboring Yorubaland, before the rise of Oyo in the seventeenth century, there were over a dozen autonomous kingdoms (Smith 1988).

As long as European demand was largely for gold and other products, political fragmentation did not constitute a serious security problem for the people and communities of Atlantic Africa. The limited numbers of captives shipped by the Europeans did expose some of the coastal villages to raids, sometimes directly by the Europeans. But affected places were limited; part of the shipment came from a diversion to Arguin of some portion of the preexisting trans-Saharan exports, and some others were prisoners from the ongoing process of territorial expansion by the Benin kingdom, made available to the Portuguese who pressed to have them on specially negotiated terms, including the military needs of the Benin state (Ryder 1969).[8] To properly comprehend what happened in the centralized states that emerged in Atlantic Africa between the mid-seventeenth and mid-nineteenth centuries, it is important to examine in some detail the economic and political significance of the early European trade in products.

It should be stressed at this juncture that commerce was a major factor in the formation of the centralized states in the savanna interior up to the end of the sixteenth century. The locations and directions of expansion of Ghana, Mali, and Songhay all indicate strongly the importance of trade, especially the gold trade, in the political economy of these states. Parts of Atlantic Africa producing kola nuts, gold, and other products demanded by the sophisticated societies of the savanna interior had been linked to the trading network of that region, which led ultimately to markets in North Africa and the Middle East. The coming of the Europeans and the development of seaborne trade both expanded the volume and relocated the centers of trade in western Africa. The export of products, which dominated the trade in the fifteenth and sixteenth centuries, produced major socioeconomic changes in several parts of Atlantic Africa. The case of the Gold Coast, which has been well studied and documented (Wilks 1977; Kea 1982), may be used to illustrate.

The central region of modern Ghana, where the savanna ends and the forest begins, had been connected to the trading centers of the middle and upper Niger valley in the fourteenth century. This led to the rise of Bighu (Begho) as a major commercial center, through which the gold, kola nuts, and other products of the Akan forest area were exchanged for products of the savanna interior, as well as imports from North Africa and the Middle East (Kea 1982, 53–55). The Akan gold trade expanded phenomenally following the arrival of the Portuguese. By the sixteenth century the general growth of trade centered on gold had given rise to the emergence of men of considerable wealth looking for opportunities for productive investment outside commerce. The positive externalities generated by export production and trade opened up many such opportunities. There is clear evidence that from the fifteenth to the mid-seventeenth centuries population grew and urban centers multiplied and increased in size. The division of labor between town and country developed as manufacturing concentrated in the towns. The growth of trade between town and country offered profitable opportunities for investment in land and agriculture which were seized by the men who had accumulated huge wealth from the trade in gold and other products. Beginning in the sixteenth century these wealthy trading families moved from the Adanse-Amanse area northward to places such as the Kwaman, Kwabre, Atwema, and Sekyere districts, where they invested their wealth in large-scale forest clearance and the creation of farmlands (Kea 1982, 85–91). These developments stimulated the emergence of a land market. "The site on which the town of Kumase was later built," Ray A. Kea tells us, "was purchased for the sum of 25,920 dambas in gold, and that on which the town of Nsuta was built cost 24,830 dambas. Only persons of wealth could have afforded to buy land" (1982, 90).[9]

Thus, the early trade in products, before and with the Europeans, produced considerable private wealth for African traders on the Gold Coast and its hinterlands. Its multiplier effects generated positive institutional change in the direction of long-term socioeconomic development. The evidence showing this has been summarized (Kea 1982, 11): "Various orally transmitted histories refer to the importance of towns, or urban centers, in many parts of the region prior to 1700. Indeed, they indicate explicitly that certain districts were more urbanized and populous than they were in the late eighteenth or early nineteenth centuries. Both archaeological evidence and contemporary written accounts support this view."

The study of Senegambia by Boubacar Barry (1992, 265, 289) suggests similar developments. Here, the most important products demanded by the early European traders were gold and hides, in that order. The leather trade peaked in the mid-seventeenth century, with an export of about 150,000 hides per year (265). This gave rise to a large-scale trade in cattle, which by the seventeenth century had made the Fulani cattle owners the richest and most powerful social group in Futa Jallon (289). The pepper and cotton cloth trade in Benin (Daaku 1970, 24; Fynn 1971, 11–12; Ryder 1969) and the copper trade in Kongo (Hilton 1985) may have produced somewhat similar effects.

The European Demand for Captives and the Exposure of Politically Fragmented Communities to Capture and Export

As the imperial powers of western Europe intensified their exploitation of the natural resources of the Americas, at the same time that the indigenous populations were almost totally wiped out by European diseases and ruthless exploitation, European demand in western Africa shifted increasingly from products to captives over the seventeenth century. Even though the problem of incomplete import data makes it impossible to state anything close to the true number of Africans imported into the Americas, the available information shows that at least 58,000 had already been landed by 1580. Between 1580 and 1640 the imports increased almost ten times, and between 1640 and 1700 they grew again by over 42 percent (Eltis 2000, 9). This mounting demand for captives seriously exposed the politically fragmented communities of Atlantic Africa and the hinterlands to capture and export. As the evidence presented above shows, in the seventeenth century Atlantic Africa and the hinterlands did not possess centralized states strong enough to prevent the internal breakdown of law and order in the face of expansive European demand for captives nor protect communities against outside raiders. The earlier European demand for products, with the multiplier effects, had created socioeconomic conditions favoring individuals with entrepreneurial aptitudes for the peaceful production and distribution of goods and services. In contrast, the growing demand for captives, with its destructive multiplier effects, created socioeconomic conditions that favored individuals with violent dispositions. As demand for products declined and that for captives accelerated, with devastating impact on production for the domestic markets, the population of bandits, operating in groups or individually, grew. This made the maintenance of internal social order in the communities with weak politico-military organizations a very tough task. What is more, the operation of these bandits across political boundaries created diplomatic complications that regularly drew the multitude of autonomous chiefdoms into wars whose prisoners were readily purchased by the Europeans. And there is clear evidence that the latter, acting alone or in conjunction with the bandits, intervened in the affairs of these chiefdoms to provoke conflicts that generated export captives.

In west-central Africa, where the Kongo kingdom was in the process of territorial expansion and consolidation of centralized authority at the time of contact, politico-military organizations were relatively too weak to withstand the onslaught unleashed by Portuguese demand for captives. The evidence is clear enough that no slave trading or chattel slavery existed in west-central Africa before the arrival of the Portuguese (Vansina 1989, 352, 353 map 3; 1990, 278; Hilton 1985, 57, 58, 78, 233 n86). Early Portuguese trade in the region had centered on copper. When the Portuguese shifted their demand to captives, the Kongo government insisted that only people from outside Kongo must be traded. But as the demand grew the Kongo state, with no standing army in the early decades of contact, was unable to prevent internal breakdown of law and order, and rampant local kidnapping of Kongo citizens for sale to the Portuguese arose. As Anne Hilton narrates, "In 1526 Afonso [the king of Kongo] complained that 'thieves and men without conscience' seized *'filhos da terra'* (people of the subject *kanda* [clan]) and *'filhos de nossos fidalgos e vassalos'* (people of the Mwissikongo [metropolitan provinces] and of the tribute submitting kanda and extra-kanda chiefs) to sell to the merchants" (1985, 58). The Kongo government appointed three judges to examine the people sold to the Portuguese to ensure that they were captives from outside the Kongo kingdom and not kidnapped Kongo citizens. With Portuguese traders spread all over the provinces, state efforts remained ineffective. The king tried to tackle the problem at its roots: "He informed the King of Portugal that he wanted Portuguese teachers and priests but he no longer wanted traders and merchants, 'for it is our will that in our kingdom there should no longer be a trade or export of slaves'" (Hilton 1985, 58). This did not work either, as the government could not keep out the Portuguese traders from all the provinces of the kingdom, including the tribute-paying provinces (ibid.).

Worse still, the Kongo state was not strong enough to protect its subjects from external bandits. Tio- or Kikongo-speaking bandits invaded the kingdom in 1568—the so-called Jaga invasion. The king, Alvaro I, confronted them, was defeated, and fled to an island in the Zaire River. He had to appeal for help to the king of Portugal, who sent the Portuguese captain of São Tomé with six hundred soldiers and the bandits were expelled from the kingdom (Hilton 1985, 69–70). When finally the threat came from the slave-raiding and slave-trading Portuguese colony of Angola in the seventeenth century, Kongo was helpless. Efforts made by King Garcia II of Kongo to develop an alternative to the slave trade with the help of the Dutch failed, as the latter were more interested in the slave trade (148–49). As the colony of Angola grew stronger and more troublesome, the king of Kongo, Antonio, in desperation mobilized the entire resources of the state and confronted the Portuguese in a battle in 1665. He summoned his people "to defend their 'lands, possessions, women and children, their lives and their liberties'" (178). The Kongo government lost everything as the Portuguese unleashed a crushing defeat.[10] Thereafter, centralized authority in Kongo dissolved, totally exposing the people to capture and export. Vansina recounts: "With the Kongo, the organization of a vast area disappeared. The structural framework of this area [west-central Africa], like that of Angola, was henceforth to be economic, with a framework of trade routes articulated by places of trans-shipment" (1992, 566).

With the demise of the Kongo kingdom, the Brazilians reorganized the slave trade from west-central Africa, operating in concert with the Afro-Portuguese, who led caravans into the interior to procure slaves. Lacking adequate capital, "the traders pressed for war as a source of captives for merchants" (Vansina 1992, 569). War was a low-cost mechanism for acquiring export captives only because there were no strong centralized states spread across west-central Africa to raise the cost of taking captives by war and raids.

On the Gold Coast, where early European trade in products was most intensive and lasted much longer, the shift of European demand to captives in the seventeenth century brought a dramatic turn of events to the orderly process of socioeconomic development that had been going on since the mid-fifteenth century. With trade in products the political institutions of the multitude of chiefdoms were adequate to keep social order and maintain peaceful relations with neighbors. This period of relative sociopolitical stability lasted up to the mid-seventeenth century. To be sure, there were some conflicts or even limited wars:

> It must be pointed out that in the first half of the seventeenth century, a period of relative political stability, there were wars on the Gold Coast. From the 1630s the Europeans reported inland wars in which they lent a few muskets to their allies. But those wars appear to have been more trade wars disputing rights of way, such as those between Abrem and Fetu, or civil wars over succession disputes. Their political effects were inconsequential, their duration short. (Daaku 1970, 149)

As the demand for captives mounted, the small chiefdoms lacked the politico-military organizations that could prevent the internal breakdown of law and order, let alone keep peaceful relations with neighbors. Daaku (1970, 149–52) believed that widespread sociopolitical instability on the Gold Coast was caused by the large-scale import of firearms by the European traders after the mid-seventeenth century. The accounts of the Dutch Company officers resident on the Gold Coast appear to imply the same. In 1679 they wrote,

> The Accanists, who are real traders, used to trade in all these areas, and they alone controlled all trade, travelling with large numbers of slaves to carry their goods through all those places. But as a result of the wars which the blacks so often start for trifling reasons, this trade is suddenly stopped . . . the passages are closed . . . and especially since musket and gunpowder have been introduced, things have become much worse, the natives having become much more war-like. . . . Consequently the whole Coast has come into a kind of state of war. This started in the year 1658, and gradually this has

> gone so far, that none of the passages could anymore be used, and none of the traders could come through. (Dantzig 1978, 17)[11]

The general breakdown of law and order continued in the first half of the eighteenth century, as the Dutch director-general reported in 1712: "Never in our memory, and as far as old manuscripts concerning events here show, has the condition on this Coast been such as it is now, when one cannot find a single little village of which it could be said that it has stayed outside the war" (Dantzig 1978, 168).[12]

If the facts observed by the Dutch company officers are separated from their interpretation of those facts, what emerges is clear. From the mid-seventeenth to the eighteenth century, European demand for captives on the Gold Coast expanded and export prices for captives increased accordingly. As a result, the Gold Coast became engulfed in widespread and persistent wars. The import of firearms increased over time. The trade in products, especially the gold trade, was virtually eliminated. In fact, the officers reported that by this time Brazilian gold was being imported into the Gold Coast and "His Majesty of Portugal had sent a proclamation to Brazil in which H. M. forbids all his subjects there, on penalty of death, to send any Brazilian minerals to this part of the world" (Dantzig 1978, 148–49).

However, the causal sequence implied by Daaku and the Dutch, with reference in particular to firearms, is not altogether accurate. A more accurate causal sequence emerges when the Dutch accounts are combined with other sources. A long-term analysis of the commodity composition of imports into the Bights of Benin and Biafra (the region covering modern Republic of Benin, Yorubaland, and southeastern Nigeria) reveals a pertinent pattern. Because these two regions were drawn into the European trade much later than other parts of western Africa (Law 1991; Latham 1973), the late seventeenth century represented the early years of intensive slave trading in both regions. The invoice records of the British companies show consistently that throughout the late seventeenth century imports into the two regions were overwhelmingly dominated by commodity currencies—cowries for the Dahomean area, and copper bars (weighing about one pound each) and iron bars for the Bight of Biafra. Firearms were rarely included. Textiles were also imported in very limited quantities.[13] In the course of the eighteenth century the composition changed radically. Textiles and firearms became the dominant products, with commodity currencies constituting a small percentage.

Combining this evidence with that of the Gold Coast, what emerges is that the seventeenth-century imports into the Bights of Benin and Biafra served the needs of a growing internal trade similar to developments on the Gold Coast in the fifteenth and sixteenth centuries. Over time, however, the growth of the trade in captives led to internal breakdown of law and order in the politically fragmented communities and to frequent conflicts and wars among them. Enclave economies developed on the coast as trade links with the interior weakened, because export captives, unlike products, were "stolen," not produced. The attendant violence shifted demand from goods employed in production and distribution to firearms and goods ready for immediate consumption. While the uncontrolled distribution of firearms in communities without strong centralized states contributed significantly to the escalation and persistence of conflicts and wars, firearms were not the initial cause. Internal breakdown of law and order and widespread conflicts among the multitude of loosely organized chiefdoms were caused in the first instance by the shift of European demand from products to captives. Contrary to Daaku's explanation (1970, 149–50) that limited importation of firearms into the Gold Coast before the mid-seventeenth century was due to legal restriction imposed by the European powers, the evidence indicates that lack of demand was the real factor. This is why firearms flooded the Gold Coast in the late seventeenth century, while they were rare in the invoices for the two bights during the same period, even though the restrictions had been formally lifted in the mid-seventeenth century.

The shift of European demand from products to captives affected the politically fragmented communities in Senegambia in ways similar to the preceding discussion. Here the internal breakdown of law and order, and the persistent conflicts and wars among the multitude of chiefdoms and petty kingdoms led to the emergence of warlords employing armies of captive recruits (the so-called *ceddo* armies; see Adama Guèye, this volume). The demand for firearms grew and their widespread distribution fueled more violence, which exposed communities and their members to capture and export. The Islamic revolutions of the seventeenth and eighteenth centuries in the region were inspired by the desire to protect communities without strong centralized states against the violence of the Atlantic slave trade (Barry 1992, 1998; M. Klein 1998; Wondji 1992).

Relatively Strong Centralized States and the Atlantic Slave Trade

The evidence presented so far makes it clear enough that, faced with large-scale European demand for captives, political fragmentation was a major factor limiting the ability of people in Atlantic Africa and the hinterlands to protect themselves against capture and export. The evidence suggests that the Kingdom of

Benin was the only state in Atlantic Africa that successfully protected its subjects from the very beginning of the Atlantic slave trade (Ryder 1969). Between the late seventeenth century and the mid-eighteenth the Oyo Empire, the Kingdom of Dahomey, and the Asante state emerged with politico-military organizations strong enough to qualify them as relatively strong centralized states. Dahomey and Asante developed under similar conditions and achieved somewhat similar outcomes. Oyo, much farther in the interior, had a significantly different history.

Oyo developed to become the most powerful state in Yorubaland in the eighteenth century. But its early history had little to do with Atlantic Africa. Although Yorubaland was politically fragmented before the emergence of Oyo, the Yoruba people were not exposed to capture and export as were the people on the Gold Coast and the Dahomean coast. This is because no ports in the area were used by the European slave traders as major export centers at the time (Inikori 1992, 28–29). Consistent with the location of the metropolitan center of the empire, its early history was linked to the Sudanese states of the savanna interior. In the fifteenth and sixteenth centuries the nascent state was subjected to frequent raids by its northern neighbor, Nupe, leading to the destruction of its capital in the early sixteenth century (Law 1977, 37–39). The state was abandoned by the rulers, to be rebuilt a century later. To protect itself against the northern raids, the new kingdom built a powerful military machine based on the use of horses (43). From the seventeenth century to the late eighteenth, Oyo expanded territorially to incorporate much of modern Yorubaland and subordinated large areas of non-Yorubaland in the north and northwest as vassal states.

The two main authorities on the early history of the Kingdom of Dahomey, Akinjogbin (1967) and Law (1986, 1991), offer conflicting accounts. According to the former, the founders of the nascent Kingdom of Dahomey migrated inland from the coast in the mid-seventeenth century to escape the rampant kidnapping in the area. The Dutch and the French had begun slave trading in the region and the weakly organized Aja states of Allada, Whydah, Popo, and Jakin could not prevent internal breakdown of law and order nor maintain peaceful relations with neighbors. Developing in the hinterland, away from regular interference by the Europeans, the Dahomeans departed from the loose state structures on the coast and evolved a centralized state system with an absolute monarchy. With its strong politico-military organization, Dahomey invaded the coastal Aja states in the 1720s to bring all of them under one strong centralized state in order to end the slave trade in the region. This conquest was carried out successfully between 1724 and 1727, and the Aja states were ultimately incorporated into the centralized state of Dahomey.

Robin Law's account is different in some important respects. Law believes that the founders of the Dahomean state were bandits who started off as raiders in the hinterland, selling their captives to coastal middlemen, who in turn sold them to the Europeans. Their motivation for conquering the coastal states, Law explains, was to have direct access to the European traders.

The contending accounts by the two authorities are both supported by European sources. For purposes of the main issues addressed in this chapter, however, the disagreement is not particularly important. More important, both accounts agree that Dahomey was a strong centralized state and its conquest of the coastal states solved the problem of political fragmentation in the area. What is more, Law agrees that the Dahomean leaders, once they established the centralized state, ceased to be bandits and became statesmen.

The fact that over the almost two centuries of European trade on the Gold Coast, from the fifteenth century to the early seventeenth, no serious attempt to develop centralized states was made until the crisis generated by the slave trade would seem to suggest a causal connection. The account by Daaku (1970, 144–81) indicates that state formation was in part a device for self-protection by weakly organized communities. The first noteworthy of these states were Denkyira and Akwamu. None succeeded in incorporating a large enough number of the numerous chiefdoms to solve the problem of political fragmentation. Rampant kidnapping, a major cause of conflict among the petty states—some were havens for bandits—persisted (Inikori 1992, 34). "Towards the end of the seventeenth and in the first few decades of the eighteenth century," wrote Daaku, "slave-raiding became an established occupation of the Akwamu, Akyem, Kwawu, Krepi, and villages bordering on the Akwamu territories sometimes became the hapless victims of Akwamu raiders" (1970, 31).

It was the development of the Asante state from the late seventeenth to the mid-eighteenth century that ultimately brought all of the Gold Coast, with the exception of the Fante, under one strong centralized state. This ended the problem of political fragmentation on the Gold Coast. As expressed by A. Adu Boahen, "Between 1670 and 1750 political revolution had taken place in the forest and coastal regions of Lower Guinea. From the thirty-eight states of the 1629 map had emerged the three large empires of Aowin, Denkyira and Akwamu, which, by 1750, had merged into the single empire of Asante" (1992, 422).

Like the relatively strong centralized states of medieval and early modern Europe, Oyo, Dahomey, and Asante restored and maintained internal law and order where previously there was chaos and disorder. They all had laws that specifically prohibited the sale of their subjects for export. In Dahomey the law applied also to the servile population incorporated into society (Law 1991, 277–78). Contemporary European visitors to Dahomey testified to the prevalence of social order in the kingdom. For example, a 1728 European report stated that the king, Agaja, "cuts off the head of whoever steals only a cowry, one travels in his country with more security than in Europe, those who find something in the roads dare not touch it, it stays there till the one who lost it comes back, travellers are not attacked" (Law 1991, 277). Hugh Clapperton ([1829] 1966) traveling in the Oyo Empire in the early nineteenth century, at a time when the government was already very much weakened, was still able to report similar general social order. The extensive literature on Asante (Fynn 1971; Wilks 1975; Arhin 1967; Yarak 1990) consistently presents the picture of a powerful state maintaining effective control over its territories.

It is thus clear that these states succeeded in eliminating the disorder that preceded them and protected their subjects to a considerable degree from the ravages of the Atlantic slave trade, to which they had previously been exposed for decades. Unfortunately for Yorubaland, at the very moment when the people most needed Oyo's protection—as the European traders moved into Lagos as their slave-trading headquarters—the politico-military organization of the empire deteriorated. Significantly, it was Oyo's efforts to stamp out widespread kidnapping in its territories, following intensive European slave trading in Lagos, that created political complications leading to the first of the series of wars in Yorubaland in the nineteenth century. With the collapse of Oyo no other state emerged to keep the peace in Yorubaland in the face of growing demand for captives by the European traders. The Yoruba became the largest single source of captives for the Atlantic trade in the nineteenth century (Inikori 1992, 26–32; Ajayi and Smith 1971; Mabogunje and Omer-Cooper 1971; Law 1977).

But, while these strong states protected their subjects against capture and export, their traders and state functionaries participated in the sale of captives to the European merchants. For this reason they have been maligned in normative debates. How do we make sense of this?

To start, it should be stressed that the people they sold were captives from outside their states, and they had no obligation for their protection. The rulers did not see themselves and the exported captives as Africans—there did not exist at the time a pan-African ideology that united all Africans sentimentally with a common African identity. That sentiment developed much later in the twentieth century. As I have argued elsewhere (Inikori 1982), the rulers of these states were not above economic considerations as they dealt in various ways with the socioeconomic and political conditions created by large-scale European demand for captives. But their actions originated from very complex historical circumstances. Again, as argued elsewhere (Inikori 1992, 25–26), simplistic explanations conceal the complexities and hamper our understanding of the historical reality.

In the first place, these states needed resources to maintain state institutions, including large military organizations. The cost of doing this had been multiplied tenfold by the extremely violent conditions, within and between states, created by European demand for captives. The main source of revenue for the states in western Africa—revenue with which to pay for vital resources—had been trade. At the very moment when state budgets were rising exponentially due to the high cost of maintaining law and order and containing external attacks, export demand for commodities was reduced to almost nothing. Gold produced in Brazil with the labor of enslaved Africans was being imported into the Gold Coast to pay for captives in the eighteenth century. The employment of African labor to produce commodities for Atlantic commerce had become such a critical element in the process of socioeconomic development in western Europe and the Americas that the main focus of European demand had become captives and very little else. In the second half of the eighteenth century the value of all products purchased by the European traders was less than 10 percent of their total purchases (including captives, which made up over 90 percent of the total) in western Africa (Inikori 1986). At the same time, the violent process of procuring the "stolen goods" (the captives) had cut off much of the precontact interregional trade in products that linked Atlantic Africa to the savanna interior and ultimately to North Africa and the Middle East.[14]

Thus, the source of revenue for the states to pay for vital imports—including military materials (firearms, horses, etc.) and the patronage luxury goods needed to maintain cohesion among the ruling elites—was reduced virtually to the sale of captives. As happened to Oyo in the late eighteenth and early nineteenth centuries, inability to procure military materials and maintain state power, under conditions of expanding export demand for captives, ultimately produced chaos, which exposed both rulers and subjects to capture and export. In an important sense, these states faced what rational-choice political theorists call the prisoners' dilemma. It is significant that the Dahomean rulers, after their conquest of the coastal states, sent to the British government a detailed proposal for the development of plantations in Dahomey to support a trade in products. It is not important to know the motive behind the proposal—whether or not it was a plan specifically designed to abolish the trade in captives (Law 1991, 300–302). All that is important for our present purpose is that the Dahomean state and the ruling elites needed some source of revenue. Were it possible economically and politically for the British and Dahomean governments, working in cooperation, to create export markets and successfully develop this alternative source of revenue for Dahomeans, the state and the ruling elites would have been economically and politically better off.

Constrained by the structure of European demand and the associated limitations of the internal market, the strong states were compelled by economic and political necessity to organize elaborate systems of tribute-paying vassal states, whose duty it was to funnel captives from weakly organized communities to the stronger states for sale to the Europeans. To illustrate, in 1744 the Asante state successfully invaded Dagomba and imposed on the king an annual tribute of two thousand captives. As Izard and Ki-Zerbo narrate, "Dagomba's future was dogged by the aftermath of this treaty, which compelled it to continually find new sources of prisoners. The main role of Dagomba warriors became one of man-hunting among ethnic groups less organized politically and militarily for which purpose mercenaries were recruited. By the end of the eighteenth century, Dagomba was no more than a channel for Asante influence which reached as far as the borders of Mogho" (1992, 339–40).

This process of establishing captive-collecting vassal states, as the foregoing shows, depended on the continued widespread existence of politically fragmented communities. Had strong centralized states like Asante, Dahomey, and eighteenth-century Oyo been spread all over sub-Saharan Africa between 1650 and 1850, the balance of power among the states, like that in Europe from the sixteenth century, would have raised the political and economic cost of procuring captives to a level that would have made their employment in the Americas less economic. As the evidence in Senegambia and other parts of western Africa shows, persistent intervention by the European traders, and the vicious cycle of violence from massive slave trading, which reproduced fragmentation in many places, severely constrained the spread of strong centralized states (Barry 1992, 266–67, 278–85).

The evidence is clear that the Atlantic slave trade was caused by European demand for captives. As shown here, European explorations brought together in the Atlantic basin economies and societies at different levels of commercial and politico-military development. The commercial and politico-military advantage of the western European nations meant that the needs of their states and economies determined what was demanded and produced in the trade relations between western Europe and western Africa. European colonization of the Americas radically transformed those needs, which in turn radically changed what the European traders demanded in western Africa—from trade in products to trade in humans.

At the time European traders first began to ask for captives, Atlantic Africa—as distinguished from the savanna interior, which had traded small numbers of captives across the Sahara to the Middle East for centuries—had no previous experience of organized slave trade. In contrast, the Europeans came from societies that had experienced it. One of the main issues addressed here, therefore, is why the demand for slave labor in the Americas focused on Africa rather than Europe. The explanation presented turned out to be contrary to the impression that has been gaining ground recently. Instead of the existence of centralized states in western Africa being responsible for the supply of captives for export, as argued in recent debates, it was their absence that facilitated the supply of captives in response to growing European demand.[15] In Europe, on the other hand, the widespread existence of relatively strong centralized states, able to maintain law and order at home and offer blow for blow to external aggressors, raised the political and economic cost of captive exports for all rulers and imposed mutual restraint on European states. Earlier in the Middle Ages and early modern times political fragmentation, similar to that in sub-Saharan Africa between the mid-seventeenth and mid-nineteenth centuries, had similarly facilitated the supply of export captives in response to demand in the Mediterranean and the Middle East.

Thus, what weakened the struggle of communities in western Africa against the Atlantic slave trade was not centralized states but political fragmentation. Hence, the emergence of relatively strong centralized states was a solution to the problem in the communities incorporated into the states. Irrespective of how the states arose, for as long as their politico-military organizations remained strong and centralized authority remained firmly in control, the subjects were protected from capture and export. Fortunately for the European traders, the vast majority of communities in western Africa did not live in these states. In fact, the European traders consciously intervened in the political process in western Africa to prevent the generalized development of relatively strong large states.

I have attempted to make sense of the apparent paradox of the strong states that successfully protected their subjects against capture and export, while at the same time participating in the export of captives from outside their political borders. In the first place, no pan-African ideology existed at the time to sentimentally constrain their action. Second, the radically transformed structure of European demand, together with the disruption of interregional trade within western Africa caused by the overseas slave trade, left little alternative sources for the procurement of resources vital to the maintenance of state power and the defense of territorial integrity. It must be remembered that trade was the *raison d'être* of many precontact states; that continued to be the case from the beginning of contact through the eighteenth century. Resources vital to the state and the ruling elites were procured through trade. The detailed evidence from the Gold Coast shows clearly that both economic and political entrepreneurs in western Africa benefited enormously from the early European trade in products. Undoubtedly, merchants and political elites would have been better off had the development process associated with the early trade in products continued. So too would the commoners have been. Kea's summary of the socioeconomic changes on the Gold Coast, following the shift of European demand from products to captives, leaves one in no doubt about this: "There occurred, then, a significant change in the 'settlement order' of parts of the region, a movement away from urbanization and town growth and toward relatively widespread deurbanization. This shift constituted a major economic and demographic upheaval, amounting in effect to a fundamental transformation in the territorial organization of the productive forces" (1982, 11).

Thus, fundamental market changes in conjunction with the new sociopolitical conditions left the states and the ruling classes little alternative if they were to function effectively. On the surface the elites appear to have benefited from the export trade in captives. But when compared with the wealth accumulated from the early European trade in products and the opportunities for the productive investment of the profits because of the multiplier effects of that trade, it becomes clear that even the political and economic entrepreneurs were ultimate losers. Much of the long-lasting wealth associated with commerce in precolonial Atlantic Africa actually came from the product trade of the nineteenth century, which not only produced profits but also generated positive multiplier effects that offered opportunities for the productive investment of surpluses from commerce. In contrast, the export trade in captives generated negative externalities that left no significant opportunity for the capitalistic investment of profits from commerce. In the end, therefore, both elites and commoners in western Africa were victims in the transatlantic slave trade.

Notes

1. Blake (1977, 16) describes the early development of Portuguese shipment of captives from Africa, which began with traders from the port of Lagos in Portugal.

Long before the Portuguese explored the coast of western Africa, these traders went with their caravels to the coast of Barbary, where they purchased slaves from the Arabs. As the coast of Senegambia was explored, the Portuguese resorted to raids in the small coastal villages to procure captives for shipment to Portugal in the early years.

2. Based on evidence showing frequent hostility to the European traders by the coastal communities in western Africa, the point has been made that the attitude of ordinary people in the Atlantic ports—people who were not traders, not government functionaries, and could not afford to own slaves—to the large-scale export of captives that they observed daily deserves detailed research. See Inikori 1996.

3. As Daniel Evans notes, "If the eastern Adriatic was not a slave export region in Roman times, there is no evidence that it became one immediately following the collapse of the *Pax Romana* in the fifth century. . . . The limiting factor on the European slave trade during these centuries [fifth and sixth] was the lack of an adequate market, the absence of areas where there was sufficient stability, sufficient surplus, for an elite class to feel secure enough to risk investment in slaves" (1985, 42–43).

4. Patrick Manning (1990) makes a somewhat similar distinction in his three-regional analysis of the slave trade's impact on Africa.

5. Estimates by the authorities, with varying degrees of uncertainty, show that as early as 1200 western Europe already had 61 million people, expanding to 73 million by 1300. Although the general crisis of the fourteenth century significantly reduced the population, growth resumed in the second half of the fifteenth century and by 1550 the figure had risen to 78 million. See North and Thomas 1973, 71. Related to the geographical area of Western Europe (Wrigley 1983, 121), these figures give average population densities of 68 persons per square mile in 1200, 81 in 1300, and 87 in 1550. (Wrigley says the area of England, 50,333 square miles, represents 5.6 percent of the total area of western Europe. The area of western Europe, 898,804 square miles, employed to compute the densities, is derived from these figures). The highest possible average densities for western Africa in the fifteenth and sixteenth centuries that can reasonably be derived from the contending estimates by the authorities would be about 20 persons per square mile (Niane, 1984a, 156; 1984b, 684; Caldwell 1985, 483; Manning 1988, 123).

6. Population expansion in medieval Europe, by raising the ratio of population to land, induced the development of division of labor within and between regions in Europe, thereby stimulating the growth of local and interregional trade in western Europe (North and Thomas 1973). Intensive involvement in world trade centered in the Mediterranean further intensified the penetration of western European economies by commerce. These commercializing economies generated forces that were an important part of the political process leading to the emergence of the nation states in western Europe.

7. Boahen (1992, 422) says the 1629 map contains thirty-eight states. Possibly some of the forty-three political entities listed were not autonomous chiefdoms.

8. The problem of compliance with the terms led to restrictions on shipments by the Benin authorities. See Ryder 1969.

9. Most of the gold was produced in and around the forested Pra-Ofin basin. In the sixteenth and seventeenth centuries the region supplied more than half the gold exported from the coastal ports and the inland commercial centers like Bighu (Begho).

The impact of gold production on the Pra-Ofin basin is summarized by Kea: "Between the mid-fifteenth century and the middle decades of the seventeenth many new towns and villages were founded in and around the basin. Rural and urban settlement formation on this scale was rooted in population growth and the expansion of trade and agricultural, craft and gold production. In short, it can be linked to developments in the division of labor and production cycles governed by the process of expanded reproduction" (1982, 85–86). The wealthy men who cleared the forests and developed farmlands employed dependent workers, as some of the gold producers also did. Initially these workers were purchased from Malian Juula merchants, who brought them from the north. But from the late fifteenth century to the early seventeenth, they were imported by the Portuguese from Benin, the Kongo kingdom, and elsewhere (105). Kea believes that the employment of these purchased people gave rise to chattel slavery. The study of Asante by Ivor Wilks shows something different. Wilks demonstrates that the employment of purchased people by the Asante in the fifteenth and sixteenth centuries did not produce a slave class. The wealthy Asante who employed purchased workers took pains to avoid the creation of a slave class. The matriclan institution was invented during the period for this particular purpose: "One of the major thrusts in Asante social 'engineering' was towards prevention of the consolidation of a slave caste: those of unfree origins were assimilated as rapidly as possible into the class of free Asante commoners and their acquired status afforded full protection of the law. . . . But the precise way in which such task forces were incorporated and assimilated into the open-textured matriclans must remain for the present a matter for speculation; all that is sure is that incorporation and assimilation occurred, and that in consequence no slave caste arose within Asante society" (1977, 523–24).

10. The account by Hilton (1985, 179) shows the magnitude of the loss. The king was killed, together with most of the principal title holders, four provincial governors, and important court officials. In all ninety-five title holders died. Kongo losses totaled five thousand, while the Portuguese losses were minimal.

11. Heerman Abramsz to Assembly of Ten (the Dutch Company's governing committee in Holland), 23 November 1679, in Dantzig 1978, 13–20.

12. Engelgraaff Robberts to Assembly of Ten, Elmina, 15 August 1712, in Dantzig 1978, 168–69; see also p. 240 for the correspondence of c. 1730.

13. These invoices are among the Treasury series (T.70) in the Public Record Office, London. They are being studied in detail for work in progress.

14. The changing structure of imports being analyzed in my ongoing research mentioned earlier in the chapter shows this clearly. For a preliminary discussion of the findings, see Inikori, "The Development of Entrepreneurship in Africa: Southeastern Nigeria During the Era of the Transatlantic Slave Trade," in Alusine Jalloh and Toyin Falola, eds., *Black Business and Economic Power* (Rochester: University of Rochester Press, 2002): 41–79.

15. See Gates (2000) for the recent debate provoked by the television series *Wonders of the African World,* which he produced. The series contains statements to the effect that the Atlantic slave trade would not have occurred had African states and their rulers not procured and sold captives. The reaction to the series by Africanists, black and white, has been overwhelmingly negative.

BIBLIOGRAPHY

Abu-Lughod, Janet L. 1989. *Before European Hegemony: The World System, A.D. 1250–1350.* New York: Oxford University Press.

Ajayi, J. F. Ade, and Robert Smith. 1971. *Yoruba Warfare in the Nineteenth Century.* Ibadan: University of Ibadan Press.

Akinjogbin, I. A. 1967. *Dahomey and Its Neighbours, 1708–1818.* Cambridge: Cambridge University Press.

Arhin, Kwame. 1967. "The Structure of Greater Ashanti, 1700–1824." *Journal of African History* 8 (1): 65–85.

Barry, Boubacar. 1992. "Senegambia from the Sixteenth to the Eighteenth Century: Evolution of the Wolof, Sereer, and 'Tukuloor.'" In B. A. Ogot, ed., *Africa from the Sixteenth to the Eighteenth Century,* vol. 5 of *General History of Africa.* Berkeley: University of California Press.

———. 1998. *Senegambia and the Atlantic Slave Trade.* Trans. Ayi Kwei Armah. Cambridge: Cambridge University Press.

Blake, John W. 1977. *West Africa: Quest for God and Gold, 1454–1578: A Survey of the First Century of White Enterprise in West Africa, with Particular Reference to the Achievement of the Portuguese and Their Rivalries with other European Powers.* London: Curzon Press.

Boahen, A. Adu. 1992. "The States and Cultures of the Lower Guinean Coast." In B. A. Ogot, ed., *Africa from the Sixteenth to the Eighteenth Century,* vol. 5 of *General History of Africa.* Berkeley: University of California Press.

Caldwell, John C. 1985. "The Social Repercussions of Colonial Rule: Demographic Aspects." In A. Adu Boahen, ed., *Africa under Colonial Domination, 1880–1935,* vol. 7 of *General History of Africa.* Berkeley: University of California Press.

Clapperton, Hugh. 1966. *Journal of a Second Expedition into the Interior of Africa from the Bight of Benin to Soccatoo.* 1829. Reprint, London: Frank Cass.

Daaku, Kwame Yeboa. 1970. *Trade and Politics on the Gold Coast, 1600–1720: A Study of the African Reaction to European Trade.* Oxford: Clarendon Press.

Dantzig, A. van. 1978. *The Dutch and the Guinea Coast, 1674–1742: A Collection of Documents from the General State Archive at The Hague.* Accra: Ghana Academy of Arts and Sciences.

Davies, K. G. 1974. *The North Atlantic World in the Seventeenth Century.* Minneapolis: University of Minnesota Press.

Eltis, David. 1993. "Europeans and the Rise and Fall of African Slavery in the Americas." *American Historical Review* 98:1399–1423.

———. 2000. *The Rise of African Slavery in the Americas.* Cambridge: Cambridge University Press.

Evans, Daniel. 1985. "Slave Coast of Europe." *Slavery and Abolition* 6 (1): 41–58.

Evans, William McKee. 1980. "From the Land of Canaan to the Land of Guinea: The Strange Odyssey of the 'Sons of Ham.'" *American Historical Review* 85 (February): 15–43.

Fynn, John Kofi. 1971. *Asante and Its Neighbours, 1700–1807.* London: Longman.

Gates, Henry Louis, Jr. 2000. "The Debate on Henry Louis Gates, Jr.'s 'Wonders of the African World.'" *Black Scholar* 30 (spring): 2–51.

Hilton, Anne. 1985. *The Kingdom of Kongo.* Oxford: Clarendon Press.

Inikori, Joseph E. 1982. Introduction to Joseph E. Inikori, ed., *Forced Migration: The Impact of the Export Slave Trade on African Societies.* London and New York: Hutchinston and Africana.

———. 1986. "West Africa's Seaborne Trade, 1750–1850: Volume, Structure, and Implications." In G. Liesegang, H. Pasch, and A. Jones, eds., *Figuring African Trade. Proceedings of the Symposium on the Quantification and Structure of the Import and Export and Long Distance Trade in Africa in the Nineteenth Century (c. 1800–1913), St. Augustin, 3–6 January 1983.* Berlin: Dietrich Reimer Verlag.

———. 1992. *The Chaining of a Continent: Export Demand for Captives and the History of Africa South of the Sahara, 1450–1870.* Kingston, Jamaica: Institute of Social and Economic Research, University of the West Indies.

———. 1996. "Measuring the Unmeasured Hazards of the Atlantic Slave Trade: Documents Relating to the British Trade." *Revue française d'histoire d'outre-mer* 83 (312): 53–92.

———. 1998. "The Known, the Unknown, the Knowable, and the Unknowable: Evidence and the Evaluation of Evidence in the Measurement of the Trans-Atlantic Slave Trade." Paper presented at the Conference on Transatlantic Slaving and the African Diaspora, Williamsburg, Virginia, 11–13 September.

———. 2002. "The Development of Entrepreneurship in Africa: Southeastern Nigeria during the Era of the Transatlantic Slave Trade." In Alusine Jalloh and Toyin Falola, eds., *Black Business and Economic Power.* Rochester: University of Rochester Press.

Inikori, Joseph E., and Stanley L. Engerman. 1992. "Introduction: Gainers and Losers in the Atlantic Slave Trade." In Joseph E. Inikori and Stanley L. Engerman, eds., *The Atlantic Slave Trade: Effects on Economies, Societies, and Peoples in Africa, the Americas, and Europe.* Durham: Duke University Press.

Izard, M., and J. Ki-Zerbo. 1992. "From the Niger to the Volta." In B. A. Ogot, ed., *Africa from the Sixteenth to the Eighteenth Century,* vol. 5 of *General History of Africa.* Berkeley: University of California Press.

Kea, Ray A. 1982. *Settlement, Trade, and Polities in the Seventeenth-Century Gold Coast.* Baltimore: Johns Hopkins University Press.

Klein, Herbert S. 1999. *The Atlantic Slave Trade.* Cambridge: Cambridge University Press.

Klein, Martin A. 1998. *Slavery and Colonial Rule in French West Africa.* Cambridge: Cambridge University Press.

Latham, A. J. H. 1973. *Old Calabar, 1600–1891: The Impact of the International Economy upon a Traditional Society.* Oxford: Clarendon Press.

Law, Robin. 1977. *The Oyo Empire, c. 1600–1836: A West African Imperialism in the Era of the Atlantic Slave Trade.* Oxford: Clarendon Press.

———. 1986. "Dahomey and the Slave Trade: Reflections on the Historiography of the Rise of Dahomey." *Journal of African History* 27:237–67.

———. 1991. *The Slave Coast of West Africa: The Impact of the Atlantic Slave Trade on an African Society.* Oxford: Clarendon Press.

Mabogunje, A. L., and J. D. Omer-Cooper. 1971. *Owu in Yoruba History.* Ibadan: University of Ibadan Press.

Manning, Patrick. 1988. "The Impact of Slave Trade Exports on the Population of the

Western Coast of Africa, 1700–1850." In Serge Daget, ed., *De la traite à l'esclavage: Actes du colloque international sur la traite des noirs.* Vol. 2. Paris: Société Française d'Histoire d'Outre-Mer.

———. 1990. *Slavery and African Life: Occidental, Oriental, and African Slave Trades.* Cambridge: Cambridge University Press.

McPhee, Allan. 1926. *The Economic Revolution in British West Africa.* Reprint, London: Frank Cass, 1971.

Niane, Djibril Tamsir. 1984a. "Mali and the Second Mandingo Expansion." In D. T. Niane, ed., *Africa from the Twelfth to the Sixteenth Century,* vol. 4 of *General History of Africa.* Berkeley: University of California Press.

———. 1984b. "Conclusion." In D. T. Niane, ed., *Africa from the Twelfth to the Sixteenth Century,* vol. 4 of *General History of Africa.* Berkeley: University of California Press.

North, Douglass C., and Robert P. Thomas. 1973. *The Rise of the Western World: A New Economic History.* Cambridge: Cambridge University Press.

Ogot, B. A., ed. 1992. *Africa from the Sixteenth to the Eighteenth Century.* Vol. 5 of *General History of Africa.* Berkeley: University of California Press.

Pelteret, David. 1981. "Slave Raiding and Slave Trading in Early England." In Peter Clemoes, ed., *Anglo-Saxon England.* Cambridge: Cambridge University Press.

Phillips, William D., Jr. 1985. *Slavery from Roman Times to the Early Transatlantic Trade.* Minneapolis: University of Minnesota Press.

Ryder, A. F. C. 1969. *Benin and the Europeans, 1485–1897.* London: Longman.

Smith, Robert. 1988. *Kingdoms of the Yoruba.* 3d. ed. Madison: University of Wisconsin Press.

Strickland, Matthew. 1996. *War and Chivalry: The Conduct and Perception of War in England and Normandy, 1066–1217.* Cambridge: Cambridge University Press.

Thornton, John K. 1992. *Africa and Africans in the Making of the Atlantic World, 1400–1680.* Cambridge: Cambridge University Press.

Vansina, Jan. 1989. "Deep-Down Time: Political Tradition in Central Africa." *History in Africa* 16:341–62.

———. 1990. *Paths in the Rainforests: Toward a History of Political Tradition in Equatorial Africa.* London: James Currey.

———, and T. Obenga. 1992. "The Kongo Kingdom and Its Neighbours." In B. A. Ogot, ed., *Africa from the Sixteenth to the Eighteenth Century,* vol. 5 of *General History of Africa.* Berkeley: University of California Press.

Wilks, Ivor. 1975. *Asante in the Nineteenth Century: The Structure and Evolution of a Political Order.* Cambridge: Cambridge University Press.

———. 1977. "Land, Labour, Capital, and the Forest Kingdom of Asante: A Model of Early Change." In J. Friedman and M. J. Rowlands, eds., *The Evolution of Social Systems.* London: Duckworth.

Wondji, C. 1992. "The States and Cultures of the Upper Guinean Coast." In B. A. Ogot, ed., *Africa from the Sixteenth to the Eighteenth Century,* vol. 5 of *General History of Africa.* Berkeley: University of California Press.

Wrigley, A. E. 1983. "The Growth of Population in Eighteenth-Century England: A Conundrum Resolved." *Past and Present* 98 (February): 121–50.

Yarak, Larry W. 1990. *Asante and the Dutch, 1744–1873.* Oxford: Clarendon Press.

CHAPTER 12
Shipboard Revolts, African Authority, and the Transatlantic Slave Trade

David Richardson

VIOLENT AND NONVIOLENT RESISTANCE by Africans against their enslavement by Europeans has during the last half century been a constant theme in the literature on transatlantic slavery. That literature has helped to put to rest, in the words of one eminent historian, "the myth of slave docility and quiescence" (Genovese 1979, xxiii). It has also been overwhelmingly concerned with slave resistance in the Americas, even in those cases when it is claimed that plantation-based revolts were but one element in a spectrum of resistance that transcended Africa, the middle passage, and the Americas (Craton 1982, 14, 27–28). A few studies of slave resistance in Africa and in the middle passage have, nevertheless, appeared. This chapter further redresses the imbalance in the literature by examining patterns of slave revolts onboard ships at the African coast and in the Atlantic crossing between about 1690 and 1810. Using new quantitative data, it also attempts to uncover explanations of these revolts and to assess their impact on the level of the slave trade as well as its structure. The analysis suggests that rebelliousness by slaves onboard ship and the resulting efforts by European carriers of slaves to curb such behavior reduced shipments below what they would have been in the absence of resistance. It also exposes, however, major variations in the incidence of revolts through time and, equally important, by coastal origin. These cannot be explained by reference to failure of European management regimes onboard slave ships but seem instead to be rooted in differences within the political economy of the various African slave supply regions. Overall, therefore, it appears that patterns of shipboard revolt shed important light on the impact of Africa and Africans on the organization and scale of the Atlantic slave trade as well as on the relationship of the trade in enslaved Africans to the development of Atlantic history.

Whether as organizers or as victims of the transatlantic traffic in slaves, Africans had a major influence on the course of Atlantic history between 1500 and 1850. African merchants retained control over the trade in slaves within Africa and thus helped to determine the magnitude and coastal distribution of shipments from the African coast.[1] Although the role of African political leaders and merchants in shaping the structure of the Atlantic slave trade is increasingly acknowledged, the position of Africans and their descendants as victims of slavery has, for obvious reasons, attracted far more attention. The scale of surpluses generated by enslaved Africans and appropriated by whites have been central to discussions of Western economic development and continue to provoke debate. So too does the resistance of enslaved Africans to exploitation and oppression by their owners. In common with plantation-based resistance to slavery, resistance by Africans to enslavement in Africa or in the Atlantic crossing has been the subject of a number of studies (Greene 1944; Mannix and Cowley 1962, 107–11; Wax 1966; Uya 1976; Piersen 1977; Rathbone 1986; McGowan 1990, 14–26; Postma 1990, 165–68; Inikori 1996, 64–74; Palmer 1997). Most focus on more than one form of resistance but all provide important evidence on shipboard revolts or mutinies, events that, according to one historian, were "vastly more serious" than other forms of noncooperation since they "came closer to a true political reaction to the socioeconomic system" (Craton 1982, 53). Notable among the features of revolts are the terror associated with them; the savage retribution exacted by ships' crews, the substantial losses of life involved, and the concentration of revolts on ships at the African coast.[2] There has, however, been no attempt to explore the relationship of shipboard slave revolts to either ethnic patterns of resistance to slavery on plantations, the structural characteristics of the slave trade (such as its coastal distribution in Africa), or their relationship to the political economy of slavery within Africa.[3]

Information relating to revolts derives primarily from European shipping records. The principal sources used are French records of slaving voyages included in the two-volume Mettas compendium (1978–84), data on revolts on Dutch ships provided by Postma (1990), and British newspapers. The last include *Lloyd's List* and various provincial publications.[4] Most of the evidence gleaned from these sources relates, as one would expect, to eighteenth-century French, Dutch, and British ships. Information on revolts is thus less representative of the Atlantic slave trade than the larger voyage set, which also includes information on Portuguese, Danish, and U.S. slaving activities. It does, nevertheless, offer a much larger sample of evidence of shipboard slave revolts and coastal incidents of violence against slave ships than any previous study. Moreover, since it shares fields of information in common with a recently published slave voyage data set (Eltis et al. 1999), one is able to make comparisons between conditions onboard ships that experienced revolts and those that appear not to have. This provides important insights into the circumstances in which revolts occurred on slave ships.

A revolt is defined as any collective act of rebellion or violence by Africans, slave or otherwise, against slave ships. It is assumed that such acts of violence involved the death of at least one person. At present, evidence exists on some 483 cases of violent actions by Africans against slave ships and their crew. They include 92 instances of attacks from the shore by apparently "free" Africans against ships or their longboats and 388 cases of shipboard insurrection by slaves. The latter are my prime concern in this chapter, though some attention is also given to shore-based attacks. The cases of insurrection involved over 360 ships, some of which experienced more than one insurrection. They also include 22 instances of planned rather than actual rebellion as well as eight cases where the distinction between insurrection and shore-based attack (or "cut-off") is ambiguous. Of the 388 insurrections, some 350 (or 92 percent) fell within the period from 1698 to 1807. Given gaps in records and the paucity of evidence on shipboard revolts on ships other than the French and British, it is difficult to determine the proportion of ships that experienced an insurrection. The evidence so far uncovered suggests perhaps as many as 10 percent did so.[5]

Predicting insurrections was difficult, but owners of slave ships were well aware of their possibility and instructed commanders to take appropriate measures to prevent them. For instance, William Barry, master of the *Dispatch,* which sailed from Bristol in 1725, was advised that as soon as he began to take on slaves at Andony in the Bight of Biafra, he should "Let the Knetting be fix'd [mast?] high fore and aft" and "keep [the slaves] shackled & hand bolte[d] fearing their rising or Leaping Overboard."[6] A common stereotype was that Igbo from the Bight of Biafra were unusually prone to commit suicide and Barry was not alone among masters intending to trade in the region to be ordered to encase his vessel with nets (Wax 1973, 395; Isichei 1976, 44). Owners also resorted to other measures to deter revolts or escapes. They included investments in firearms, swivel guns, and cannon and in extra crew to supervise slaves.

Although revolts by slaves occurred on perhaps one transatlantic voyage in ten, almost all the ships affected still managed to reach the Americas with a large proportion of their original captives. While insurrections occasionally produced heavy loss of life among slaves and their captors and the number of deaths varied widely, the mean number of slaves killed in insurrections was about twenty-five—or probably no more than 10 percent of those onboard when uprisings occurred.[7] These figures do not, of course, allow for injuries and the loss of market value of the slaves surviving an uprising. Perhaps no more than one percent of slaves entering the Atlantic slave trade in between 1500 and 1867—or one hundred thousand Africans—died in revolts at the African coast or in the Atlantic crossing. This was one-fifteenth of all those who died in the middle passage between Africa and the Americas.[8]

While the direct cost to traders of shipboard slave revolts was modest, it would be wrong to assume that such events—or even the threat of them—had little or no effect on the level of slaving activities. That slave revolts were common enough to induce traders to invest in preventive measures meant that the costs of slaving voyages were higher than they might otherwise have been. Crucial factors in driving up the expense were the cost of barricades and other fixtures on ships and of the extra crew typically carried by such ships. Crew numbers on slave ships were normally 50 percent higher than on produce carriers of similar size and largely accounted for the fact that about 18 percent of middle passage costs were attributable to the potential of slaves to revolt in transit. The latter figure in turn suggests that, from 1680 to 1800 at least, without shipboard or coastal resistance the number of slaves shipped across the Atlantic would have been perhaps 9 percent greater than it actually was. Put another way, Africans who died resisting slave traders as well as those who resisted unsuccessfully and survived to work on plantations saved perhaps six hundred thousand other Africans from being shipped to the Americas in the eighteenth century or one million during the whole history of the trade (Behrendt, Eltis, and Richardson 2001).

The conditions that increased the propensity of slaves to rebel are difficult to identify. Mannix and Cowley argued that "as long as a vessel lay at anchor, the slaves could dream of seizing it," but the "opportunity was lost as soon as the vessel put to sea." (1962, 111).[9] Palmer, by contrast, claims "many Africans resisted enslavement during the voyages" (1997, 32). My data tend to corroborate the latter view. Indeed, they suggest that insurrections could occur at more or less any time. Furthermore, just over half of revolts occurred while ships were moored off the coast, just over a tenth between the end of loading and the start of crossing, and about a third on the middle passage.[10] The higher incidence during embarkation suggests that ships often experienced revolts before they were fully loaded. It might also seem to endorse contemporary suggestions that slaves were more inclined to rebel while they were still in sight of Africa. Loading times of ships in Africa, however, were normally at least twice as long as passage times across the Atlantic (Eltis and Richardson 1995, 478). This implies that revolts were slightly more likely in the crossing than during the African phases of voyages and that proximity to the African shore made little difference. As far as enslaved Africans were concerned, conditions that offered opportunities to escape from captivity seem to have been seized upon wherever and whenever they presented themselves.

Further light can be cast on those conditions by comparing ships that experienced a revolt with those that did not.[11] This comparison suggests that ships experiencing revolt tended to be larger and to lose more crew to disease in Africa and in the Atlantic crossing. On the whole, larger ships took longer to complete their loading and thus had more exposure to risk of revolt. The same applies to ships on which the crew was decimated by disease and where, as a result, management presented exceptional difficulty.

More surprising findings emerge, however, when one begins to look at revolts in the context of regional patterns of slaving activity. Comparing again ships that experienced revolts with those that did not, those trading south of Upper Guinea that had revolts had proportionately more women than normal among their captives. Why this was so is unclear. Men normally led revolts and also suffered much higher levels of casualties in such incidents than women, but the role of women in supporting or encouraging revolts has perhaps not been fully appreciated (White 1985, 63–64).[12] The management of female slaves onboard ship seems, nevertheless, to have provided opportunities for them to participate in revolts. Unlike men, women were rarely shackled, even at the African coast. Moreover, though usually housed separately from adult males, women were often accommodated close to the officers' quarters as well as to weapon stores. Because women were subject to sexual abuse by the crew, they may also have had better access to information vital to the planning of revolts. While tentative explanations of women's involvement in revolts are possible, why this exhibited regional variations still remains obscure.

TABLE 12.1

Regional Shares of Violence and of Transatlantic Slave Departures, 1519–1867 (percent)

	Senegambia	Sierra Leone	Windward Coast	Gold Coast	Bight of Benin	Bight of Biafra	West-central Africa	Southeast Africa
Slave revolts	22.0	9.3	5.2	16.2	19.7	13.0	11.3	3.2
All violent incidents	21.5	12.3	7.3	14.4	18.0	13.2	10.4	2.8
Slave departures	4.5	3.7	1.7	9.4	18.4	13.7	44.2	4.4

Source: Shares of violent incidents calculated from Eltis, Behrendt, and Richardson n.d.; share of slave departures from Eltis 2001.

Even more striking variations emerge when the focus shifts from gender to concentrations in the incidence of revolts by region of trade. Evidence on the geography of revolts is given in Table 12.1. This shows that the incidence of revolts varied remarkably according to trading location in Africa, with four areas of trade—Senegambia, Sierra Leone, the Windward Coast, and Gabon–Cape Lopez—being associated with much higher rates of shipboard revolt than others. Compared, for example, to the Slave Coast (or Bight of Benin), revolts were up to eight times more likely on ships trading at Senegambia and Gabon–Cape Lopez and two and a half times more likely on those trading at Sierra Leone and the Windward Coast. The differentials are, moreover, even more remarkable if one takes west-central Africa or ports such as Bonny and Calabar, in the Bight of Biafra, as benchmarks. Compared to ships trading at these places, those trading at Senegambia and Gabon–Cape Lopez were fourteen to thirty times more likely to experience a revolt. Overall, rebellions on ships trading at places to the north of the Gold Coast and at Gabon–Cape Lopez were about four times greater than one might have expected from their share of slave shipments from Atlantic Africa to the Americas.[13]

Regional variations in the incidence of shipboard insurrections are not explained by loading times of ships or crew mortality rates. Ships trading at Senegambia, Sierra Leone, and the Windward Coast tended to spend longer at the coast, but differences in mean loading times throughout the coast were modest and variations in loading times within the three regions noted were not exceptional (Eltis and Richardson 1995, 477–78). More significant, ostensibly, was crew mortality, which exhibited much greater levels of regional variation (Behrendt 1997). Mortality rates on Liverpool ships at the African coast in 1770–75 averaged 39.1 per thousand crew months, but the range of mortality rates among trading centers was wide, ranging from 11.8 to 85.0 per thousand crew months. Moreover, Gambia and the Windward Coast were among the places with the highest mortality rates. Although this finding might seem to offer some explanation for the higher incidence of slave insurrection on ships leaving these areas, inspection of crew mortality levels in other regions questions its significance. For example, while ships leaving the Bight of Benin experienced relatively few revolts, mortality rates of crew on ships trading there matched those of Gambia and the Windward Coast. In addition, mortality of crew on ships trading at Sierra Leone, a region associated with high levels of shipboard insurrection, was lower than on ships trading to the Bight of Biafra, which had some of the lowest levels of insurrection. Although high rates of crew deaths or sickness on individual ships leaving Africa may have been important in prompting insurrections, death rates of crew in themselves are insufficient to account for the higher rate of insurrection on ships leaving from places north of the Gold Coast.

European shippers believed that some ethnic groups were more prone to rebel than others. In 1790 Bristol trader James Fraser suggested that security for slaves from Bonny, in the Bight of Biafra, had to be greater than for those from Angola.[14] Writing three decades later, John Adams drew further distinctions between rebellious slaves shipped at Bonny when commenting on the Ibibios or "Quaws," said by Adams to have "a ferocious aspect." Ibibio were, he suggested, "always . . . found to be the ringleaders" when insurrections took place on ships from Bonny. Indeed, he argued, they were "often the only slaves concerned in such events, "the Heebos [Igbo] remaining passive spectators" (1966, 132). Writing of the Danish slave trade from the western Bight of Benin, Paul Isert made similar distinctions in the propensities of slaves of different ethnic backgrounds to rebel. Observing that the "Krepees" (Ewe) were ringleaders of a revolt onboard the ship on which he left the coast in 1785, he noted that the Dunko on the same ship were from "a most well-mannered nation" (1992, 177).[15]

In 1753 a group of Liverpool merchants instructed the master of their Gambia-bound ship to "keep a watchfull Eye over you[r] Slaves to prevent any insurrections, which has too often been the Case, especially amongst those of Gambia."[16] Thirty years later a French captain trading in Senegal tried to distinguish Bambara from Wolof. Echoing reports of a revolt on the English ship *Brome* in 1693

(Eltis 2000, 229–30), the Frenchman claimed that, though it was not necessary to shackle the Bambara when ships were in the lower river, "one, and even two pairs of irons is scarce enough for every single captive of the Yolofs [Wolof]."[17] According to this captain, while on the lower Senegal River the Wolof "were still too near the confines of their own country to let any opportunity of recovering their liberty to escape them," whereas the Bambara, "who come from the interior parts of Africa . . . never think of making their escape." Similarly, a shipmaster with experience of trade at Sierra Leone and Sherbro claimed that slaves coming from "the country immediately upon the sea coast" tended to be fettered well into the middle passage, whereas those from inland "are liberated as soon as the ship leaves the Coast of Africa."[18] Whether true or not, European traders seem to have singled out slaves from Senegambia and parts of Upper Guinea as being prone to rebellion.

The picture of the scale and trend of slave exports from Senegambia to America in the eighteenth century has recently undergone radical revision. Earlier estimates based on contemporary comments suggest that less than two hundred thousand slaves were exported in the century after 1711. They also suggest that exports peaked at about three to four thousand slaves a year before 1740, before declining modestly during the following two or three decades. A brief recovery was then thought to have occurred during the 1780s before exports fell precipitately during the 1790s and remained at very low levels thereafter (Curtin 1975, 164–66). Calculations based on shipping data, however, now reveal that some three hundred thousand slaves were carried away from Senegambia for America between 1701 and 1800 (Eltis 2001, 44). Moreover, whereas earlier studies suggested exports declined after 1740, the new data show that there was a major surge in exports in the third quarter of the century, with shipments throughout much of the later eighteenth century being two to three times greater than previously assumed. Contrary to what was previously thought, therefore, Senegambia was a significant net contributor to the overall rise in slave shipments from Africa to America after 1750. This rise in both Senegambian and global exports took place against the background of an Atlantic-wide inflation in slave prices. As Table 12.2 shows, the mid-century surge in Senegambian exports also coincided with a general rise in shipboard revolts. This raises two questions. First, how did suppliers in the region meet this increased transatlantic demand for slaves? Second, was increased supply of slaves for export connected with shipboard revolts, and if so, how?

Though drought periodically helped to generate slaves, warfare and raiding were the principal sources of slaves shipped from Senegambia to America. In-

Table 12.2
Shares of Violence and of Transatlantic Slave Departures by Quarter Century, 1651–1867 (percent)

	1651–75	1676–1700	1701–25	1726–50	1751–75	1776–1800	1801–25	1826–67
Slave revolts	0.2	3.6	12.5	19.9	36.7	20.7	4.6	1.8
All violent incidents	0.2	3.1	10.3	19.0	40.8	20.0	5.2	1.4
Slave departures	2.3	5.0	9.3	12.7	18.5	18.7	15.6	17.8

Source: Same as Table 12.1.

deed, some historians argue that slaving activities in western Sudan, including Senegambia, became inextricably intertwined with the militarization of states in the region. Armies, or "raiding forces of professional warriors"—mostly employed by "warrior states" such as Kajoor and Bawol near the coast or by Muslim states in the far interior such as Segu, Bundu, Futa Toro, and Futa Jallon—were vital to the generation of slaves (Klein 1992, 27–30; Barry 1998, 61–125). It is also argued that from the late seventeenth century inland states became increasingly important as sources of slaves for the Atlantic traffic, with Muslim trade networks being crucial to the delivery of slaves to the coast.[19] Some of the slaves exported from Senegambia were victims of religious wars, or jihad, though it appears that as the eighteenth century progressed religion often became a pretext for war, the principal purpose of which was to procure slaves to exchange for imported goods, including arms.[20] Such developments, together with the gender composition of slave shipments, have inclined historians to claim that in the eighteenth century most slaves shipped from Senegambia to America originated in the far interior, with only small proportions being supplied from areas near the coast (Curtin 1975; Klein 1992; Searing 1993). This suggests that a spatial separation of the more violent initial enslavement processes from those related to marketing of slaves began to occur in Senegambia from the late seventeenth century onward.

It is possible—even probable—that, as Senegambia's involvement in the Atlantic slave trade rose after 1750, the processes promoting separation of enslavement from marketing of slaves were arrested or perhaps reversed as suppliers near coastal areas sought to gain from the burgeoning American demand for labor. Some scholars acknowledge this possibility. Curtin has observed that the supply of "Bambara" from the interior "dropped off" when the king of Segu, Mamari Kulubali, died in 1755 and then remained low in the 1760s and 1770s. As a result, he suggests, the slaves shipped from both Gambia and Senegal in this period "came from sources closer to the coast" (Curtin 1975, 180). Similarly, Searing (1993, 32–33) has estimated that in most years between 1700 and 1790 slaves from the lower Senegal River constituted no more than 10 percent of all transatlantic exports from Senegambia but that in some years the proportion rose to 30 percent. The last figure seems to have applied to the periods of famine in 1750–56 and other years in the second half of the eighteenth and early nineteenth centuries. Both Curtin and Searing made such claims, however, without fully appreciating that slave exports from Senegambia were increasing sharply during the period in question or that rising prices may have given incentives to near-coast, intramarginal suppliers, even in areas that were relatively depopulated, to expand their activities. The latter perhaps presupposes a lack of political authority capable of regulating or restricting entry into slave raiding and trafficking, a position that seems to accord well with the historical literature. Despite the comments of Curtin and Searing, historians still seem to have underestimated levels of enslavement activities and their attendant violence in lower and middle Senegal and Gambia after 1750.

Evidence is emerging of a growth of slave procurement in areas in Senegambia closer to the coast after 1750. Data on the ethnicity of slaves arriving in Louisiana from Senegambia between 1723 and 1820 show that throughout this period Wolof and Mandinga comprised larger proportions of arrivals than Bambara from the far interior of the region. Wolof speakers from near the coast were particularly important in the late 1760s and again in 1777–93, and were not the only near-coast group from Senegambia to be identified in Louisiana records (Hall 1999).[21] This evidence is consistent with data on the age and gender of slaves entering the transatlantic trade in eighteenth-century Senegambia.[22] Across the century, of the slaves shipped from Senegambia to America, 68.5 percent were male and 17.0 percent were children. Before 1750, however, child ratios were substantially lower than the eighteenth-century average, while the ratio of males shipped in 1726–50 was as high as 78.7 percent. By contrast, child ratios among slaves from Senegambia rose sharply after 1750, reaching 34.6 in 1766–70 and remaining above 20 percent in most years through to 1790, while ratios of males generally fell below 70 percent and reached a low of 56.9 percent in 1766–70. The last were years when Wolof apparently comprised the largest single group of slaves shipped from Senegambia. As children normally fetched lower prices than adults at the coast and—compared to adults, particularly men—could not bear the higher transport costs to the coast associated with seizure far inland, the sharp rise of child ratios after 1750 is consistent with intensification of enslavement activity near the coast. On the available evidence, the peak of such activity may have occurred around 1770, when Senegambian exports were at their height, but near-coast slave procurement seems to have remained important throughout the late eighteenth century.

Other patterns of trade-related activities in Senegambia are not only consistent with an intensification of near-coast slaving activities after 1750 but also reveal some of its possible consequences. On the evidence of export figures, local production of gum, which was concentrated to the north of middle and lower Senegal and on the Mauritanian coast, underwent a major decline in volume between the 1730s and 1780s (Curtin 1975, 216, 331).[23] This is difficult to explain in demand terms since the price of gum rose sharply during the same period, thereby offsetting the fall in physical exports. It is more likely, therefore, that other factors inhibited shipments of gum. These probably included restrictions on labor supplies for gum production arising from competing demands for slaves for export. One British trader noted in 1766 that "the King of Brack [Walo] finding the slave trade to answer better to him than the Gum, has quarrelled with his Neighbours, and obstructed the Moors from bringing any [gum] down for fear of being sold for Slaves." Unable to buy gum, the trader decided "to Pick up as many Slaves as I could get and Sail away."[24] Other British traders also seem to have experienced problems in purchasing gum at this time, taking in slaves instead. The relative profitability of slave trafficking after 1750, therefore, may have encouraged merchants of lower or middle Senegal to switch to slave production, with apparently important repercussions, if the report of the "king of Brack's" quarrels with his neighbors is accurate, for levels of local political conflict.[25] The spread of such conflict in turn had repercussions for the security of European ships trading on the river, as the complainant against the "king of Brack" noted. It was, he observed, "very dangerous to go up and down the River [Senegal], being Shot at from the two opposite shores." Remarks such as these are underlined by statistical evidence, which shows that shore-based attacks by Africans leading to the loss of European ships were up to twenty times more likely on the Senegal and Gambia Rivers than elsewhere in Atlantic Africa. Such attacks were, moreover, heavily concentrated from 1750 to 1790, reflecting perhaps increasing lawlessness along the lower parts of the rivers as expanding slaving activities promoted political instability.[26]

Senegambia was not alone in depending on enslaving people from near-coast areas to sustain the surge in its exports after 1750. Large proportions of the slaves taken by European traders from Sierra Leone and the Windward Coast probably came from near the coast, though some also came from far inland.[27] These regions emerged as major sources for America only after 1750, whereas Senegambia had longstanding links to the Atlantic slave trade dating from the seventeenth century or earlier. In this respect, Senegambia's involvement was similar to that of the Gold Coast, the Slave Coast, the Bight of Biafra, and Angola. In these regions, however, rising American demand after 1750 seems to have been met more by extending enslavement frontiers inland than, as in Senegambia's case, by intensifying slaving activities nearer the coast.[28] The response of suppliers in Senegambia to transatlantic demand in 1750–75 was, therefore, perhaps unusual, prompting closer identification geographically between enslavement and slave-marketing functions. Was the peculiarity of the political economy of slaving in Senegambia in this period linked to revolts on ships leaving the region?

Answering this question invites speculation, but contemporary remarks relating to the higher propensity of slaves from near-coast societies to revolt and to the resentment of such slaves at being separated through sale to Europeans begin to provide the basis of an answer. Implicit in such remarks was the central issue of who, among Africans, might and might not be sold to Europeans. It is widely agreed that those groups involved in enslavement activity, including Muslims, typically sought victims from outside their own ethnic group or "nation." As a result, some states or warlords sustained themselves by war against, and enslavement of, "outsiders." Some might be sold directly into the export trade.[29] Others were retained or absorbed into family structures as domestic slaves, thereby augmenting the large servile populations in Senegambia and the western Sudan more generally that were born into slavery. Domestic slaves were employed in the household as well as in commercial activities such as grain, textile, and gum production. Where they were not directly employed in productive activities, they could be employed as *ceddo* or *tonjon* (or elite warriors). Persistently troublesome domestic slaves or those found guilty of crimes might be sold, but there were constraints on this, especially in Senegambia.[30]

Although religious wars may have contributed to creating insecurity in eighteenth-century Senegambia, the political instability accompanying sharply rising exports after 1750 conceivably weakened or undermined local conventions protecting domestic slaves or free peoples from being sold to Europeans, thereby breeding the resentment to which contemporaries referred. Precisely who was affected is difficult to say, but the fall in gum output between the 1730s and 1780s raises the possibility that slaves or even traders associated with gum production were seized and sold to European traders.[31] A similar fate probably befell occupants of some slave villages, or *runde,* raids on which were also reported at this time. Those seized in this fashion were said by some contemporaries to have been prone to insurrectionary behavior.[32] Perhaps, however, the most dramatic changes in circumstances were reserved for elite slaves, notably those who served in the armies of warlords, the activities of which almost certainly increased in lower and middle Senegal and Gambia in these years. As ceddo regimes lived by slave raiding and selling slaves for arms and other goods, it is not surprising to find warriors taken prisoner in wars or raids among those entering European ships. Such slaves were, moreover, seen by some as highly likely to rebel on shore or on ship, the cause of such rebelliousness being attributed, among other things, to the discredit that their sale to Europeans brought to their lord. The leaders of one revolt planned by former soldiers were, indeed, said to have preferred an honorable death on the battlefield in the service of their king to being sold to Europeans (Pruneau 1789, 109).[33] The loss of honor felt by such slaves provides, therefore, perhaps one bridge between shore-based disorder in Senegambia and rebellion on ships leaving the region in the second half of the eighteenth century. Put another way, it suggests that rebellions onboard ship may have reflected a breakdown of political order within Senegambia arising from increased export demand for slaves after 1750.

Although revolts probably occurred on no more than one slaving voyage in ten, this figure gives a misleading impression of their significance in relation to the scale and structure of the Atlantic slave trade and its impact on the social history of the Atlantic world. This chapter has drawn attention to two sets of issues concerning the relationship between slave rebelliousness and the Atlantic slave trade. The first concerns the management of slaves onboard ship, the difficulties of sustaining it, and the implication of the cost of defending ships against revolts by their "human cargo." Estimates of such costs suggest that if enslaved Africans had been more docile or quiescent, some 10 percent, or over one million, more may well have been shipped across the Atlantic than actually were. In percentage terms, this figure may appear modest but the number involved was almost equal to the total of slaves shipped from Senegambia, Sierra Leone, and the Windward Coast combined or from the Gold Coast during the whole history of the Atlantic slave trade. Even if revolts largely failed to secure freedom for those directly involved, they ultimately reduced the numbers of Africans forced into slavery in the Americas. This in turn perhaps moderated the impact on African societies of the Atlantic slave trade.

The second set of issues also revolves around relationships between slave revolts and African societies, but in this case concerns the impact of the political economy of slave supply within Africa upon variations in the incidence of shipboard revolt through time and by region of trade. At the heart of this set of issues is the finding that, in comparison with other places, there was a much higher incidence of revolts on ships leaving Sierra Leone, the Windward Coast, Gabon–Cape Lopez, and, above all, Senegambia. This feature of revolts cannot be explained by failure in the management of slaves onboard ship. It demands, instead, an African-centered explanation. Variations in the propensity of particular ethnic groups to rebel were recognized by European traders, but these do not correlate neatly with regional patterns of shipboard revolts. A fuller explanation of shipboard revolts requires, therefore, analysis of the particular conditions and circumstances under which Africans were sold to Europeans. At this stage of research, any arguments linking slave supply conditions with shipboard revolts must be tentative. A preliminary analysis of the background to revolts on ships leaving Senegambia, however, shows that rebelliousness reached unprecedented levels after 1750 and was associated with a previously unrecognized surge in slave exports after 1750. Unlike most other regions, where increased slave exports may have been accommodated by extending slaving further inland, at Senegambia it was probably based in 1750–75 at least by intensification of enslavement activities in lower and middle Senegal and Gambia. This, in turn, may have contributed to a breakdown of political authority, allowing warlord (ceddo) regimes to increase in these areas and prompting attacks by these and other groups on ships trading on the rivers. A further possible outcome of this process was the weakening of local customs or conventions inhibiting the sale of certain groups to Europeans and a violent response by those who became its victims. In this respect, disorder spread from shore to ship as slave exports from Senegambia reached exceptional levels after 1750.

Whether or not this particular explanation of shipboard revolts at Senegambia proves sustainable, historians can no longer rely on arguments based on management failure by European carriers to explain shipboard revolts by Africans. Such revolts were as much a part of African history as the very processes that culminated in the sale of enslaved Africans to Europeans in the first place. Indeed, patterns of shipboard revolt provide a window through which to view those processes and their consequences for social and political order within Africa. It is often claimed that the Atlantic slave trade had socially and politically regressive effects on Senegambia as well as Upper Guinea more generally (Rodney 1970; Barry 1998, ch. 8). The relatively high incidence of revolts on ships leaving these regions may be seen as consistent with such claims. By the same token, however, the generally lower incidence of revolts on ships leaving the Gold Coast, Slave Coast, Bight of Biafra, and west-central Africa suggests that increasing slave supply in these regions was perhaps more easily accommodated within existing structures of political order, especially in near-coast areas. In volume terms, these regions were much greater suppliers of slaves to the Americas than Senegambia, Sierra Leone, and the Windward Coast. They also included the major African slave-trading ports.[34] While historians have been preoccupied with the damage inflicted on Africa by the slave trade, slave traders themselves tended to congregate at places where, on the evidence of shipboard revolts, political authority remained largely intact, even in the face of rising slave exports. Understanding why exports could increase without breakdown in political authority in some regions or places but not others is surely important if we are to explain not only shipboard slave revolts but also the ethnicity of those arriving in the Americas and Africa's integration into the Atlantic world.

Notes

This chapter was originally published in the *William and Mary Quarterly* 58 (January 2001), 69–92. Reprinted and abridged by permission of the author and publisher. I am grateful to David Eltis, Robin Law, and Philip Morgan for comments on an earlier version of this chapter. The usual disclaimer applies.

1. Some merchants and states "remained consistently indifferent or hostile to the Atlantic slave trade" and "reacted with great ferocity to Africans or Europeans who attempted to enslave them" (McGowan 1990, 8). They were, however, in a minority.

2. According to Genovese, "No slave revolt that hesitated to invoke terror had a chance" (1979, 11).

3. The analysis presented in this chapter relies on a data set developed by David Eltis, Stephen Behrendt, and Richardson (n.d.) that is linked through some common fields of data with the recently compiled slave voyage data set that they have published (Eltis, Behrendt, Richardson, and Klein 1999). The new data set contains records of shipboard slave uprisings or mutinies as well as attacks on ships and their crews from the African shore. Some of the latter caused ships to be lost or, to use the contemporary phraseology, "cut off" at the coast. Events such as these have been the subject of recent papers by McGowan (1990) and Inikori (1996), but the data on which this chapter relies are both more extensive and detailed than those underpinning earlier studies. As the new data set is linked to the published voyage data set, it is also possible to highlight features of slave revolts and other attacks on slave ships in Africa that other studies have neglected.

4. Series of *Lloyd's List* have survived for 1702–4, 1741, 1744, 1747–53, 1755, 1757–58, 1760–77, and from 1779 onward. Not all the issues published in these years have survived. There are also details of slave rebellions and coastal attacks on ships by Africans in other eighteenth-century newspapers. A list of those consulted is to be found in appendix A of the introduction to Eltis et al. 1999.

5. See Behrendt, Eltis, and Richardson 2001 for the numbers of cases in each category and the assessment of the proportion of ships experiencing revolts. The former differ slightly from those given in the original version of this chapter published in *William and Mary Quarterly,* while the latter differs from that made by Postma (1990, 165–66), who notes that on fifty-eight "carefully examined" slaving voyages of the Middelburg Company there were at least eleven reported rebellions. Extrapolating from these figures, Postma claims that up to three hundred revolts possibly occurred on Dutch ships alone. The data set on slave revolts underpinning the current paper has thirty-six fields, four of which relate to the identification of ships, enabling this data set to be linked to the published voyage data set (Eltis et al. 1999). Another eight relate to the sources consulted. The remaining twenty-four fields provide data on specific aspects of shipboard insurrections or shore-based attacks. They include details of the initial source of the incident, the phase of the voyage, and time of day when it occurred, the numbers of slaves and crew killed, and the fate of the ship and captives. These data refer to revolts on identifiable ships, but there is evidence of revolts on ships that so far have escaped identification. Willem Bosman (1967, 365–66) reports an uprising on an unnamed Dutch ship in which about twenty slaves died and also notes that the Portuguese were more unlucky than the Dutch, having lost four ships "in this manner" in four years. The unnamed Dutch ship may have been the *Son Vergulde* (Eltis et al. 1999, voyage nos. 10288, 10289), which was the only Dutch ship known to have had revolts onboard from 1696 to 1705, but the Portuguese vessels to which Bosman alluded are unknown. Similarly, a Danish traveler reported that in 1785 a Dutch ship and five hundred of its slaves were lost during a shipboard revolt off the Gold Coast and that in the same year an English ship and all its crew were lost in a revolt off the same coast (Isert 1992, 176). The Dutch ship may have been the *Neptunis* (voyage no. 10890), which was reported to have lost a hundred and fifty slaves in a revolt on the Gold Coast. We have, so far, no other reference to an English ship lost on the Gold Coast.

6. Hobhouse papers, Jefferies Collection, Avon County Library, Bristol.

7. On losses of slaves in revolts, see Behrendt, Eltis, and Richardson 2001.

8. For data on slave mortality, see Klein and Engerman 1997.

9. Other historians have reiterated this view (Wax 1966, 9; Postma 1990, 167), thereby echoing claims by some contemporaries (see Isert 1992, 176).

10. For a summary of the data on the timing of revolts, see Behrendt, Eltis, and Richardson 2001.

11. For further details see ibid.

12. The data suggest that, for each woman killed in revolts, seventeen men also died.

13. All the data in this paragraph derive from Eltis, Behrendt, and Richardson n.d.

14. James Fraser, Minutes of Evidence, February 1790; in Lambert 1975–76, 71:38.

15. The Dunko came from north of Ashante. Isert had earlier described the Krepees (Ewe) as having been "notorious for so many years" (51) and, in terms of physique, among the strongest of "Black nations" (57).

16. William Davenport, Lawrence Spencer, and Robert Cheshire to Samuel Sacheverall, 26 July 1753, Letterbook of William Davenport, Raymond Richards Collection, University of Keele Archives, Keele, Staffordshire.

17. *Voyages to the Coast of Africa by Mess, Saugnier and Brisson* (London, 1792), 336; cited in Searing 1993, 54.

18. Evidence of Peter Whitfield Branker to House of Lords, 24 April 1793, in F. W. Torrington ed., *House of Lords Sessional Papers, 1792–93,* vol. 1 (New York, 1975), 310. Branker himself reported that he had made eleven voyages to Africa in 1772–91, including three to Sierra Leone, Sherbro, and "the country adjacent."

19. Klein 1992 provides a useful summary of the recent literature on these issues.

20. Firearms constituted a relatively high proportion of the trade goods imported into Upper Guinea, including Senegambia (Richardson 1979).

21. The use of ethnic labels by Europeans in the context of the slave trade remains the subject of debate. This is particularly so in relation to the term Bambara; see Caron 1997, 98–121. Caron's analysis suggests that Louisiana records overstate the importance of "Bambara" slaves and thus the far interior as a source of slaves shipped from Senegambia.

22. The following data are based on Eltis et al. 1999.

23. See also Curtin 1981, 93. Curtin's figures suggest exports fell by almost 25 percent by volume.

24. *S. Farley Bristol Journal,* April 19, 1766, Avon County Library, Bristol. The "King of Brack" is the king of Walo, "Brack" being the title conferred to the sovereign of Walo.

25. There are other examples of the demand for slaves by Europeans prompting local violence in areas near the coast. In April 1790 the Swede Charles B. Wadström, who was in Africa in 1787–88, claimed that mulatto merchants from Gorée went "up to the kings of the country, when they are in want of Slaves, and excite the kings to such pillages, which has been told me by the Mulattoes themselves (who do not make any secret of it) as well as by the French officers" (in Lambert 1975–76, 73:24). The relationship between the slave trade and wars in Africa was, of course, a major issue in debates in Parliament and elsewhere over abolition of the trade.

26. Evidence on attacks by Africans on ships comes from Eltis, Behrendt, and Richardson n.d. The fact that the British seized control of Senegal from the French in 1759 may have created additional problems for trade relations in the river by disturbing established political alliances. The French recovered control in 1779.

27. John Matthews, who resided at Sierra Leone in 1785–87, claimed that Fulah inhabitants of the interior were responsible through wars "for the propagation of their religion" for furnishing "a great number of the slaves which are sold in these parts" (1788, 94). On the sources of slave supplies in Sierra Leone and the Windward Coast in general, see Rodney 1970, ch. 9–10.

28. One indication of this is to be found in trends in proportions of children among slaves exported from the Slave Coast, the Bight of Biafra, and west-central Africa, which

in the eighteenth century fell in each quarter century after 1725, in some cases quite sharply. Child ratios among slaves taken from the Gold Coast during the same years fluctuated between 17.5 percent and 20.6 percent per quarter century. See Eltis et al. 1999.

29. It has been argued that it was "the pool of captives recently enslaved and lacking any social identity" that "was tapped by the Atlantic and trans-Saharan slave trades" (Klein and Lovejoy 1979, 186).

30. For one contemporary comment, see Moore 1738, 33.

31. Figures compiled by Hall (1999) show that Nard (or Maures) comprised significant proportions of Senegambian arrivals in Louisiana after 1750.

32. Wadström, for example, claimed that domestic slaves sold or threatened with sale into the export trade were prone to revolt (in Lambert 1975–76, 73:35). That domestic slaves were prepared to rebel against changes in their circumstances was noted by Matthews, who noted that a revolt by slaves within Upper Guinea in 1785 was triggered by their "extremely cruel" treatment by their Mandingo owners and by the "opportunity, when the principal fighting men were out upon an expedition, to attack their masters" (1788, 154). More generally, it has been claimed that rebellion by slaves within Upper Guinea, including Senegambia, "was a constant reality." Starting "in the hinterland, it continued during the coastal transition, and remained a real possibility throughout the long middle passage" (Barry 1998, 123).

33. Pruneau went on to indicate that two leaders of the failed revolt were executed onshore. The rest of the five hundred captives involved in the revolt were sold to a vessel commanded by Captain Avrillon. A few days out to sea, the slaves revolted. In the ensuing struggle, 230 of the captives were reported killed.

34. Eltis, Lovejoy, and Richardson 1999, where it is argued that the factors favoring concentration of slaving at a few ports included "the impact of local political conditions on trade relations" (23).

Bibliography

Adams, John. 1966. *Remarks on the Country Extending from Cape Palmas to the River Congo.* 1823. Reprint, London: Cass.

Barry, Boubacar. 1998. *Senegambia and the Atlantic Slave Trade.* Trans. Ayi Kwei Armah. Cambridge: Cambridge University Press.

Behrendt, Stephen D. 1997. "Crew Mortality in the Transatlantic Slave Trade in the Eighteenth Century." *Slavery and Abolition* 18:49–71.

Behrendt, Stephen D., David Eltis, and David Richardson. 2001. "The Costs of Coercion: African Agency in the Pre-Modern Atlantic World." *Economic History Review* 54:454–76.

Bosman, Willem. 1967. *A New and Accurate Description of the Coast of Guinea.* 1704. Reprint, London: Cass.

Caron, Peter. 1997. "'Of a Nation Which the Others Do Not Understand': Bambara Slaves and African Ethnicity in Colonial Louisiana, 1718–60." *Slavery and Abolition* 18:98–121.

Craton, Michael. 1982. *Testing the Chains: Resistance to Slavery in the British West Indies.* Ithaca, N.Y.: Cornell University Press.

Curtin, Philip D. 1975. *Economic Change in Precolonial Africa: Senegambia in the Era of the Slave Trade.* Madison: University of Wisconsin Press.

———. 1981. "The Abolition of the Slave Trade from Senegambia." In David Eltis and James Walvin, eds., *The Abolition of the Atlantic Slave Trade.* Madison: University of Wisconsin Press.

Eltis, David. 2000. *The Rise of African Slavery in the Americas.* Cambridge: Cambridge University Press.

———. 2001. "The Volume and Structure of the Transatlantic Slave Trade: A Reassessment." *William and Mary Quarterly* 58:17–46.

Eltis, David, Stephen Behrendt, and David Richardson. n.d. "Slave Ship Revolt Data Set." Unpublished.

Eltis, David, Stephen D. Behrendt, David Richardson, and Herbert S. Klein. 1999. *The Trans-Atlantic Slave Trade: A Database on CD-ROM.* Cambridge: Cambridge University Press.

Eltis, David, Paul E. Lovejoy, and David Richardson. 1999. "Slave-Trading Ports: Towards an Atlantic Wide Perspective." In Robin Law and Silke Strickrodt, eds., *Ports of the Slave Trade (Bights of Benin and Biafra).* Stirling, U.K.: University of Stirling.

Eltis, David, and David Richardson. 1995. "Productivity in the Transatlantic Slave Trade." *Explorations in Economic History* 32:465–84.

Genovese, Eugene D. 1979. *From Rebellion to Revolution: Afro-American Slave Revolts in the Making of the Modern World.* Baton Rouge: Louisiana State University Press.

Greene, Lorenzo J. 1944. "Mutiny on the Slave Ships." *Phylon* 5:346–54.

Hall, Gwendolyn Midlo, ed. 1999. *Databases for the Study of Afro-Louisiana History and Genealogy on CD-Rom.* Baton Rouge: Louisiana State University Press. Louisiana slave database, 1723–1820.

Inikori, Joseph E. 1996. "Measuring the Unmeasured Hazards of the Atlantic Slave Trade: Documents Relating to the British Trade." *Revue française d'histoire d'outre-mer* 83:53–92.

Isert, Paul Erdmann. 1992. *Letters on West Africa and the Slave Trade.* 1788. Reprint, trans. and ed. Selena Axelrod Winsnes. Oxford: Oxford University Press.

Isichei, Elizabeth. 1976. *A History of the Igbo People.* London: Macmillan.

Klein, Herbert S., and Stanley L. Engerman. 1997. "Long-Term Trends in African Mortality in the Transatlantic Slave Trade." *Slavery and Abolition* 18:36–48.

Klein, Martin A. 1992. "The Impact of the Atlantic Slave Trade on the Societies of the Western Sudan." In Joseph E. Inikori and Stanley L. Engerman, eds., *The Atlantic Slave Trade.* Durham, N.C.: Duke University Press.

———. 1998. *Slavery and Colonial Rule in French West Africa.* Cambridge: Cambridge University Press.

Klein, Martin A., and Paul E. Lovejoy. 1979. "Slavery in West Africa." In Henry A. Gemery and Jan S. Hogendorn, eds., *The Uncommon Market: Essays in the Economic History of the Atlantic Slave Trade.* New York: Academic Press.

Lambert, Sheila, ed. 1975–76. *House of Commons Sessional Papers of the Eighteenth Century.* 145 vols. Wilmington, Del.: Scholarly Resources.

Mannix, Daniel P., and Malcolm Cowley. 1962. *Black Cargoes: A History of the Atlantic Slave Trade, 1518–1865.* New York: Viking.

Matthews, John. 1788. *A Voyage to the River Sierra-Leone.* London: B. White.

McGowan, Winston. 1990. "African Resistance to the Atlantic Slave Trade in West Africa." *Slavery and Abolition* 11 (1): 5–29.

Mettas, Jean. 1978–84. *Répertoire des expéditions négrières françaises au dix-huitième siècle.* Ed. Serge Daget. 2 vols. Paris: Société Française d'Histoire d'Outre-Mer.

Moore, Francis. 1738. *Travels into the Inland Parts of Africa.* London: E. Cave.

Palmer, Colin A. 1997. "The Slave Trade, African Slavers, and the Demography of the Caribbean to 1750." In Franklin W. Knight, ed., *The Slave Societies of the Caribbean,* vol. 3 of *General History of the Caribbean.* Paris: UNESCO.

Piersen, William. 1977. "White Cannibals, Black Martyrs: Fear, Depression, and Religious Faith as Causes of Suicide among Slaves." *Journal of Negro History* 62:147–59.

Postma, Johannes M. 1990. *The Dutch in the Atlantic Slave Trade, 1600–1815.* Cambridge: Cambridge University Press.

Pruneau de Pommegorge, Antoine. 1789. *Description de la nigritie par M. P. D. P.* Amsterdam: Maradan.

Rathbone, Richard. 1986. "Some Thoughts on Resistance to Enslavement in West Africa." *Slavery and Abolition* 6:11–22.

Richardson, David. 1979. "West African Consumption Patterns and Their Influence on the Eighteenth-Century English Slave Trade." In Henry A. Gemery and Jan S. Hogendorn, eds., *The Uncommon Market: Essays in the Economic History of the Atlantic Slave Trade.* New York: Academic Press.

Rodney, Walter. 1970. *A History of the Upper Guinea Coast, 1545–1800.* Oxford: Clarendon.

Searing, James F. 1993. *West African Slavery and Atlantic Commerce: The Senegal River Valley, 1700–1860.* Cambridge: Cambridge University Press.

Uya, Okon E. 1976, "Slave Revolts in the Middle Passage: A Neglected Theme." *Calabar Historical Journal* 1:65–88.

Wax, Darold D. 1966. "Negro Resistance to the Early American Slave Trade." *Journal of Negro History* 51:1–15.

———. 1973. "Preferences for Slaves in Colonial America." *Journal of Negro History* 58:371–401.

White, Deborah Gray. 1985. *Ar'n't I a Woman?: Female Slaves in the Plantation South.* New York: Norton.

Epilogue

Memory as Resistance

Identity and the Contested History of Slavery in Southeastern Nigeria, an Oral History Project

Carolyn A. Brown

The historiography of Africa has yet to capture the horror and terror that accompanied the African dimension of the slave trade. Within world history it is the narrative of those who became African American slaves that has taken pride of place and come to exemplify a universal chronicle of suffering, pain, and eventual triumph. However, the contemporary political agenda of African descendants within the Americas has led historians to shy away from tackling the complex and contradictory narrative of the circumstances under which these people were enslaved as well as the story of those enslaved Africans who did not end up in the Americas, across the Sahara, or in the Indian Ocean but remained within the continent. In other words, this haunting silence creates a void where the voices and experiences of Africans on the continent should be articulated. Historians are confronted with a number of evidential problems that make it especially difficult to complete the narrative of the trade with the voices of these communities who remained. Nonetheless, the narrative of the trade is incomplete without the presence of these voices.

This chapter describes a pilot project that is seeking to document the ways that these experiences are remembered by communities in an area that was intensely involved in the slave trade.[1] Secondarily, it compares these memories with archival and recent statistical studies of the trade to determine the extent to which oral history can be a useful tool for historical reconstruction. The findings are not considered to be typical of any general lived experience of slavery on the African continent but merely a partial chronicle of the experience in one specific area of West Africa—the Biafran hinterland. The preliminary findings of this project give anecdotal verification of some of the gendered patterns of enslavement for the area. Only in the Bight of Biafra did the number of women enslaved reach near parity with that of men.

Southeastern Nigeria and the Slave Trade

The interior of the Bight of Biafra is inhabited by the Igbo people and a smaller number of other ethnolinguistic groups. It was one of the most important sources of enslaved Africans sent to the Americas in the eighteenth and early nineteenth centuries. It is estimated that 1.5 million Africans were exported between 1660 and 1841. Although the literature on the impact of the slave trade on Africa has grown over the last twenty years, historians are only beginning to grasp the objective and subjective impact on African societies of the seizure, sale, and abduction of the large numbers of men, women, and children swept into New World slavery. Given the sheer numbers of people taken from the Bight of Biafra, it is no surprise that there was scarcely a village, kin group, or family that did not lose a relative to the trade. Despite the possibilities that this region offers as a site for an in-depth study of the impact of the trade on an African community, we historians have not really begun to document the subjective "costs" of this "loss" or to capture the psychological trauma that it undoubtedly produced throughout the area.[2]

Between 1740 and 1807 two-thirds of all slaves came from this area. Unlike other areas of the coast, where the numbers of male slaves exported far exceeded that of women, in the Bight of Biafra they reached near parity. We found anecdotal confirmation of this fact in our oral history project. The conventional explanation for the lower proportion of women exported from most of the coast is that women captives were retained on the continent and therefore constituted the bulk of slaves held internally by African societies.

We have not yet been able to explain this statistical variation. We do not know whether it was caused by demand or supply. We cannot yet determine whether this disparity was caused by a preference for Biafran women among European slavers or by the resistance to their sale by African merchants.[3]

Because of archival evidence of their role in the slave trade as well as the presence of suitable interview subjects, four states in southeastern Nigeria were chosen as the location of the first phase of the project:

- Anambra State, located near the market town of Onitsha, which was connected to Bonny, the key slave entrepôt;
- Enugu State, specifically the Nkanu area, near the city of Enugu, where former slaves continue to battle with their erstwhile owners for equality;
- Abia State, the Cross Rivers area, location of the Aro people, the primary slave dealers throughout Igboland, and source area for Calabar. Here interviews were conducted in two villages that had major slave markets: Bende and Uzuakoli;
- Imo State, center of the palm belt, where many prosperous traders built huge multistory mansions.

Four interviewers were recruited from among the university staff of each area. In most cases they were quite familiar with the villages and acquainted with oral traditions about the slave trade. Each selected the villages in which to hold interviews—both video- and audiotaped—based on previous knowledge that these villages were either involved in the trade as merchants or victims or were the site of ongoing conflict between former slaves and freeborn people. Between December 1999 and July 2000 some thirty-five interviews—each between ninety minutes and two hours long—were collected about the slave trade, internal slavery, and contemporary social problems rooted in the heritage of slavery.

Memory and Igbo Society: Preliminary Findings

The interviews far exceeded our expectations and graphically underscored the historical value and urgency of the project. The memories recounted in the interviews speak to several themes that are of increasing importance to the project. As women were a large percentage of the enslaved, oral accounts of women being kidnapped, victimized, and sold were much more prominent than stories of men. One researcher, Nneka Osakwe, was able to capture a number of valuable accounts that focus on the place of women in the trade.[4] Her interviews were conducted in Anambra State. The towns (groups of villages) are all believed to have been founded by descendants of a common ancestor and are considered the original home areas of the Igbo. They are spread out along the northeast axis toward Onitsha, the major market town along the Niger River. The area is somewhat under the political influence of the Nri people, a sacerdotal clan of the Igbo. Despite their sacred functions and status, they were active slave merchants. They were believed to be second only to the Aro in their involvement in the slave trade.[5]

Several themes reappeared in a number of the key interviews. One was especially haunting: it spoke to the current significance of the slave trade as it is evoked to explain contemporary misfortune. In a number of villages, informants mentioned that particular families were cursed because a relative sold a daughter into slavery. The practice of selling a girl child was deemed especially abhorrent as it violated the terms of kinship. In this case, informants mentioned that the family had been confronted with a range of personal and family disasters and had found that they were victimized by a curse that often appeared as a spate of deaths, financial loss, or other misfortune. An oracle attributed this to the sale of a daughter generations ago.

In one interview, the actual sale was recalled in a way that expressed, despite the generations of separation, the anguish felt by a mother: "In her father's family there were two of such female members—Akuabate and Nwiru. Their sale was traumatic. They were forcefully taken away by their uncles from their mother, who was a widow. Their widowed mother was said to have cried until she went blind! She eventually died from the agony she suffered."[6]

While the interviews revealed that widows and their children were most likely to be enslaved, they raised complex problems both about the historical trajectory of the trade as well as women's acceptance of gender ideologies. First, because we are unable to determine with sufficient accuracy the time period in which these sales occurred, we cannot say if this practice coincided with an erosion of family ideologies of kinship or if it was considered by the majority of the rural community to be an antisocial practice. First, the fact that the Nri priest–slave traders were participants suggests a degradation of local mores and customary practices about kinship. Second, some of the accounts suggest that enslavement was a reaction to a more widespread expression of social resistance by women. There were instances of enslavement of a particularly "troublesome" girl or a transgressive woman who broke a gender taboo. Such a case was recounted by one Mrs. Akuinyi Hampo, who noted that a woman considered rebellious in the village of Ezeagu violated convention by picking a pod of kola nuts from a tree.[7] We do not know if her action was an individual instance of rebellion or whether she was part of a more generalized process of resistance by women against offensive practices. This can be determined only with further interviews and further exploration of archival accounts.

These interviews also revealed that in certain areas the heritage of slavery was especially salient and was expressed in persistent discrimination and persecution of people descended from indigenous slaves. In at least one case this persecution created a coalition of slave descendants who became a formidable political force in the early twentieth century. The slave-freeborn dichotomy was especially significant in the towns near the city of Enugu, in the southern Nkanu area, on the northern frontier of Igboland. Here in 1922 whole settlements of slaves, locally called *ohu,* heard of emancipation and launched a violent civil war to force the freeborn community to permit them to participate in the sacri-political life of the village.[8] Interviews in this area capture the continuing struggles waged by these communities against persecution and were circumscribed by suspicions that the interviewer, a "freeborn" descendant, would not be sympathetic. This was expressed in the interview of one Mary Ebiem of Ugwuaji, Nkanu. In the 1920s the establishment of her village, Ugwuaji, was the British response to the frustrated demand of ex-slaves for land of their own beyond the control of their erstwhile owners. Today's memory is a pivotal part of the identity of this community, as they proudly recall the conditions that led to their demands for a separate village. Mrs. Ebiem passionately recounted the pivotal incidents that sparked the revolts of the 1920s—the kidnapping and sale of four adolescent ohu (slave) girls going to market—as if it had recently occurred. She also recalled the case of a man whose niece was kidnapped and sold and who became the first ex-slave to actually shoot the "freeborn" perpetrator. Memories of resistance play an important role in the consciousness of these communities. In the 1930s they succeeded in getting the government to outlaw the use of the term ohu and to replace it with *awbia,* a more ambiguous term meaning "stranger." Nonetheless, the community found that a semantic shift did little to secure equal rights and social acceptance. While the experience in southern Nkanu may not be typical, it does raise questions about the heritage of slavery and indicates a new area for contemporary research.

In many ways, the project raises more questions than it answers and uncovers additional frustrations for the historian. However, it does speak eloquently and passionately of the centrality of the slave trade in collective memory. That people would attribute present-day misfortune to events that happened several generations before suggests that the slave trade continues to hang in a troublesome way in popular imagination. Moreover, the fact that we can still locate informants eager to tell stories of the trade raises interesting questions about the memory of ill-fated ancestors in kin-based societies. As Osakwe has noted in several conversations, people who disappear in families leave a hole that is never filled. And this void is passed down from generation to generation. Fortunately for the project, many of these people remain in the adjacent area and can quickly recall the circumstances under which an ancestor fell into the Atlantic or domestic trade.

This project was not designed to be comprehensive but to demonstrate what is possible in documenting the history of the area's involvement in the slave trade. It is hoped that it will stimulate other scholars, both local (Nigerian) and foreign, to continue searching for the intricacies of the impact of the slave trade on this area. We have identified a series of hypotheses that have an impact on the topic. While they are necessarily preliminary, the following conclusions come to mind.

The project tells us that this area is an ideal site for the collection of folklore and community histories of the slave trade. The prominence of the memory of the slave trade is a further indication of the pivotal role it played in the development of the Biafran hinterland. Oral data will help to fill a gap in the literature on the actual experiences of the men, women, and children who were swept up into the slave trade. We anticipate conducting an additional one hundred interviews in several new areas as well as returning to old sites.

It is entirely possible that we can actually locate these historical experiences in time. By coordinating documentary data with family histories and personal recollections we can approximate time periods. We can test this anecdotal information against the macro material collected, for example, from the Cambridge slave-trade database.[9]

Finally, the enslavement experiences of Africans, both those captured and deported as well as those internally held in bondage, are a central element of the transatlantic experience of the continent. Scholarly documentation of their stories, their experiences, and their pain are a crucial dimension of the greater Atlantic narrative of African people. This should be the foundational narrative of all current diasporic studies.

NOTES

1. The project, which began in late 1999, was jointly supported by the Faculty of Arts and Sciences and the Center for African Studies, Rutgers, The State University of New Jersey; the York/UNESCO Nigerian Hinterland Project of Canada; and the Schomburg Center for Research in Black Culture of the New York Public Library. It was coordinated by the Enugu Historical Documentation Center, whose director, Anayo Enechukwu, a local historian, served as the site director. All contributed financially while the director, Carolyn A. Brown of Rutgers University, supervised the project.

2. I owe this observation to Austin Ahanotu, whose paper at the conference cited below argued that this involvement had a traumatic impact on the psyche of the peoples in the area, an impact that has not even been broached in the historiography of the region. "Slavers and Historical Memory: Should the Village Remember," paper presented at a Rutgers University, York University Nigerian Hinterland Project conference, "Repercussions of the Atlantic Slave Trade: The Bight of Biafra and the African Diaspora," Nike Lake, Enugu, Nigeria, 10–14 July 2000.

3. For an earlier discussion see the essays in Claire Robertson and Martin Klein, eds., *Women and Slavery in Africa* (Madison: University of Wisconsin Press, 1983).

4. The following account is from Nneka Osakwe, "Haunting Tales of Loss and Enslavement: Finding Women's Voices in the Oral History of the Slave Trade From The Bight of Biafra," part 2, "An Overview: Examples from the Interviews of the Project Memory and the Atlantic Slave Trade," paper presented at the conference Atlantic Crossings: Women's Voices, Women's Stories from the Caribbean and the Nigerian Hinterland, Dartmouth College, 18–20 May 2001.

5. The Aro are a clan of the Igbo whose "homeland" is near the Cross Rivers area of southeastern Nigeria. In the seventeenthth century they organized a complex trading network that gave them a near monopoly on importing European goods into the hinterland and in selling slaves to Europeans on the coast. This control spanned the colonial period. They accomplished this through the "colonization" of a vast periodic market system throughout southeastern Nigeria and the manipulation of a local oracle, Ibini Ukpabi, used to adjudicate disputes in the area. There is an extensive literature on the Aro. See especially K. Onwuka Dike and Felicia Ekejiuba, *The Aro of South-Eastern Nigeria, 1650–1980: A Study of Socio-Economic Formation and Transformation in Nigeria* (Ibadan: Ibadan University Press, 1990); David Northrup, *Trade without Rulers: Pre-colonial Economic Development in South-Eastern Nigeria* (Oxford Studies in African Affairs. Oxford: Clarendon Press, 1978); and K. Onwuka Dike, *Trade and Politics in the Niger Delta, 1830–1885: An Introduction to the Economic and Political History of Nigeria* (Oxford: Clarendon Press, 1956).

6. Ogechukwu Nwigbo, interview by Nneka Osakwe, Nwafia, Njikoka, Local Government Area, 4 July 2000.

7. Akuinyi Hampo, interview by Nneka Osakwe, Amansiodo, Ezeagu, 5 July 2000.

8. For a discussion of this revolt, see Carolyn A. Brown, "Testing the Boundaries of Marginality: Twentieth-Century Slavery and Emancipation Struggles in Nkanu, Northern Igboland, 1920–1929," *Journal of African History* 37 (1996): 51–80.

9. David Eltis, Stephen D. Behrendt, David Richardson, and Herbert S. Klein, *The Trans-Atlantic Slave Trade: A Database on CD-ROM* (Cambridge: Cambridge University Press, 1999). The database, which covers the trade from 1595 to 1866, includes more than twenty-seven thousand slave-ship voyages and approximately two hundred fields of information.

Contributors

THIERNO MOUCTAR BAH, a native of Guinea, studied at Dakar University and received his Ph.D. at the Sorbonne. He is professor of history at the University of Yaoundé, Cameroon. He is an expert in the military history of Africa, and was editor (1972–95) of the pan-African historical journal *Afrika zamani.* He has published numerous articles on precolonial African history, with a focus on the military dimension and the foundation of a peace culture. He is a consultant for UNESCO.

CAROLYN A. BROWN, associate professor of history and director of the Center for African Studies at Rutgers University, is author of *We Were All Slaves: African Miners, Culture and Resistance in the Enugu Government Colliery, Nigeria, 1914–1950.* She is currently working on the oral history of southeast Nigeria and on a social history of the nationalist struggle in a major Nigerian town: *Cowboys, Letterwriters, and Dancing Women: Identity and Struggles over Space in a Colonial Town: Enugu, Nigeria, 1914–1955.*

DENNIS D. CORDELL is professor of history and associate dean for general education at Southern Methodist University, Dallas. He is the author of *Dar al-Kuti and the Last Years of the Trans-Saharan Slave Trade,* coeditor of *African Population and Capitalism: Historical Perspectives,* and coauthor of *Hoe and Wage: A Social History of a Circular Migration System in West Africa.* He is now working on studies of social reproduction and the Saharan slave trade and of new African immigrant communities in France and the United States.

SYLVIANE A. DIOUF is the author of *Servants of Allah: African Muslims Enslaved in the Americas,* named an Outstanding Academic Book in 1999 by *Choice.* She has published studies on the African Diaspora, West African Muslims, and African migrations to Europe and the United States. She has edited a volume on American migrations and has written several books on African and African American history for younger readers and numerous articles for international magazines.

ADAMA GUÈYE pursued her studies at Université Cheikh Anta Diop in Dakar, Senegal. She has conducted oral history projects and archeological digs in several sites linked to the slave trade, including Gorée Island. She teaches history at the University of Djibouti.

WALTER HAWTHORNE received a Ph.D. in African history at Stanford University in 1998. On a Fulbright Fellowship he conducted research among Balanta and other societies in Guinea-Bissau. Currently an assistant professor at Ohio University, he is working on a book to be published in the Heinemann Social History of Africa series.

JOSEPH E. INIKORI is professor of history at the University of Rochester. His research and teaching focus on the evolution of the current world economic order from the sixteenth century. He has published many articles on the economies of the slave trade in various journals and anthologies and is author of *Africans and the Industrial Revolution in England: A Study in International Trade and Economic Development*, *The Chaining of a Continent: Export Demand for Captives and the History of Africa South of the Sahara, 1450–1870*, and *The Atlantic Slave Trade*.

MARTIN A. KLEIN has done extensive research on the history of slavery in West Africa. Among other books, he is author of *Slavery and Colonial Rule in French West Africa*, editor of *Breaking the Chains: Slavery, Bondage, and Emancipation in Modern Africa and Asia*, and coeditor of *Women and Slavery in Africa*. He is recently retired from teaching at the University of Toronto.

PAUL E. LOVEJOY, Distinguished Research Professor of history, York University, Toronto, is a Fellow of the Royal Society of Canada. He has published over fifteen books and sixty papers and articles on African economic history, slavery, the slave trade, and the African diaspora. He is director of the Harriet Tubman Resource Centre on the African Diaspora and holds the Canada Research Chair in African diaspora history.

John N. Oriji received his Ph.D. in African history at Rutgers University. He has taught in both Nigerian and American universities and is currently professor of African history at California Polytechnic State University, San Luis Obispo. He has authored two books in African history and twenty-five journal articles.

Ismail Rashid, a Sierra Leonean, is assistant professor of history and Africana studies at Vassar College. He received his Ph.D. at McGill University, Montreal. His research includes slave resistance, rural protests, and anticolonialism in Sierra Leone and contemporary conflicts in West Africa. He has recently published "'Do Dadi nor Make Dem Carry Me': Slavery and Resistance in Sierra Leone" and "Escape, Revolt, and Marronage in Eighteenth- and Nineteenth-Century Sierra Leone Hinterland."

David Richardson is professor of economic history and deputy dean of the faculty of social sciences, University of Hull, United Kingdom. He has published a four-volume series on Bristol and the African slave trade and is coeditor of *The Trans-Atlantic Slave Trade: A Database on CD-Rom.* He is currently working on studies of the British slave trade, shipboard revolts (with David Eltis and Stephen Behrendt), and the slave trade and the history of the Bight of Biafra (with Paul E. Lovejoy).

Elisée Soumonni teaches history at Université Nationale du Bénin, Cotonou. He is a member of the International Scientific Committee of the UNESCO Slave Route Project and the head of the Beninese Institute of Study and Research on the African Diaspora (IBERDA). A former Fulbright Research Scholar at Emory University, he has published several articles on the slave trade, including "The Historiography of Dahomean Yorubaland," "The Compatibility of the Slave and Palm Oil Trades in Dahomey," and "The Administration of a Port of the Slave Trade: Ouidah in the Nineteenth Century."

Index